The EVERYTHING
Landlording Book

Dear Reader:

Reasons for wanting to become a landlord vary. Some of you want extra income to supplement your retirement money. Some want to purchase a multifamily home and build equity for a single-family home, instead of paying rent to a landlord. Others may want to develop a new career and realize that starting off with a small rental property, such as an owner-occupied duplex, is a good way to learn the business.

Whatever your motivation, when you go into landlording you will be starting a complex and rewarding new business and should approach it as such.

I'm delighted you've selected *The Everything® Landlording Book* to help you get started. Although landlords in owner-occupied dwellings are exempt from many state and federal laws, I've tried to present an overview of the ones you need to know about, what it takes to be a landlord, as well as information about starting and running your business. I hope you'll find this book full of practical advice that will help you launch a successful career.

Judy Tremore

The EVERYTHING® Series

Editorial

Publishing Director	Gary M. Krebs
Managing Editor	Kate McBride
Copy Chief	Laura MacLaughlin
Acquisitions Editor	Eric M. Hall
Development Editor	Christina MacDonald
Production Editors	Jamie Wielgus
	Bridget Brace

Production

Production Director	Susan Beale
Production Manager	Michelle Roy Kelly
Series Designers	Daria Perreault
	Colleen Cunningham
	John Paulhus
Cover Design	Paul Beatrice
	Matt LeBlanc
Layout and Graphics	Colleen Cunningham
	Rachael Eiben
	Michelle Roy Kelly
	John Paulhus
	Daria Perreault
	Erin Ring
Series Cover Artist	Barry Littmann

Visit the entire Everything® Series at www.everything.com

THE
EVERYTHING®
LANDLORDING
BOOK

An all-in-one guide
to property management

Judy Tremore

Adams Media
Avon, Massachusetts

An Everything® Series Book.
Everything® and everything.com® are registered trademarks of F+W Publications, Inc.

Published by Adams Media, an F+W Publications Company
57 Littlefield Street, Avon, MA 02322 U.S.A.
www.adamsmedia.com

ISBN: 1-59337-143-8
Printed in the United States of America.

J I H G F E D C B

Library of Congress Cataloging-in-Publication Data
Tremore, Judy.
The everything landlording book / Judy Tremore.
p.   cm.
(An everything series book)
ISBN 1-59337-143-8
1. Rental housing--Management. 2. Real estate management. 3. Real estate investment.
4. Landlord and tenant. I. Title. II. Series: Everything series.
HD1394.T74   2004
333.5'4--dc22   2004013352

This publication is designed to provide accurate and authoritative information with regard to the subject matter covered. It is sold with the understanding that the publisher is not engaged in rendering legal, accounting, or other professional advice. If legal advice or other expert assistance is required, the services of a competent professional person should be sought.

—From a *Declaration of Principles* jointly adopted by a Committee of the American Bar Association and a Committee of Publishers and Associations

Many of the designations used by manufacturers and sellers to distinguish their products are claimed as trademarks. Where those designations appear in this book and Adams Media was aware of a trademark claim, the designations have been printed with initial capital letters.

Forms on pages 270–282 used by permission of U.S. Legal Forms, Inc.

This book is available at quantity discounts for bulk purchases.
For information, call 1-800-872-5627.

Contents

Acknowledgments

Thank you to the people who generously contributed to this book. Andrea Soule, a landlord for nearly thirty years with her husband David M. Soule, spent hours reading, commenting on, and adding to the book. And thanks to David, who also manages a multifamily complex.

Michael Lillo, owner of a Farmers Insurance Group of Companies agency, and several of his colleagues generously gave professional advice.

Clay B. Powell, director of the Grand Rapids, Michigan, Rental Property Owners Association (RPOA), served as a resource as well.

Frank D. Edens, J.D. and CEO of U.S. Legal Forms, Inc., Brandon, Mississippi, graciously contributed most of the landlord-tenant forms found in Appendix B.

Dan and Deb Zondervan shared their experience about converting a home into an owner-occupied dwelling. In the 1980s they renovated their first rundown Victorian house, putting two rental units on the second floor.

Thanks also to Paul Leer, owner of small rental properties, for his advice on financial records.

Top Ten Things
Every Landlord Should Know

1. Landlording the right property in a good location makes all the difference when it comes to finding the tenants you want.

2. Find inexpensive ways to fix up your property and make an apartment attractive.

3. Take the time to understand the laws, codes, and permits affecting landlords and tenants before getting started.

4. Learn about insurance and liability issues and what is needed to avoid lawsuits.

5. Be sure to determine a competitive rental rate that will cover expenses and bring in a return on investment (ROI).

6. Figure out what it takes to find and keep the best possible tenants, and then do it.

7. Learn to avoid discrimination complaints when marketing and showing the property.

8. Develop systems for recordkeeping, documenting all contacts with applicants and tenants, and using legal forms.

9. Learn how to do your own maintenance and repairs and how to improve tenant safety.

10. Know when and how to legally evict troublesome tenants.

Introduction

▶ Some people go into landlording assuming that it's an easy job. If you have an apartment and a tenant, then all you need to do is collect rent each month and in a short time you'll be raking in the cash. Right? The truth is that although just about anyone can go into landlording, to be a success you have to make an investment, and that doesn't mean just money.

You have to be willing to invest in yourself. You should go into landlording with an open mind and a willingness to learn everything you can about the business—before you start and long after you have experience.

As you're just starting out, you'll want to read *The Everything® Landlording Book* and then devote many more hours to educating yourself by learning from other landlords and through seminars, workshops, and other books. It's best to begin your education immediately, before you renovate your home into an owner-occupied dwelling or purchase your first duplex.

You'll also want to find out about federal, state, and local landlord-tenant legislation, as well as local building codes and zoning laws. State and local regulations and the forms that you'll use as a landlord can vary in each community, and you don't want to inadvertently include language in your lease or advertisements that can lead to legal hassles.

To avoid trouble, you'll want to develop a thorough understanding of fair housing laws. Not all of them apply to small landlords in owner-occupied dwellings, but you'll need to know what the laws are when it comes to advertising your unit, talking to people who apply to rent the apartment, and dealing with your tenants.

You'll also want to know what you can do to reduce the risk of getting a problem tenant—and what your options are for getting rid of one.

It will also help if you look at landlording as a business—one that will take an investment of your personal time. Knowing how to keep records and books that will satisfy Uncle Sam at tax time is just one facet. The other is to know how you can increase your long-term "profit" by using all the tax advantages available to landlords. These include your ability to deduct legitimate business expenses from your personal income, the tax advantages of depreciation on your dwelling and the improvements you make to your property, and the equity you'll build up, as well as the increased valuation you'll realize if you ever decide to sell your home.

The Everything® Landlording Book will help you with all of these things. You will find suggestions about how to adapt your home into an owner-occupied dwelling or buy a rental property. You'll get tips about fixing up your property and learn about the laws, codes, and permits that pertain to rental properties. You'll get tips on marketing your space, showing your property, finding the right tenants, providing a "perfect" home, and making money off your property.

You'll find two chapters dealing with insurance and liability issues. The fact is that landlords have to be aware that they are prime targets for liability claims, and it behooves them to know what steps they can take to eliminate the risk.

You'll get the nuts and bolts of rental applications, rental agreements, leases, tenant's checklists, collecting and increasing rent, and recordkeeping. You'll find out what you should do about maintenance and repairs, simple tasks you can undertake that can save you money, and how you can improve your tenants' safety.

And in Appendix B you'll find samples of some of the forms from various states that landlords use in their business. You can use them as guidelines, but be sure to get forms that comply with landlord-tenant regulations in your state.

The Everything® Landlording Book will give you a good foundation upon which you can build your new career. It provides an overview of the business from the first time you think seriously about going into landlording to the first time you may have to evict a tenant. It's meant to lead you to the other resources that will help you launch a challenging, rewarding career as a landlord.

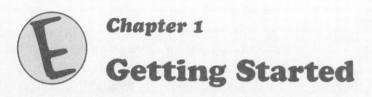

Chapter 1

Getting Started

Y ou have a lot to think about and learn if you want to become a landlord. You'll need to take a look at your weaknesses and strengths, how much you're willing to put into landlording, and whether you can sustain your energy and enthusiasm over the long term. Landlords who succeed treat landlording as a serious business and are willing to invest both time and capital.

Is Landlording Right for Me?

Anyone can be a landlord, right? All it takes is having an apartment and finding a tenant and then you're all set. Well, it's not quite that easy. Landlording is a complex business that is best run by a multitalented person who likes people and can work with his hands as well as his head. If you enjoy challenges and are willing to learn new skills, being a landlord in an owner-occupied dwelling can be rewarding.

As a novice, however, don't jump into it too fast. First find out what you'll be getting into. Read this book, then check out some of the other books, magazines, and Web sites listed in Appendix A. Talk to other landlords and ask them what they like most about their job and what bothers them the most. Go as a guest to a professional meeting or seminar. Listen and learn as much as you can.

You also need to honestly consider how landlording will affect your personal life. How does your family feel? Do you have family commitments that are a priority? Does your family back your decision to become a landlord? After all, this is a job that will affect their lives, too.

If you plan on working on your duplex after working at a full-time job, will you have enough time, energy, and interest to come home to more chores? You don't want to burn out. When landlords get to that point, they let their property deteriorate until the only tenants they can attract bring along more problems. Anyone can spend a few months working around the clock, but it's not easy to sustain that pace for a year or two. Are you up to the challenge?

FACT

Don't go into landlording half-heartedly. If you would prefer being on a golf course on weekends and watching ball games every night, you might start resenting your tenant. Over time your resentment will escalate and make you feel miserable and then you might let things slide.

Maintaining an owner-occupied dwelling might not be a full-time job, but it can be time consuming. You won't be able to go to Florida to escape three months of ice and snow if you have a tenant, unless you're going to hire someone else to do your work. Are you willing to make that commitment? If you buy a fixer-upper—and have a full-time job—getting away for a vacation will be a dream, not reality, for quite some time.

The Qualities of a Successful Landlord

To keep your expenses low and increase your income, you'll want to do most of a landlord's tasks yourself. This is especially important if you are thinking of landlording because you want to supplement retirement income or build equity in a starter home. If you were going to have others do all the work, you'd have to hire a lawyer, a bookkeeper, an accountant, a secretary, a plumber, an electrician, a handyman, a painter, a designer, a marketing agency, a mediator, yard-care and cleaning services, and, in some cases, a collection agency.

How motivated and committed do you feel about going into landlording? Have you always dreamed of owning your own business? If you are excited about becoming a landlord and absolutely certain you'll be good at it, you'll be able to sustain interest in your work. Read the following sections carefully, and be honest with yourself about whether you have the qualities necessary to be a successful landlord. Then if you still think landlording is for you, go ahead—start converting your home into an owner-occupied dwelling or start looking for a duplex.

Personal Qualities

It's very important for a landlord to be committed and motivated. It also helps if you like people and treat them with fairness, honesty, and respect—you want to be friendly with your tenants. A good landlord is flexible and can stay calm, even though he or she might be angry or upset. A sense of humor helps, too. Do you laugh when you make a mistake and then learn from it? If you tend to lose your temper when you're frustrated by things going wrong, you might be better off in another job.

A good landlord has good communication skills and a great deal of patience. Are you assertive? Can you make a point without becoming aggressive or belligerent? Are you able to stay optimistic and enthusiastic even when you're overtired or having to deal with a tenant's problem late at night?

ALERT!

Before you leap into landlording, try to honestly assess your limitations and strengths. Be realistic. If you don't like doing paperwork or don't want to tinker with a lock or a leaky faucet, how long will it take before you're putting more of your own cash into hiring help than you're getting out of your apartment?

Natural Management Skills

It helps to have management skills. Landlords need to organize and prioritize all sorts of tasks and set goals. Are you good at keeping things straight and solving problems under pressure? Do you get flustered if someone interrupts your work, or can you set it aside and come back to finish the job later?

As a rule, are you patient or impatient? When you're looking for a duplex to buy or a new tenant to live in it, can you take time to find the one that's exactly right? If you rush into purchasing property, you may end up with something in a neighborhood that's decaying. If you aren't careful about checking a prospect's background, you may find that you've given a one-year lease to a problem tenant. Both rash decisions will have a negative impact on your income.

Business Skills

Landlords need to be assertive when a tenant is late on a rent payment or breaks a provision in the lease or rental agreement. They have to make decisions based on common sense and good business practices. If you aren't getting rent because a tenant lost a job, you have to start eviction proceedings. Can you do that and can you do it diplomatically?

In evictions or any other tenant disputes, you have to stay calm and not lose your temper. A landlord should act professionally at all times and never argue or verbally attack the tenant. It takes focus and a sense of purpose. After all, you're pursuing what's rightfully yours—the rent.

If you are willing to learn, you'll be able to pick up all the skills necessary for running your business: advertising, marketing, maintenance, accounting, bookkeeping, and the legal skills that pertain to landlording.

That also means learning about the federal, state, and local regulations governing landlord-tenant relationships.

The bottom line is that if you aren't getting the rent, you lose two ways: the rental income and the money you're shelling out to pay your property bills. A landlord needs to be able to collect the past-due rent or find a new tenant who will pay on time, every month.

Handyman Skills

Landlords take on simple plumbing and electrical work, carpentry, and furnace and water heater maintenance. They know how to do small repairs and make the unit attractive to tenants. They handle all their own painting and cleaning to keep expenses low.

If you have to hire someone every time a toilet needs to be unplugged or a lock doesn't work properly, you'll be spending most of your rental income on repair services. If you don't know how to use a hammer and other tools, or get frustrated when you have to spend hours repainting and cleaning every time a tenant moves, you probably shouldn't become a landlord. If you don't have the time or really dislike these chores, can you afford to hire someone to do them, and for how long?

It's not necessary to have handyman experience before going into landlording, but it's essential that you're willing to learn how to become proficient in many different tasks. You can get simple instructions off the Internet, or in how-to-fix flyers, brochures, and books. You can always learn from experienced friends and relatives. If they do all their own work around the house, ask them if you can watch (or help) while they work so that you can learn how to do it, too.

Bookkeeping Skills

Ask yourself how much you enjoy paperwork. Some people handle numbers with the ease of an accountant; others hate balancing their checkbooks. Do you understand financing, interest rates, credit reports, bookkeeping, filling out and filing your business reports, and preparing income tax returns? Are you good at budgeting and putting money aside for taxes or do you tend to spend more than you should? In general, do you make good decisions about spending money?

FACT

Tenants move around a lot—one landlord says turnover occurs every year to eighteen months. The national average for length of stay is less than a year. With a parade of tenants moving in and out—which is hard on an apartment—you might find yourself thoroughly cleaning and painting it twice or more in a period of a few years.

Financial Stability

Look at your own finances and credit history. Do you have money set aside that can be used for emergencies? Are you able to get a short-term loan if you need one? Will you be able to cover expenses if the apartment stays vacant for a couple of months? Can you afford to hire someone to do the jobs that you don't have enough experience to do or don't want to do?

Why Landlords Fail

The most common reasons landlords fail are:

- They don't know how to run and manage a business.
- They didn't learn about it beforehand.
- They didn't stop to analyze whether income from their property would cover expenses.
- They purchased property in the wrong neighborhood or paid too much for it.
- They can only attract low-income tenants because of the location.
- Their tenants have to be evicted for nonpayment of rent and/or breaking terms of the lease.
- They won't take time to improve and maintain their property.
- They go overboard and spend too much on appliances, fixtures, cabinets, etc.

Can I Make Money?

The first few years of landlording are generally the hardest. Some landlords say it takes five to seven years for a rental property to create a healthy cash flow. You may do better than that if you put in extra hard work. Or perhaps there will be a poor economy when you start out, but then it will improve and rental rates will go way up. Landlording can be a risky business, but generally it's much more stable than the stock market. Just be patient.

If you purchase a small duplex at a good price and charge enough for rent, you'll have help in paying the mortgage. But there may be expenses that have to be paid out-of-pocket, especially if the previous owner neglected to keep up the property. To keep these expenses down and profits up, for the first few years concentrate on doing low-cost and no-cost improvements that will make the building and unit more desirable. Delay expensive repairs if you can. (Chapter 5 can help you decide which repairs are emergencies and which are okay to hold off on.)

Don't forget that the value of your property will increase as you improve it and pay off your loan. It will appreciate as the neighborhood improves. Your owner-occupied dwelling will be a valuable asset if you ever decide to purchase more rental properties or sell it to another landlord.

You also have to remember that finding the perfect tenant takes time. All the time you spend getting the apartment ready for a tenant, advertising, and checking into the backgrounds of those who look promising is downtime. The apartment is sitting vacant and you won't be getting any rent until someone moves in.

Generally it takes more than one rental unit for a duplex owner to produce income. But remember that you're getting help with the mortgage and building equity in the dwelling that you can later use to purchase a single-family home. And don't overlook the tax advantages you get when you own rental property. They'll help reduce your taxable income.

Renting Out Part of Your Home

If you add an apartment to your own home, you'll be in a better position to get income from your property—if you don't go overboard on expenditures and don't take out a huge high-interest loan.

Be careful as you plan the details of your renovation. Installing the best appliances and fixtures isn't necessary and it can have a negative impact on your income if you do put them in. Remember that if you tear out walls and ceilings, you pay for demolition as well as reconstruction. If you begin to tinker with the plumbing and electrical systems, you run the risk of creating new and costlier problems, especially in older homes. All of this can raise construction costs.

The other factor to consider in converting your home into a two-unit building is how you will finance the project. Will you take out a home improvement loan, borrow on the equity in your house, or use personal savings? How much you borrow and how quickly you replace it will affect income, too.

Tax Breaks

But there's more than one way to make money. As a landlord you'll have tax benefits that a homeowner doesn't get, especially once the mortgage is paid off. Capital improvements on rental property, such as putting on a new roof or rebuilding the front entrance, raise the value of your property. In addition, as a landlord you have tax breaks on your tax returns; take every one that you can.

Depreciate the cost of capital improvements (see Chapter 8). Deduct your expenses—the cost of running your business and repairing your property for such things as normal wear and tear. Keep track of mileage when you go for supplies. Record all your expenses, and at tax time, report them. Take all the deductions allowed. It will reduce your taxable income.

Gathering Resources

It takes the same resources to go into landlording as it does to buy or remodel any home. You need equity in a home or a down payment and closing costs. A good credit rating is essential because it affects your ability to get the loan. And lenders like to see that you have a savings account or other assets, such as stock, bonds, life insurance with a cash value, pension funds, and longevity on the job.

FACT

Sometimes you can avoid paying points on a new mortgage if you agree to a loan with a higher interest rate. That can reduce your upfront costs and distribute them over the length of the loan. But don't do it unless you know for sure you can collect enough rent each month to cover the mortgage and higher interest payments.

If you're going to buy property, you need to be able to spot good deals and price real estate realistically. If it's a fixer-upper, you need to assess whether it's structurally sound, how good the roof is, and what shape the windows are in.

You also need savings. This is essential so you can have a rainy day fund that can help pay for unforeseen expenses and to cover times when a vacant apartment is not pulling in rent.

You'll need business cards, a variety of rental forms, a second phone line that's dedicated exclusively to business, an answering machine, and a cell phone. Set up a home office. Do you have a computer and printer? Where will you store records and forms? Find a box or other place to store spare keys to the unit. You'll also need space for tools, spare parts, and cleaning and painting supplies and equipment.

Your resources should include books, magazines, newsletters, and Internet sources so you can keep building up your knowledge about landlording. Don't overlook the benefits of joining a professional organization, where you can tap into the wealth of information that the organization itself and its member landlords have. Professional organizations also offer seminars and meetings where you'll be able to learn more.

Setting Goals

Every business needs good business planning. Think strategically before you get started in landlording. What do you have to do immediately?

What has to be accomplished in the first year? And where would you like to be five years down the road? Put it down on paper.

Identify and prioritize your goals. For instance, which of the following goals are factors in your decision to become a landlord, and how important are they to you?

- Receiving extra income from the monthly yield off your property
- Building up equity to purchase the home of your dreams
- Making a long-term investment in the current rental property
- Using the equity from your first duplex to buy more property
- Building up your business so you can eventually be a full-time landlord

Think about the rental market you would like to target. Decide who your ideal tenants would be—for instance, students, young professionals, small families, Section 8 tenants, or empty nesters—and how you can attract them. You can't predict who will come to your door, but the amenities you offer, the apartment's location, where you choose to advertise your vacancy, and the cost of rent will have an effect on who decides to sign the lease. Think also about your long-term goals—do you eventually want to have better tenants? What will it take to get them?

QUESTION?

How can I learn more about landlording in my area?
Listen to landlords and real estate professionals. They'll have tips that come from long experience. Go to seminars and workshops for landlords, and join a professional association. Every community has its own unique personality. You'll learn what works with tenants in your area and what doesn't.

Write down three short-term goals. Then write down a half-dozen or so long-term goals. Look at them from time to time to remind yourself what you hope to accomplish and to find out whether you've achieved any of them. If you haven't, get yourself back on track.

How Do I Get Started?

Experts say you shouldn't buy the first property you like or jump into landlording without a great deal of thought and accumulated knowledge. But at some point, you have to make a decision. Establish a plan for finding property, financing it, fixing it up, selecting the right tenant, getting insurance, and collecting rent. And then go for it!

Buying Property

If you decide to buy property to rent out, give yourself a deadline—say six months to a year—to do so. Start looking at property immediately. You need to develop a keen eye for what you can get at various prices, and it will take time to recognize a good bargain. Meanwhile, keep educating yourself so that as you get near your deadline, you'll be ready to make a decision. Try not to procrastinate beyond that point or you might be doing so forever.

As you look at property, consider what has to be repaired, what has to be replaced, and what it will cost. Consider whether you can attract your "perfect" tenant to that neighborhood. Look at "Income property for sale or trade" ads. As you're driving through neighborhoods, watch for signs that say "For sale by owner." You might be able to make a better deal with an owner because you won't be paying any real estate commissions.

Adding an Apartment to Your Home

It's not easy to estimate what it will cost to renovate your home, but you might come close if you start out by getting prices on new construction, then add on a contingency factor for the extra work of putting things back together. You'll also have to factor in extra funds for unpredictable problems you might uncover once you start electrical work or plumbing.

To come up with an estimate of your renovation costs, find out what an electrician would charge to wire a new house of approximately the same square footage as the apartment you plan to create. Also ask a carpenter what it would cost to build that house. If you're adding a bathroom, find out what a plumber would charge to install one. Add up the prices, then add on a contingency factor for the unforeseeable extras that might run up the price.

Finding Extra Money

If you're short on money for fixing up your property, you can trade a newer car for an older, reliable model. You can use the equity in your home to get a loan. You can take out the cash value of a life insurance policy and reinsure yourself with a term life policy for the same amount of insurance as you had before. Term life premiums are not expensive and they don't tie up your savings. As a last resort, is someone in your family willing to back your venture? You won't know unless you ask.

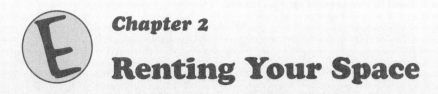

Chapter 2

Renting Your Space

Your house was great for raising kids. But they've got families of their own now and there's simply too much room. Now you're thinking about renovating your home into a two-unit dwelling. Then you can get a tenant and use the income from rent to supplement your retirement funds. In this chapter you'll find out what you should think about before you decide to take on a tenant and hire a contractor to convert your building.

Legal Considerations

If you want to renovate your home into an owner-occupied dwelling, you can't just go ahead and do it. There are a number of legal issues to be aware of before you begin.

Zoning and Building Codes

It's absolutely necessary for you to start at city hall. You need to go to the zoning department to find out if the zoning in your neighborhood permits multifamily use. If not, you have to apply for a zoning variance. In some communities, a variance will not be granted and you simply will not be allowed to have a tenant in a single-family zone.

City hall also can tell you what local building codes apply to owner-occupied buildings. Some communities have very stringent building and housing codes that tell landlords exactly what they can and can't do and how to do it. Others take a softer approach. They may have a few requirements that you have to meet.

Find out what your community stipulates in the building code. Does the code establish minimum square footage? Will you need a building permit if you make extensive renovations? Will the work be inspected, and if so, at what stages? Do you have to register your rental property or pay an annual licensing fee? Be sure you get all the details before spending time and money on big plans for renovation.

When you visit the building department, introduce yourself to the building inspector and explain what you want to do. In addition to knowing the building codes, he or she probably can give you a few tips about doing the project.

Fair Housing Laws

The federal government has set up fair housing laws to protect tenants. Many states and communities have defined their own fair housing regulations and enforce them more stringently. (See Chapter 4.)

However, as the owner of an owner-occupied dwelling you do not have to follow the fair housing laws. If you don't want to rent to someone in a protected category, that's your choice. You also can have a smoke-free apartment. But you still may want to check with the state and visit city hall, the county, or your township or village offices before you start to advertise. Find out what they have to say about advertising for and finding a tenant.

Your Right to Enter

Once your tenant signs the lease or rental agreement and moves in, the apartment belongs to him or her. Even though you retain a separate key, you have no right to enter without the tenant's permission. Whether you want to make repairs, do routine maintenance, or show the apartment to prospective tenants because yours is moving out, you have to clear it with your current tenant in advance. It's a good idea, therefore, to include a phrase in your lease or rental agreement that the landlord has the right to enter—after giving notice—for routine maintenance and repairs and when there is an emergency

ALERT!

Be aware that the terms "rental agreement" and "lease" are not synonymous. Although they both spell out rental terms between a landlord and a tenant, they have some important differences. You'll learn what these differences are in Chapter 14.

Abandoned Property

When tenants are evicted, they often leave things behind. Find out what your community's code says about abandoned property. You need to know what you can do about possessions left behind and exactly how much time you have to give tenants to collect their belongings before you throw anything out. These rules will vary in each community.

Other Things to Consider

Once you've got all the legal basics covered and have decided you can handle the demands of landlording, you have other kinds of rental space–related decisions to make before your tenant moves in.

Terms of the Lease or Rental Agreement

Since you will be potentially sharing part of the building you live in with tenants, you need to think carefully about what you will and will not allow. Consider the following questions in advance, and include the appropriate stipulations when you draw up your lease or rental agreement.

- Are pets allowed?
- Who will supply appliances?
- Are laundry facilities included?
- Who pays for garbage pickup?
- Is smoking allowed?
- Who will shovel snow?
- Will you allow satellite dishes and other technical devices such as a DSL line for Internet?
- What utilities are included?

The best way to find out what the project will cost is to make a detailed plan, shop around for competitive prices on supplies and materials, and get quotes from at least three licensed builders and other professionals. Put a budget together and go from there.

Are Licensed Professionals Required?

If you're doing extensive remodeling, you may need to find licensed builders, plumbers, and electricians to do the work. If so, will you hire them yourself or do you plan to have a builder or general contractor in charge? General contractors usually have licensed plumbers and electricians that they work with. But you'll probably save money if you do most of the remodeling yourself and hire your own licensed professionals, because then you won't have to pay the contractor's fee.

Will Rent Cover Your Extra Expenses?

You have probably thought about how much you'd like to realize each month in rent. But have you also thought about the extra expenses that you'll have to pay? You'll have extra insurance premiums, interest on any money you borrow, and times when you're not collecting money because the unit is empty. You may have to pay higher utility bills. There will be repairs, legal and accounting fees, advertising, and other out-of-pocket expenses to pay.

Will the rent you charge cover those extras? The only way to find out is to estimate the costs, figure out how much income you'd like each month, and calculate how much rent you'd have to charge to cover costs and have income left over. Then look at some classified ads or speak with a realtor. Is the amount you came up with a realistic figure for rentals in your neighborhood? Once you have a list of expenses and an ideal rental price in mind, your first task is to set up a working budget. It will help keep you on track.

Finding the Extra Space

The next thing to consider is how you can carve an apartment out of the unneeded space in your home. With some houses, it's fairly obvious. In a two-story home, the apartment can be upstairs. In a ranch-style house built on a slope, the full basement can be converted into an apartment. It's particularly easy if your basement floor is at ground level and you can walk straight out into the backyard.

In large Victorian homes, there is usually one staircase near the front door and narrow back stairs off the kitchen. Either stairway could be used as access to an upstairs apartment. All you'd have to do is partition off the hallways with drywall and doors. If you have a trilevel house, a cozy apartment can replace what you formerly used as a family room and office. All you need to do is figure out where to construct an outside entrance.

You might even split your house in half down the middle, having an apartment in front and another in back, or one on the left and one on the right. Then both you and your tenant could have bedrooms upstairs. If your garage once was a stable with a high loft area, it can be converted into an apartment—if zoning in your community permits that use. If your home sits on a huge lot, adding on to your house might be the best solution. The possibilities are endless and a good builder or architect might have other ideas.

Where's the Kitchen?

Occasionally a house was built with two kitchens, but this is rare, and your tenants won't want to cook on a hot plate. So where should the kitchen go? If you plan to purchase a gas stove, the least expensive choice is to put the new kitchen above, below, or near yours so it will be close to the gas line. Same with the kitchen sink—you want it to be close to the water pipes.

If you are going to provide an electric range, you'll probably have to hire a licensed electrician to add a 240-volt line. Ask the electrician whether the new line will also be able to handle a microwave and an air conditioner or if a second line will be necessary.

Remodeling or Adding a Bathroom

Does the space you're remodeling have a half bath? If so, enlarging the space so you can add a shower or tub should be fairly easy. You can put up a couple of new walls, tap into existing plumbing, and let water flow into the existing drain.

Starting from scratch will be more expensive; this involves putting in all new water lines, sanitary and drain pipes, a ceiling vent or fan (required by many local building codes), electrical wiring, bathroom fixtures, lighting, a cabinet and mirror, towel rods, a door, and a shower door or tub enclosure. If the space requires a whole new bathroom, you should also consider adding a separate water heater and separate meters for water and electricity. Then if your tenant likes long hot showers, you won't have to pay for them.

Find out what your local building code requires for bathroom remodeling or additions. Some codes stipulate that you must hire a licensed plumber. Also find out whether the bathroom will have to be inspected. Will there be an inspection fee?

Moving Walls

Will the space you want to rent have to be reconfigured? Will you have to tear down and rebuild walls? Widen doors and a hallway? Put in some closets? What does your local building code say about exits? Some communities require landlords to provide two separate means of egress (exit). How much will it cost to buy lumber and drywall? Do you know how to do the work yourself or will you have to hire a carpenter or builder? Keep in mind that any extensive work may require that you get a permit from the building department at city hall.

Wiring

If you have an older home, is the wiring sufficient to handle today's demands? A hundred years ago one outlet per bedroom was not uncommon, but if those bedrooms are converted into a living area or kitchen, it's definitely not enough. Tenants today come with lamps, TVs, DVD players, VCRs, stereos, computers, printers, electronic video games—the list goes on and on.

Today's tenants also want access to cable TV. If you don't provide cable, don't be surprised if your tenant asks to put up a satellite dish. Many of them today are twenty-four inches or less in diameter and are unlikely to cause any damage to the structure.

You can't snake multiple extension cords into the sole outlet in each room. Even if the tenant wouldn't mind, your local building code probably won't allow it. The code also may require that you hire a licensed electrician to do any rewiring.

It may be in your best interest to rewire your home anyway, however, since your tenant may be apt to overload existing electrical outlets, and that could cause temporary blackouts or, in extreme cases, a fire. Your other option is to consider restrictions on such things as window air conditioning units and additional freezers. Restrictions should also be considered when there's only one electricity meter and you are paying the bill for the whole house.

Utilities

Gas, electricity, water, sewer, and garbage disposal are becoming major household expenses. In some parts of the country, fresh water is scarce. In others, prices for natural gas may be much higher than average.

What happens when your demand for utilities goes up because your dwelling now has two households? Is it practical to add a second water heater and meter? And what about electricity and gas when there's only one furnace and all the power flows through one electricity meter? If you can't separate utilities, figure out how much you will have to add to the monthly rent to cover your tenant's usage.

What are my responsibilities for heating the apartment?
As a landlord you may be required to provide a minimum level of heat in cold weather to comply with state or local housing codes. Most tenants will be comfortable if you keep the thermostat set at seventy degrees.

Laundry Facilities

Will you provide access to laundry facilities—either by letting tenants use your washer and dryer or by installing coin-operated appliances for laundry? Laundry privileges are a nice touch and one that tenants appreciate. But you must decide whether it's worth the expense and calculate the wear and tear on your appliances. Perhaps your tenant would be willing to pay a surcharge each month for laundry privileges. At $10 a month, you'll have $120 more in your pocket.

You also need to figure out what the guidelines will be for when and how the laundry area can be used. What hours and days would work best with your own schedule, and will you permit tenants to dye or dry-clean fabric?

If you have to buy new appliances to make laundry privileges an amenity, be sure to buy a brand that's not too expensive. Cheaper appliances do the job just as well as the expensive ones. The only difference is that they don't have all the bells and whistles.

Maintaining Your Privacy

Two families living under one roof: they're neighbors, acquaintances, and landlord-tenant. Tenants don't want someone always watching over them and you don't want them to feel so cozy that they'll say, "Gee, I'm a little short of money this month. Can I give you the rent in two weeks?"

If you have to remodel your home, find a way to let your tenants have a separate entrance. It will help each of you keep a little distance in the relationship. Tenants would rather not go through shared space, whether it's an empty hallway with several closed doors or your own front door. When they unlock their apartment, they want to go directly into their own space. It increases their sense of security.

With separate entrances you can more easily maintain your business identity. Separate doors cut down on chance meetings and idle chitchat that might mislead your tenant into thinking of you as a friend. You are not your tenant's friend—keep your relationship as businesslike as possible.

ALERT!

The biggest mistake landlords make is to become friends with their tenants. Maintain a business relationship at all times so you don't confuse your tenants by being a landlord one time and a friend another. If they think you are a friend, they may be more apt to take advantage of you.

Will You Be Happy Sharing Space?

Any way you look at it, when you have a tenant in an owner-occupied dwelling you're inviting a person to share your home. You can make sure a prospective tenant has a good credit history, stable employment background, and solid references. But people have different lifestyles and habits and you'll have to adapt to that.

What can you do to protect your peace and quiet and avoid small irritations that might escalate into something bigger? Don't worry. First of all, most people looking for an apartment feel the same as you do. If they think a lifestyle involving sharing walls with a landlord might cause problems, they'll opt not to rent.

But no matter who wants to rent from you, the best way both of you can avoid stepping on toes is to have the tenant sign a very detailed lease agreement. You want it to clearly state your expectations—how much noise you'll tolerate from tenants, whether they can throw parties, or if they can work on their car in the backyard.

It's up to you to figure out exactly what habits and behaviors you can tolerate and what will drive you round the bend—*before* applicants come knocking. You'll get more information about using leases and rental agreements for stipulating acceptable and unacceptable behaviors in Chapter 14.

Dealing with Difficult Tenants

Some landlords never have to face the hard fact that sometimes tenants can cause problems and their leases have to be terminated or they have to be evicted. Dealing with difficult tenants is bad enough. Having to take them to court to get rid of them or collect unpaid rent or damages is even more unpleasant. It costs money to hire a lawyer and go to court. Cleaning up after unruly tenants costs, too—your time and your money.

FACT

A landlord with one apartment in an owner-occupied building is exempt from nondiscrimination laws. That means if you do not want to rent to someone in a protected category, you don't have to offer a lease. But you should still be careful about what you put in ads and say to people hunting for an apartment. Find out what the nondiscrimination laws pertaining to advertising say before you place your first vacancy notice in the paper.

But the largest toll can be taken by your reaction to these aggravating situations. Are you strong enough to handle evictions? Can you distance yourself and think of the eviction only as an unpleasant, but necessary, side of being in business? If you think it's not possible to keep yourself from getting involved emotionally, perhaps you should think twice about becoming a landlord.

What to Do if You're Not Sure

Once you start meeting potential tenants, you may find yourself unsure about a particular applicant. Even though he or she appears to have good credentials, a good job, and the ability to pay rent on time every month, you may hesitate to offer a lease. When you're not sure a tenant will work out, it might be intuition telling you not to lock yourself into a lease that will be in force for a full year. You can structure the term of a rental agreement any way you want it. Rather than a full year-long or even six-month lease, offer a month-to-month rental agreement instead.

If you let the applicant move in on a month-to-month basis, neither of you will be obligated if things don't work out. If anything is bothering you, just tell them that their tenancy expires at the end of the month. You have to give thirty days' notice, but you don't have to offer any explanation on a month-to-month agreement. And if things work out well with the tenant and it turns out that you worried about nothing, you can always offer the fixed-term lease after he or she has been there a while. Better to be cautious rather than sorry.

Chapter 3

Buying a Space to Rent

If you're just starting out, it makes a lot of sense to purchase rental property. Tenants help pay the mortgage while you build equity in a home. Starting a landlording business also makes sense as a long-term investment when wages are stagnant, jobs aren't secure, you need more cash to support a family, and it's harder to save for retirement. In this chapter you'll learn where to look for your first property, and how to find a great deal.

Selecting a Rental Property

As values of single-family homes escalate, so do down payments and the monthly mortgage payment required to buy those homes. If you're yearning to get into owning property, but feel you can't quite swing a house, buying a duplex might be your answer. With a duplex, you can live in one unit and rent the other to a tenant.

By living in a duplex, you eliminate your own rental payments and have help purchasing your property. Your tenant helps you pay the mortgage, which allows you to build equity much more quickly. Then when it's feasible, you can use that equity to buy a single-family home for yourself.

Having a duplex is a simple way to start a part-time small business as a landlord. If you find the landlording business satisfying, when you're ready to move out you can get a second tenant for your space. You'll also have the option of selling the duplex, which will have appreciated during your ownership, and using the money for your new home or to purchase a multiunit rental property.

Duplexes are commonly scattered throughout every community, many of them on the edges of single-family neighborhoods. These duplexes are more affordable than the neighboring single-family homes, especially if you get a good deal. Look for a duplex that:

- Is a fixer-upper needing minimal repairs
- Needs to be painted and cleaned
- Is not too large
- Has separate utilities
- Is located in a thriving neighborhood and community
- Is structurally sound
- Will bring in sufficient income
- Has a land contract
- Can be resold easily

Start Big or Start Small?

All first-time landlords have a learning curve and it's easy to make mistakes during this period. Since it takes more skill to manage a multiunit building, buying that type of structure gives you more opportunities to make errors. In addition, managing multiple units is a full-time job, not something that can be handled after a regular workday. The potential for you to burn out and give up will be greater if you try to take on too much.

So if you're thinking of landlording in your spare time, get a small duplex to start off. It will be easier to learn the skills you need, and you'll also have an opportunity to build tenant relationships gradually, one tenant at a time.

FACT

If the duplex has separate utilities so that your tenant pays his or her own bills, the rent you collect can help you pay off your mortgage and set aside money for repairs. Your tenants will have to deal with the cost of using too much water or setting the thermostat too high and for routine utility cost increases.

Large buildings also cost more and require more money for maintenance and repairs. Most small duplexes are very affordable when you're just starting out, and you can find one easily because there are more of them on the market than larger multifamily buildings.

After you've mastered the learning curve, then you can go out and purchase a building that has six or eight units. When managing that becomes easy, then you can tackle something even larger if that's what you want.

How to Determine a Property's Value

For your purposes a property's value is not determined by the owner's asking price or the assessed valuation. You want to find a low-priced building in a good neighborhood or a neighborhood that's on its way up. Avoid properties needing extensive repairs unless you can do all the work yourself and have an inside track for getting good discounts on materials.

You want property that will appreciate (become more valuable) after you've fixed it up so that you can sell it at a profit later. As mentioned previously, be careful to judge the neighborhood carefully. If houses are abandoned, boarded up, or decaying through lack of care and if yards are littered with junk, it tells you that no one is willing to invest in the area. So even if you get your building into tiptop shape, you'll have difficulty finding a buyer, let alone a good tenant.

Finding the Right Location

Some neighborhoods are too expensive for first-time buyers. You may get more rent for your unit, but expenses will be higher, too, including the down payment, closing costs, mortgage, and taxes. A deteriorating neighborhood where the value of housing is depreciating is costly, too. Although prices will be affordable for getting started, you'll have a hard time attracting good tenants and the property will be difficult to resell.

Once you find a likely duplex, check the zoning. Will there be noise problems because of traffic or airplanes? Are the gutters, curbs, and streets in good condition, and does the area in general seem to be free of crime? Is the property near a river that occasionally floods? These are all things to consider when you're thinking about getting rental property.

Housing and Areas to Avoid

Avoid abandoned duplexes with a lot of structural damage, boarded-up or missing windows, damaged ceilings, floors, and walls, and vandalized plumbing and wiring. Look for, and stay away from, rotted wood. What kind of condition are the roof and the siding in? Watch for areas where water may be seeping through and causing mildew problems.

Don't buy property in neighborhoods where yards are filled with junked cars and trash. Take a good look at the other houses—are they rundown or cared for? Is the city or community itself viable or are young people moving out in droves to find jobs elsewhere? Drive around the neighborhood at different times during the day to find out what's going on after school and at night. Can you spot a lot of suspicious-looking activity on the street and gangs of teens just hanging around? If you don't think you would feel comfortable living in a certain neighborhood, chances are your ideal tenant wouldn't either.

Where to Search

Look for good buys in stable neighborhoods or neighborhoods coming back after years of neglect. How can you tell if a neighborhood is getting better? Watch for signs that young adults and young families are moving into the area and fixing up homes. You'll see recently improved homes and yards intermingled with rundown property. The low prices of those neglected homes are attractive to young, energetic couples.

Are owners fixing up their property by painting, cleaning up yards, and putting in new landscaping? It's infectious. Their improvements and yours will spur others in the neighborhood to fix up their property. As homes in the neighborhood improve, so will property values.

ALERT!

While a neighborhood is in transition, homes sell for less money and that makes them more affordable because of lower mortgage payments. Be certain, however, that the neighborhood is on the upswing and not going the other way. Get a report from the Chamber of Commerce. It will tell you about local businesses, industry, and jobs.

Considering Repair Costs

Is the building you're considering structurally sound? Take a close look at the roof. Does it sag or is it curling along the edges? A roof might sag because the rafters are too small. The shingles might be curling because they're old and need to be replaced. Always look for water stains on the ceilings and walls. Find out how old the roof is, how many layers of shingles it has, and how soon it will have to be replaced. It costs upward of $5,000 to take off old shingles and put on new. Replacing a roof on a Victorian home might cost upward of $20,000.

There are many potential problems to be aware of when it comes to floors, as well. When you check out the floors, make sure they are level. If floors are sagging or bouncy, the floor joists may be too small for the span. There may be bearing walls without adequate support. And there might be problems with the foundation on which the building rests.

Look at the plumbing and wiring. If they are in bad shape, it will be a big expense to redo them. How are the windows? Are they hard to open and close, are they drafty? Again, replacing windows is very expensive. Take the cost into consideration.

You might have to pay for large repairs such as roofing out-of-pocket because the bank that gave you a mortgage might shy away from giving you another loan, especially when you haven't built up equity in the property. And if you don't realize any income from the property during that first fix-up year, can your budget handle all of the expenses?

Also find out whether the title on the property is clear or if there are any outstanding taxes or liens that have to be paid to clear it. Contractors place liens on property when they haven't been paid for their work.

When setting rent, keep in mind that the unit has to bring in enough income that you can make the mortgage payment and also set aside some money each month to pay for property taxes and repairs. If the rent just barely covers your monthly expenses, you may have trouble finding the cash for semiannual and annual bills.

Finding Great Deals

If you take your time, talk to a lot of people, and are patient, you'll eventually find a deal that's just right for you. At this point, focus on the particulars of the deal, not the property, even though you're sure a particular building is "meant for you." When you talk to owners, try to maintain a take-it-or-leave-it attitude. You don't want to look eager because then the owner might not come down on the price quite as much.

Buying from the Owner

Landlords who want to retire from the business may give you a good deal on vacant dwellings they own that need work, especially if they don't want to spend the time or money to fix them up. Some will accept a land contract that gives them a regular monthly income—your payments—on their property. (See below for more information on the benefits of land contracts and how they work.)

Working with an Agent

If the property is sold through a real estate agent, be sure you are getting the best deal. Did the owner and agent inflate the asking price? Find out what other duplexes in the neighborhood are selling for. If those prices are much lower and the owner you're talking to won't come down, find another duplex that has a more realistic price.

Handyman Specials

If you get a handyman special (also known as a fixer-upper), figure out what you'll need to do the work and how long it will take you, and then shop around for best prices for materials and supplies. If you plan to hire skilled workers, such as a plumber, an electrician, or a carpenter, get at least three quotes from licensed professionals. If all these costs plus the asking price add up to less than the cost of similar properties in the area, you've found yourself a good deal.

If you are unable to do the work yourself, it would be better to buy property that needs only minimal repairs. The added bonus for buying something that only needs some cleaning up and painting is that you can get a tenant more quickly and then have immediate help paying for the mortgage, taxes, and monthly bills.

Fire-Damaged Property

Sometimes a building that's had a fire can be a good deal for a person who is handy around the house. The owners have collected insurance money and if they don't want to bother with fixing up the house, they might be willing to sell it for less so they can just move on and get a new house. You can always ask the owner. But before you do, make sure that you can handle the repairs and that the price is low enough to make it worth the time and money you'll have to put into fixing it up.

If you don't have the skills or time to repair major structural damage or install the new furnace, roof, or siding yourself, do you have money available to hire skilled workers? That can be expensive if you're on a tight budget.

Bank Foreclosures

Sometimes when banks want to get rid of property they've accumulated through foreclosures, they're willing to make a deal. They might waive closing points, the appraisal, and possibly even inspections. Perhaps you can get generous financing terms. You might enlist the help of a real estate agent or two to find foreclosures, or a landlord you know might hear of one. Keep your ears open. Also read the legal notices in the large general-circulation newspaper in your area.

Auctions

Auctions also must be advertised in a large-circulation newspaper or a local legal publication. They are generally held at the county courthouse or office building. The notice will state a minimum price at which bidding will start, based on the dollars owed for unpaid taxes and other accumulated expenses. The property is then sold as-is to the highest bidder, who generally has to pay for the property with cash or a cashier's check. (The rules vary in each state or county.)

ALERT!

If you buy property at an auction, you still might not get the property if the owner comes in and pays the taxes owed before the sale. You should also realize that creditors can add a lien on the property after the auction takes place. Unless they are federal or state liens, they generally are removed when you get the tax deed. Ask your county about the rules governing auctions.

Estates

You can often get great deals on property that has to be liquidated quickly, such as when a couple gets a divorce and wants to divide assets as quickly as possible. Sometimes heirs to an estate want their share of the property right away and ask the executor to sell it immediately. Write to people who own or are handling an estate and say you're interested in helping them sell the property. You might be surprised at the interest they show. When you purchase estate property, you pay any taxes owed, plus interest, penalties, legal fees, court and title costs, and any other fees that have accumulated. Sometimes the deceased party accumulated state liens for unpaid taxes, so be sure to take this into account.

Rural and Farm Communities

Look beyond the city and suburbs for property. Property taxes in small towns and rural areas are usually lower and property is not as expensive as what you'll find in or near town. Some people want to live "in the country" and are willing to commute to work. But make sure you find a community that is viable enough to appeal to commuters. If Main Street has too many boarded-up stores and too few pedestrians, it may not be a good idea to purchase property there.

HUD Sales

The Department of Housing and Urban Development (HUD) will sell a house if the owner has defaulted on a loan through an FHA (Federal Housing Authority)-approved bank. When that happens, the government pays off the bank and the property reverts back to the government agency. To sell these properties, HUD sets a minimum price and the house goes to highest bidder.

HUD has its own rules for such things as closing costs, down payments, transfer taxes and recording fees, and using a real estate agent to handle everything. Usually the property offered will have been vacant for some time and needs a lot of work. If you can do the work yourself and meet the qualifications, you can often get a very good deal this way.

Get the Word Out

While you're looking for a good deal on property, let people know you're looking. Some landlords run ads and hand out flyers stating that they are looking to purchase rental property. They tell neighbors and friends. And eventually a tip comes along that yields a good deal. Figure out how to make friends in the local real estate community and establish your own network for leads.

FACT

When you want to purchase a duplex on a land contract, offer the owner the full asking price. You can do your negotiating to determine the interest rate and term of the contract. But if you aren't willing to pay the asking price, the property owner will just walk away and look for another buyer.

What to Ask For

Once you start looking around for starter property, you'll find that there are more possibilities than you once would have thought. You can find the best deal by doing your research on the neighborhood and asking questions. When you find property you're interested in buying and are ready to make an offer, find out the answers to three key questions:

- Can the property be purchased on a land contract?
- Will the seller take no or low money down?
- Will the seller take a discount for obvious necessary repairs?

Negotiating a Land Contract Sale

When you find a suitable dwelling, ask the owner to consider a land contract purchase—also called a contract for deed, installment plan, or conditional sales contract. If you can get a land contract, you don't have to go to the bank for a mortgage or pay closing costs or points. With a land contract, the owner retains the title to the property and essentially finances your purchase for a predetermined number of years. Your monthly payments, at the mutually agreed interest rate, go directly to the owner. When you've made all the payments, you get title to the property. To negotiate a land contract, you and the owner have to agree on the rate of interest and length of the seller's loan. Some sellers will also ask for a small down payment.

Land contracts are a good way to buy income property, often with no money down. And you bypass the necessity of getting a loan from the bank, and paying closing costs and real estate fees. The important thing is to make certain you'll get enough income from the property to pay for the expenses and the mortgage, plus cover any time that the unit is unoccupied and not bringing in rent.

If the property can be purchased on a land contract, go ahead and negotiate with the owner on the interest and the length of the loan and try to reduce or eliminate the down payment. Often an owner is willing to forgo that money and simply collect the monthly payments. The price itself, however, is not negotiable. Always offer the advertised or listed price when entering into a land contract.

Making an Offer on a Handyman Special

If you want to purchase a fixer-upper, don't offer the asking price. It usually is more than the owner expects to get and includes a commission. If the sale is being handled by a real estate agent, some landlords say you should offer no more than sixty percent of the asking price, others say seventy-five percent.

FACT

If a real estate agent is involved, always start with a very low bid. You can negotiate by going higher, but decide in advance how much you want to spend. Your research on housing and the neighborhood will tell you where to set your limit. Keep it in mind while you are negotiating for the property.

If it's obvious that the dwelling needs immediate work, such as putting on a new roof or installing a new furnace, ask if the seller will give you a discount on the purchase price. Sometimes owners will make a deal because they want to get the property off their hands as quickly as possible and not worry about scheduling repairs.

Just make sure the purchase price is low enough that you'll have money to spare for materials and supplies. If there is structural damage, be sure you can do the work yourself. Figure out what materials you'll need, and get cost estimates before you finalize the sale. Add those numbers to the purchase price. If everything adds up to less than what similar properties in good condition are selling for in the neighborhood, then you know you've found yourself a deal. Make your offer and get to work.

Can You Do It on a Shoestring?

There are several ways to find rental housing that doesn't require a lot of upfront cash, especially when you buy a small two-unit dwelling. It takes patience to find such properties, however, and a willingness to walk away from negotiations if you can't get exactly the deal that you want.

Start out by carefully reading the classified ads every day, looking for income property sold by the owner. Drive around neighborhoods that once were depressed but are now picking up. Look for signs that say, "For Sale by Owner."

Get to know other landlords by joining a rental property owners association. They might know a landlord who wants to sell some smaller properties; perhaps the people you meet are thinking of selling some of their own property.

Occasionally if an owner has not held a property for long and has not built up equity, you might be able to assume the loan after making a low down payment to the owner. If you have access to money, try making a cash offer at sixty or seventy percent of the value of the property. Sometimes owners are eager to sell and willing to get out for ready cash.

The keys to starting out on a shoestring are to:

- Negotiate with the owner—find out if he or she is willing to make a deal.
- Never purchase a property at the full asking price unless it's on a land contract.

- Be willing to walk away from a property—even if you love it—if the owner won't budge.

When to Pull In Experts

You can do a lot for yourself as a potential income property owner, but there will be times when it is to your advantage to pull in experts. You may need help finding the right property, and a real estate agent has access to most of them. You also might be able to find someone in the loan department of a bank or an insurer who has information about what's coming onto the market. You may also find yourself needing advice or assistance from other professionals, such as lawyers and insurance agents. Don't fail to ask your contacts to let you know if they hear of anything that might be up for sale in the near future.

Real Estate Agent

Real estate agents have access to computerized listings in your area and some will be willing to spend time on less expensive properties even though they know up front that their commission will be lower. If you can find a couple of agents willing to work with you, ask them to be on the lookout for property that has potential as a rental.

One of the best things you can do for yourself when you're entering the landlording business is find an experienced landlord willing to give you advice and guidance. The person you choose as your mentor will be flattered to help you out. Best of all, it won't cost you anything except, perhaps, a few business lunches.

Real Estate Lawyer

Anytime you're negotiating a land contract and don't have a real estate agent working for you, you'd be wise to have your lawyer look at the contract before you sign it. He or she can spot wording or conditions that might cause problems down the line, and can help you get ownership that is unquestionably legal. Lawyers also can search for liens filed on the property; if there are any, the property is not free and clear. And a lawyer can find out whether the property owner has any pending court cases or previous bankruptcies, or if he or she repossessed the dwelling on a previous land contract.

Title Company Representative

The best way to find out if the owner has a clear title to the property you've agreed to purchase is to have a title company search the records. If you're dealing with a mortgage company, you won't have an option; they'll require it. But it's money well spent. You don't want to find out later that an heir or prior owner has a claim on the house you thought was yours.

Appraiser

The best way to find out exactly what a property is worth is to have it valued by an appraiser. Again, if you're going to have a conventional mortgage, that will be a requirement. Otherwise, you can hire one on your own.

Insurance Agent

A good insurance agent will help you find affordable insurance policies, keep you abreast of premium increases, and answer your questions about riders and changes in insurance coverage. You need to find out such things as whether a separate policy for flood insurance is required, whether you need additional liability coverage in your area, and whether your policy includes full replacement costs.

Chapter 4

Laws, Codes, and Permits

Before you decide to rent space in your house or buy rental property, you should find out about the federal, state, and local laws that pertain to landlording. Each level of government prohibits discrimination and requires landlords to provide units that are safe and habitable. In this chapter you'll get an overview of government regulations, landlord-tenant relationships, how to avoid discrimination complaints, and where you can go for more information.

Federal Fair Housing Laws

Title VIII of the Civil Rights Act of 1968, also known as the Fair Housing Act, prohibits discrimination in housing. Enforced by the Department of Housing and Urban Development (HUD), these laws protect minorities living in the United States from being excluded from housing. The Fair Housing Act and 1988 Amendments, as well as the Americans with Disabilities Act of 1990, further define protected categories.

The landlord of an owner-occupied dwelling with four or fewer units is exempt from the federal Fair Housing Acts, but may be included in state or local laws prohibiting discrimination. Your best bet as a landlord is to understand the laws governing landlords and tenants and follow the intent of the legislation. That's the best way to avoid the headache of having to answer a discrimination complaint filed by someone looking for an apartment or by one of your tenants. The Fair Housing Acts prohibit discrimination based upon:

> race
> color
> religion
> national origin
> family status (includes those with children under eighteen, pregnant women, and the elderly)
> disability or handicap
> sex
> sexual orientation

Based upon the above-listed protections, discriminatory practices by landlords are prohibited by the legislation and can include:

- Advertising or saying anything that indicates preferences or limits housing opportunities to exclude those in protected categories. (This applies to all landlords no matter how many units they have.)
- Falsely stating that the unit is rented
- Setting restrictive standards in selecting tenants
- Refusing to rent to members of a protected group

- Setting different terms, conditions, or privileges before or during a tenancy
- Inconsistency in treatment of tenants, such as requiring some to pay larger deposits
- Inconsistency about late payments
- Terminating a lease for discriminatory reasons

Federal Laws Protecting the Disabled

The Americans with Disabilities Act of 1990 includes protections for people with physical, mental, hearing, visual, and other sensory disabilities. It also protects people with certain medical conditions (such as HIV-positive status or asthma), recovering alcoholics, and former drug users. Although the Act pertains mostly to owners of multiunit buildings, other landlords may be affected.

FACT

If you have a visually impaired tenant and want to give him or her anything in writing, you must first read it aloud so that he or she understands what you are trying to communicate. It is not up to the impaired tenant to find out what the document contains.

If you are renting an apartment to a person in a wheelchair, you may have to provide a spacious parking place that's located near the unit. Guide dogs for visually impaired tenants must be allowed, even if your policy is to allow no pets. Hearing-impaired tenants also must be allowed to have dogs that alert them to doorbells, ringing phones, and fire sirens. And some people with psychological problems such as depression or anxiety disorders are beginning to ask landlords to allow their pets because the animal provides emotional support.

Landlords may also be required to let a tenant modify the unit so that it meets his or her specific needs. Someone in a wheelchair may want countertops that are lower than standard height or want to build a ramp to the entrance. If opening doors and turning on faucets is a problem, then you should allow the tenant to change the existing knobs to a more manageable fixture. Tenants should always get your approval first. If modifications would not be acceptable to another tenant, then the tenant must restore the unit to its original condition when he or she moves out.

Exemptions for Owner-Occupied Property

Landlords who have owner-occupied dwellings are generally exempt from the federal fair housing standards and can reject applicants in protected categories. Other properties exempted in the federal Acts include single-family houses rented without using discriminatory advertising and without the help of a real estate broker, housing operated by a religious group or private club (which can be restricted to members), and housing that exclusively serves senior citizens, sixty-two or older, if all occupants are seniors. (There also is a fifty-five-and-older housing exemption; at least eighty percent of the units must be occupied by at least one person who is fifty-five or older.)

ALERT!

Keep in mind that all landlords must follow HUD's nondiscriminatory advertising guidelines, and your state and local government may have fair housing codes that apply to small property owners. It is essential that new landlords understand the fair housing laws in their state and community to avoid violating those housing codes.

Discrimination Complaints

People can file complaints with HUD or with state or local housing authorities if they suspect a landlord has discriminated against them. A complaint filed with federal and state fair housing agencies typically is investigated. If the complaint is not dismissed, the agency will try to have both parties reach a compromise. If an agreement to compromise fails, then an administrative hearing is held before a judge.

Tenants and prospective tenants also can sue landlords in a federal or state court. Landlords determined guilty of discrimination, either in an administrative hearing or in a state or federal court, may be subject to penalties.

Penalties for Discrimination

The courts can order a landlord to rent a particular unit to the tenant or pay the tenant for damages. Damages include rent paid by the applicant for another apartment after tenancy was denied, damages for humiliation and emotional distress, and punitive damages and costs for the plaintiff's attorney. If the person is disabled, a landlord may be ordered to renovate the unit to accommodate disabled tenants or to set up an escrow fund so that future improvements can be made.

Landlords also can be ordered to pay a civil penalty to the federal government—currently more than $10,000 for a first violation. For three violations within seven years, the penalty would be more than $50,000. Some states also invoke penalties.

FACT

If a party files a discrimination complaint or sues in federal or state court, some landlords do their own legal research, others get a lawyer. A complaint before HUD can go on for up to ten years before it is resolved.

State and Local Laws and Regulations

Before you buy income property, you should find out what legislation your state has enacted in regard to rentals and landlording, because they might prohibit exemptions given to small landlords in the federal Fair Housing Acts. Similarly, you need to know what local authorities require. Put this task high on the list of things you have to do.

States have rules governing landlord-tenant relationships, fair housing, landlord responsibilities and rights, and a tenant's responsibilities and rights. They also have a strong voice on health and safety laws governing rental property.

Fair Housing

When it comes to fair housing protections and nondiscrimination, many states have clauses that mirror the federal legislation, but also add age and marital status to the list. For fair housing regulations, call your state fair housing agency or go to the Web site maintained by the National Fair Housing Advocate Online (✍ *www.fairhousing.com*). Your state's consumer protection agency also can provide information about landlord/tenant relationships. Local and county codes also address discrimination and may be more stringent than the federal and state legislation. They may prohibit discrimination based upon age and divorce as a category of the family status protections.

Health and Safety Standards

Local housing codes and zoning ordinances establish health and safety standards for tenants. Zoning determines which uses are permitted in particular neighborhoods in the community. Building codes address structural issues—roofing, flooring, egress (exits), and minimum window size. They may prohibit renting a unit if the windows are boarded up or blocked.

States also protect the health and safety of tenants, using an "implied warranty of habitability" standard. Housing regulations vary from state to state, so it is essential that you know what your state requires. For a list of all the state agencies, go to the Federal Consumer Information Center. (See Appendix A.)

ALERT!

Always start with local housing codes and zoning ordinances because they may be more stringent than state and HUD guidelines. Sometimes the requirements may seem contradictory, but try to get a good understanding of how they mesh.

Health and sanitation issues are also covered by local ordinance and include such things as heat, electricity, hot and cold running water, and plumbing. Local codes may stipulate how quickly landlords must repair frozen water pipes because that affects a tenant's ability to live in a habitable dwelling. Local codes specify that units be free of rodents and bug infestations. You may have local codes that apply to lead-based paint, mold and mildew, and asbestos in rental units.

It is essential that you understand and comply with the regulations so that you can avoid prosecution if someone files a complaint. You can get information about them from local housing authorities or city hall.

Local Fire Codes

In many communities you'll find fire codes that pertain to the health and safety of tenants. They prohibit landlords from renting units where the windows have been painted shut. They may specify that each apartment carved out of a single-family home have two means of egress in case of fire or emergency. If so, landlords may have to convert a window into a second door; in some cities, they may be required to construct stairs leading from the unit directly into the yard. Windows that are not blocked by furniture can also be used for egress if tenants need to get out in a hurry.

You may want to provide an emergency exit for tenants even if it is not required by local codes. Not only will it keep the tenants safer, the emergency exit helps protect you from liability should a fire break out, and it will very likely reduce the premium on your insurance policy.

Smoke Detectors

Local codes may stipulate that landlords must provide smoke detectors in the unit. In some cities, the code also specifies where they should be placed and what kind of detector should be installed.

FACT

One Michigan community requires a hard-wired smoke detector system or a ten-year sealed lithium battery unit. Nine-volt battery-operated detectors no longer meet the code because the city discovered that tenants took down smoke detectors, did not replace dead batteries, or removed the batteries and used them for something else.

Some cities require landlords to install one detector in each bedroom, another outside bedroom doors or anyplace else tenants might sleep, and one additional detector on each level of the unit. Cities may also have guidelines for mounting the detectors outside doorways on ceilings and walls and inspecting and cleaning the face and grillwork once a month. Landlords are warned not to paint smoke detectors; paint decreases their reliability.

Animals

Local housing codes may also address pets and other animals and require occupants and owners to remove any unsafe, odorous, or unsanitary conditions. Tenants may be required to repair property damage caused by a pet. Codes often prohibit farm animals and wild animals in the city unless the owner obtains a permit. Animals that are often banned include alligators, wild birds, ferrets, lizards, opossums, raccoons, venomous snakes, and poisonous spiders. Find out what animals your local government allows people to have as pets, but remember that you can ban any or all of them in your lease.

Occupancy Regulations

Your state and local government may have established occupancy standards for rental housing. Municipal codes generally cover how many people can occupy a unit, based on fair housing standards and the health and safety of occupants. Occupancy also may be addressed in the zoning ordinances, as well as building codes.

FACT

Landlords cannot arbitrarily decide that they want their units to be occupied by one, two, or more people and turn anyone else away. Try to use other standards for accepting and rejecting applicants.

Federal guidelines for occupancy allow "reasonable" restrictions on tenants. That has been interpreted as two persons per bedroom. But the Department of Housing and Urban Development guidelines permit two-plus-one—two people occupying one bedroom and another person sleeping on a daybed in the living room. HUD also describes other factors that should be considered, such as the size of the unit and the age of children. You can get more information about federal occupancy standards on the HUD Web site in Appendix A or by calling the Fair Housing Clearinghouse (📞 800-343-3442).

Local codes and ordinances may limit occupancy to two people per bedroom for health reasons, basing the decision upon the square footage of a bedroom. When a bedroom is very large, local codes may permit more than two occupants.

What About Children?

There are federal, state, and local occupancy standards that pertain to renting to families. They may seem to be contradictory. To avoid any problems you should abide by the least restrictive standards when you rent to a family with children.

Under local, state, and federal standards, landlords cannot discriminate against single parents or refuse to rent a two-bedroom unit to a parent who has four children—someone can sleep in the living room. And landlords cannot say an apartment isn't suitable because a boy and girl would have to share a bedroom and they are "too old." Who sleeps in the bedrooms is the parent's decision, not the landlord's.

Student Housing

Don't turn students away. They are not protected by the federal Fair Housing Acts, but you may be setting yourself up for a discrimination complaint if you routinely turn away all students for no reason other than that they go to school or you are worried they may have too many parties. But in considering them, you also have to be aware of city housing codes. Local codes often restrict the number of unrelated people that can live in one unit.

When you're ready to set occupancy standards for your unit, base them on state and local laws. Have those standards in place before you start talking to prospective tenants so that you can't be accused of discriminating against families or students.

To avoid problems, find out what your local codes say about occupancy. Then establish standards for selecting tenants that all applicants must meet. If you have standards in place before you talk to prospective tenants and stick to them, you'll have legitimate reasons for selecting one tenant over the rest.

Zoning Ordinances

Most cities, villages, and townships have enacted zoning ordinances to determine whether an owner, tenant, or business is using the property as permitted by local law. Zoning ordinances also may address occupancy standards in addition to the occupancy standards in the local building code. It's your job to discover whether your unit complies with local regulations.

The letter and number zoning designations may differ in various communities, but classifications are similar, such as:

R-1: Single-family residential
R-2: Mixed residential use, which permits both single-family and multifamily buildings
B-1: Business
B-2: Mixed business and residential use

ALERT!

If you apply for a zoning variance, prior to the hearing you will have to submit a copy of your plan and diagrams of the work you want to do. You'll also have to pay a fee to the city. You can handle this yourself or have your builder or carpenter go with you.

Before you start remodeling your home for an apartment or purchase property that you can rent to tenants, it is absolutely essential that you go down to your local zoning department to find out what uses are permitted in the neighborhood. If you live in an R-1 zone, you will have to go before the zoning board of appeals to request a variance. If it's granted, the variance will allow you to construct that second unit and lease or rent it to tenants.

Notices of the variance hearing are sent to neighbors in the immediate vicinity, as you may know if you've ever received such a notice. Neighbors might object to your request because they don't want increased traffic, parking problems, or possible noise problems. If the zoning board agrees with them, your variance may be denied.

Even if you find a building that already contains two or more units, check into how the property is zoned. You may discover that the zoning commission "grandfathered" the multifamily use into a single-family zone simply because the apartments were there before the zoning ordinance was written. Grandfather clauses sometimes restrict the special use permit to the original property owner, or they may have expired if the building was vacant for a year or more. Don't purchase any property until you know what zone it's in and what uses are permitted under that zoning.

In-law apartments very often are not zoned for two-family use. Check out how the property is zoned and what uses are permitted before you finalize the purchase. Don't take anything for granted.

Building Codes

Anytime a property owner makes a structural change to a building or residence, he or she must get a building permit from the city or local building department and pay a fee. To get a permit, you must provide a drawing or sketch of the work you want to do. You can sketch an outline yourself or hire an architect, contractor, or builder to draw up a plan.

Building Inspections

As work on your unit or building progresses, you'll get visits from a building inspector. Inspectors are paid to enforce local building codes. They look at such things as the structural soundness of an addition and whether electrical, plumbing, heating, and ventilation requirements are being met according to code.

Building inspectors also inspect existing buildings to see if they meet statutory standards. If they don't, the inspector can issue fines to the property owner or close the building.

To prepare yourself for the inspector, you can get copies of local health, safety, and fire codes from the county office and at city hall or the housing authority. If you live in a rural area, check with your township office to find out if the board has fair housing regulations and what is required by local building and zoning codes.

Lead Paint

If you have an older building, you must give your tenants a lead paint disclosure form, as well as the federal Environmental Protection Agency (EPA) booklet "Protect Your Family from Lead in Your Home." If the dwelling is known to have been constructed before 1978, the Department of Housing and Urban Development (HUD) requires that you do so. Disclosure should also be written into every lease and rental agreement.

Exceptions to Disclosures

Disclosure forms and the EPA booklet do not have to be handed out to tenants if they are:

- In a zero-bedroom studio
- Occupying the property for less than a hundred days
- In designated elderly housing, with no children
- In housing designated for the disabled, if there are no children
- In an apartment that was certified by an inspector as free from lead

State Action

Forty-one states have adopted laws concerning the hazards of lead. In addition to prohibiting use of lead-based paint, they require property owners to monitor and maintain existing lead-based paint and building materials that contain lead, such as solder on copper water pipes. Some children love to chew on windowsills. Others eat flakes of paint off the walls and woodwork. If the paint is old, they could easily be eating lead. Lead causes brain damage, retardation, learning difficulties, hearing loss, developmental delays, and hyperactivity. If a child gets ill after ingesting lead, many communities hold landlords liable.

Many states are in the process of adopting a Model Lead Exposure Reduction Act. If they do pass the legislation, it will presume that any house built before 1978 has lead in it and that, as the landlord, *you know about it.*

QUESTION?

How do I know whether the paint on the walls has lead in it or not?
If the house was built before 1978, it's safest to assume that all gloss or semi-gloss paint that has been used is a lead-based paint. But don't try to remove it unless it's peeling or flaking. Just keep the painted area clean and repaired.

If you suspect you have lead in your building, have the area tested. Then, if results are positive, remove peeling or flaking paint or other sources of lead. Yes, it will be costly, but in the long run, less costly than what you'll have to pay if a court decides you are liable for the lead that led to the illness of a tenant's child. Get as much information as you can from your state and local government and figure out what your obligations are.

Mold, Mildew, and Other Concerns

First people worried about asbestos in buildings, then lead paint. Now mold and mildew are grabbing environmental hazard headlines as causing the latest strain of "sick building syndrome" in offices and homes; very frequently excessive mold is the culprit. But don't panic. You can find mold in just about any building; that doesn't necessarily mean it will cause a problem that aggravates the health of occupants.

Some people are allergic to mold, others may experience a toxic reaction. But generally, these incidents occur in buildings that have had serious water problems in the past. Typically the wallboard, ceiling tiles, or wood never dried out and once the fungi appeared, it multiplied over an extensive area.

There are no federal or state regulations covering mold and mildew, but communities are beginning to issue guidelines on how to treat the problem. New York City was the first. In 1993 the city described four levels of severity based on how many square feet of a building was affected and specified who should take care of removal.

As a landlord operating a small owner-occupied dwelling, you probably won't have more than occasional mold and mildew problems in a bathroom or basement. Nevertheless, don't ignore them, especially if your tenant thinks it's affecting the health of someone in the family. Treat the first signs quickly so the problem area doesn't become larger.

FACT

Mold and mildew are fungi. They grow everywhere if conditions are right. And even when you think you've gotten rid of fungus, it can flare up again after being dormant for months. All mold needs to grow is nutrients (such as wood, ceiling and grouted tiles, oil-based paints, and concrete), moisture, and temperatures between forty and one hundred degrees Fahrenheit.

Be proactive. Tell your tenant what can be done to prevent mold or keep it from recurring. You and your tenant can:

- Monitor moisture.
- Keep surfaces clean.
- Let air circulate freely.
- Move furniture that is obstructing air vents.
- Remember that appliances can be a source of the problem.
- Use dehumidifiers.
- Use a mildew-resistant latex paint.

Asbestos

If there's asbestos in your house—perhaps used to insulate the heat ducts or water pipes in your basement—and it's in good condition, don't remove it. You can coat the asbestos with paint to prevent particles from floating in the air.

The EPA also offers the booklet "Guidelines for Controlling Asbestos-Containing Material in Buildings." You can get more information on the EPA Web site.

Rodents—and Other Critters

State and local governments say rodents, insects, and even birds can destroy property and be a health hazard. Your local housing code most likely requires property owners to keep structures and exterior property free of nests and infestations. Should they appear, the owners and landlords must have them exterminated, clean up the premises, and prevent future infestations.

Your tenant should be involved in keeping the premises sanitary. Tenants can keep surfaces clean and free of clutter, and not let food sit on counters, stoves, and tables. If the apartment should need treatment by an exterminator, the tenant will need to make all the affected corners, windows, screens, and plumbing accessible to the exterminator.

Once your property has been visited by the exterminator, to avoid further infestations look for and repair holes in the foundation and around windows, check for and fix leaking plumbing, and repair attic and basement windows when you see they need it.

Requirements for Landlords and Tenants

When tenants rent an apartment, they expect the unit to be habitable—that means safe and clean. They expect their landlord to repair and maintain the property and keep it in good condition. Landlords, in turn, expect tenants to meet terms of the lease, pay rent on time, take care of the property and not run it down. They also expect tenants to use the property responsibly, not illegally.

Landlords' Responsibilities

Many states and local governments now require landlords to provide buildings that are safe, sanitary, and structurally sound and to comply with all health and safety codes. That means units must have:

Heat
Electricity
Hot water
Toilets and plumbing that work
Doors that lock
Unbroken windows with screens
No rats or insect infestations

Tenants have the right to privacy, quiet, and possession of a clean, livable unit. If anything breaks or doesn't work, the landlord must fix it in a timely fashion. Landlords have to maintain the property; if they don't, tenants can report any violation to health or housing authorities.

Do You Need to Be Licensed?

Landlords who are just starting out usually do not have to be licensed. But they very likely have to register income property with local officials and they may have to renew that registration a year or so later. Some cities routinely inspect rental properties to see that they comply with local housing and safety codes; others may inspect only if they receive a complaint about the apartment or building.

You should take care of the registration as soon as you are ready to look for a tenant. City officials will not take it kindly if they find out you have tenants after a neighbor calls to complain or someone in the building department lets another department employee know that you remodeled extensively and converted your property into two units in order to collect rent. You will want to deduct legitimate business expenses and declare income from your rental unit to city and state tax authorities, so it's better to follow all necessary and recommended local business procedures.

Tenants' Responsibilities

When tenants sign a lease, they are expected to keep the unit, fixtures, and appliances in a good and sanitary condition. They must take out the garbage and put it in trash containers and keep the apartment and disposal area clean and sanitary.

F A C T

If your tenant breaks a window or door, he or she has to repair or replace it. Your responsibility is to fix windows and doors before the tenant moves in. If you fix a window broken by your tenant, you can deduct the expense from the tenant's security deposit.

Tenants also have to be responsible about how they act. They should:

- Be quiet, not a nuisance to neighbors
- Not use the property for illegal purposes, such as selling drugs
- Comply with terms of the lease or rental agreement
- Not run a home-based business without landlord approval
- Pay rent as the lease or rental agreement requires
- Behave reasonably
- Not damage or destroy the unit
- Not alter or add to the unit without landlord approval
- Not slander other tenants or the landlord

If your tenant is irresponsible or behaves unreasonably, you have the right to evict him or her. However, you must be able to prove the irresponsible behavior. The key to proving your case is to keep good records of everything that transpires and how you handled it.

Whenever a tenant breaks a rule, send notification that it was a violation of the lease. In eviction proceedings, a judge will expect that the tenant received at least three notices from the landlord before coming to court. (If the tenant signed a rental agreement, you can terminate the tenant after giving thirty days' notice.)

Be a Knowledgeable Landlord

As a landlord, you want to conduct your business professionally. That means knowing the law and applying it every step of the way in deciding who will be your tenant. Before you advertise, determine exactly what objective criteria are most important to you and how you will apply them in the process of weeding out prospective tenants within the guidelines of the law.

You might decide, for instance, that every prospect to be considered must have a sound credit history. Your next requirement might be that they have a good employment history. Your third requirement might be that they have an income level that allows them to pay the rent. Or you might base your decision on what their previous landlords told you.

If you rate every prospective tenant in the same order and use only those three to five objective reasons to eliminate the undesirable prospects, you'll be protecting yourself from discrimination complaints. Be sure to put your rating system in writing—documentation is the key ingredient in a successful landlord-tenant experience.

A good business practice is to document every decision you make and every communication you have with your prospects and tenants. Take notes on all conversations and write down the date and time you talked to them. Keep a duplicate of every letter, notice, and agreement in your files.

Avoiding Discrimination Complaints

The best way to prevent discrimination complaints is to be a proactive landlord. Go a step or two beyond what any antidiscrimination act requires. If you have to extensively renovate your unit, think about modifying the apartment so that it is accessible to people with handicaps. When you advertise or talk to prospective tenants, be scrupulous about what you put in writing or say to them.

Remodeling Projects

If you're rebuilding a wall, door, or hallway, make it wider so that people in wheelchairs can get through it easily. Provide toe room underneath counters. And if you have enough space in the kitchen, put in one countertop that's lower than the rest so a tenant in a wheelchair can comfortably work there.

Install mirrors that are large enough to accommodate people sitting down as well as tall tenants. Add a safety bar or two to the bathroom and put solidly fastened handrails on stairs. Make sure you install faucets and doorknobs that don't have to be rotated; the old-fashioned levers and one-unit controls are easier for anyone with a physical disability or arthritic fingers. And if you're putting in new carpets, limit your choices to those that are tightly woven and have either no nap or a very low nap. Don't use thick padding because plush carpeting makes it difficult for a person in a wheelchair to get around.

If mold and mildew tend to thrive in the bathroom, basement, or entryway, treat it quickly. Consider installing a better bathroom fan or vent. A dehumidifier also helps remove excess moisture. But be sure your tenants know how to use it and will empty it regularly.

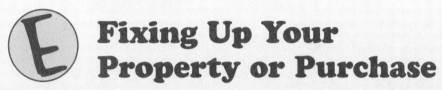

Chapter 5

Fixing Up Your Property or Purchase

Once you've decided to rent out space in your home or purchase your first rental unit, take a good look at what you must do to get it ready. Your obligation as a landlord is to provide a habitable, safe dwelling for your tenant. In this chapter you'll learn what you have to do to meet building codes, what projects are a good investment, and how to spruce up your property so it appeals to prospective tenants.

The First Steps

Whether you renovate your home into an owner-occupied dwelling or purchase a starter with two or three units, you must start at city hall. Once you've found out what the zoning regulations and local building codes require, you'll get a clear idea of what you must do, what you want to do, and what you shouldn't do because it's not cost effective. Assigning each possible project to one of those three categories will help you figure out your priorities.

Must-Do's

Using your building as permitted by local zoning and making sure the structure complies with local building codes tops the list. Building codes were enacted to ensure the health and safety of occupants. Each municipality has its own codes, but they generally pertain to state guidelines for habitability. (See Chapter 4.)

A landlord is obligated to provide tenants with a safe, habitable dwelling. That means that as a landlord, you must repair things that break or don't work properly, maintain the property—keep it up to standards—at all times, respond quickly to emergencies, and keep the dwelling free of rodents and insect infestations.

If you are converting your home into an owner-occupied dwelling, you will have to follow the local building code when you renovate or add an apartment. If you purchased a fixer-upper, you will have to meet codes that may have been ignored by previous owners.

ALERT!

Always do the work and repairs required by the state and local government. Keep records of what was repaired and when. Then if someone gets injured on your property, you'll have a better defense if a liability claim is filed.

Want-to-Do's

Want-to-do's are the tasks you do to make your property appealing to tenants. They include cleaning the exterior and inside of buildings, applying fresh paint, cleaning bathrooms, kitchens, and appliances. Perhaps the unit will look better to prospects if you put in a new carpet.

Spruce up the outside, too. Planting low-maintenance evergreens, bushes, and flowers at the entrance is always a plus.

Maintenance contributes to the economic viability of your dwelling. The better it looks, the more easily you will find good tenants. A clean and attractive exterior and grounds send the message that the apartment will be clean and attractive, too, because the landlord cares about the property and the tenants living there.

Shouldn't-Do's

What you should not do are costly, unnoticeable renovations. They won't pay for themselves because you can't charge enough rent to cover the cost of the project or improvement. For instance, you don't want to purchase top-of-the-line appliances when less expensive models will be just as efficient, or relocate walls for the sake of gaining a few extra square feet in a room.

Officials don't care if a kitchen or bath is remodeled; they just want hot and cold water running through the faucets. Likewise a landlord does not have to tear down a wall to make a room larger or put in a new door to change the traffic pattern. Improvements like these may make the property look and function better, but they are not required by law and might not pay for themselves in the rent you collect.

When you go into landlording, decide what color you want to use in the apartment. Most tenants prefer white or off-white walls. They're neutral and whites are easily touched up when the wall gets dirty. Some landlords store left-over latex paint in a big can and keep adding to it until there's enough to paint another room or hallway.

Even new carpeting can be too extravagant if you purchase high-quality wool. Carpets stain and hold moisture and odors, and tenants often don't care what happens to them. If flooring is an issue and needs to be replaced, consider putting in hardwood floors in the living areas and carpeting only the bedrooms. Initially a wood floor will be more expensive than a new carpet, but you'll never have to replace the floor. In the end, it's more cost effective for a rental unit. In addition, bare wood floors are very much in vogue today.

It simply doesn't make sense to spend too much on appliances and carpets in a rental unit, especially when you can't recover the cost in what you charge for rent. Most experienced landlords will tell you not to waste your money.

Repairing Versus Maintaining Property

Leaky roofs, damaged stair treads, malfunctioning furnaces and water heaters, broken entry locks and windows, and frozen pipes all need to be fixed. If you don't repair them your unit is not habitable, and possibly not safe. You also might be cited with violating local and state building codes if you don't arrange to do the work within twenty-four to forty-eight hours.

Compare that to leaky faucets and running toilets. They also have to be repaired, but you can delay putting in new washers or a rubber seal for a bit. It's necessary to do the job, but it's not an emergency. No one can be hurt.

FACT

You can't avoid doing maintenance and repairs. Make your job easier—and your time more efficient—by purchasing the tools you'll need and a quantity of washers, light bulbs, and other supplies well in advance. Then you won't have to run to the store every time you have to replace something.

In most states landlords have a legal obligation to maintain their property after the tenant moves in so that it continues to comply with state and local housing codes. This means that the landlord must make any repairs that are not the fault of a tenant. The landlord also is obligated to maintain the building, grounds, appliances, utilities, and anything else you and your tenant agreed to in the lease.

Maintenance Is Essential

As a landlord, maintaining the property—the dwelling, appliances, equipment, and utilities—is an important part of your job. Peeling paint, dirty hallways, greasy stoves, worn carpets—they need tending to. If you want to attract the kind of tenant you'd like to have in your home, you should provide a clean, livable apartment. Cleaning up and maintaining the unit, while desired and appreciated by most tenants, benefits you, too. If your unit and home look good, you'll be able to charge more for rent. Chapter 16 includes more information on property maintenance.

QUESTION?

How quickly do I need to repair things for my tenant?
When your tenant calls about minor repairs, you may not be required to respond immediately. But if you want a happy tenant who will renew the lease, you'll be wise to take care of it quickly. A week or so is reasonable; just don't put it off for a month.

Your Responsibilities as Landlord

You are responsible, by code, for anything that affects the habitability and safety of your unit. In Michigan, for example, if a tenant is injured on your property and the condition that caused the injury, such as an unsafe stair, existed before the accident, you can be determined liable for personal injury.

A gas leak, flooding, or major structural damage is considered an emergency and threat to health and safety. It must be repaired, usually within twenty-four hours.

Defective water heaters, clogged drains, or problems with an air conditioner affect the quality of your tenant's life, but don't pose immediate danger. These problems don't have to be fixed right away, but you should plan on repairing them within a couple of days. Do not go any longer than that. You can take care of minor repairs—such as leaking faucets or a light fixture that doesn't work—as your schedule permits.

Will You Have to Hire Help?

If you can handle most repairs and maintenance around the house, you won't have to worry about hiring someone to do the jobs. But if you're all thumbs, you'll have to set aside some of the rent money each month just to cover those expenses.

You should decide what jobs you can do yourself. Do you have the right tools and enough time to handle these chores? Do you even want to do them? If not, perhaps your tenant is handy and has the skills for most household jobs. Find out if your tenant is willing to do the repairs in exchange for a reduction in rent for a month or two. But make sure agreements such as these are in writing.

In the meantime, ask friends and neighbors if they can recommend anybody who does odd jobs. Then start making a list so that when you need someone you know who to call.

Valuable Inexpensive Renovations

A clean, attractive apartment is more appealing to prospective tenants than one with dirty, smelly rooms, and it only takes a little elbow grease to make it look better. If you spend time cleaning and painting, and making certain inexpensive improvements, you can ask more for rent. In addition you'll be much more likely to attract good tenants—the kind of people who will take pride in caring for their new home.

No-Cost Improvements

It doesn't cost anything except for the collection fees and an afternoon or two of your time to remove trash, clean up the yard, trim trees and shrubs, pull out weeds, cut the grass, and dig out unsightly, overgrown bushes. Edging around a driveway or sidewalk will have a positive impact on a prospective tenant, too.

But don't stop outdoors. Take a good look at what's in your basement. It's probably filled with junk that's been there for years. Toss all of it out. Then clean out any other trash or rubbish that you or a tenant has accumulated. Install bright lights and consider painting the concrete to reduce dust.

FACT

Never forget that the apartment is your asset. You should want to keep it in good repair and make it as attractive as you can without spending unnecessary money. Usually that's possible with elbow grease, paint, and routine yard work.

Once the basement is cleared out and clean, look at the front entrance and halls. Cleaning and painting those walls will also improve the appeal of your property and will help make sure that prospective tenants get a good first impression of the property at the moment they step inside the front door.

It should go without saying: thoroughly clean the apartment before you show it. Think of your grandmother when she tackled spring cleaning and turned the house inside out. She scrubbed the kitchen and bathroom walls, baseboards, windowsills, shower, tub, toilet, sinks, mirror, and medicine cabinet (inside and out).

She cleaned under the sinks, washed the fixtures and lights, and turned out closets and cabinets, making sure the shelves were spotless. She cleaned the oven and burners, degreased the hood, and carefully washed all the appliances.

She took down blinds, curtains, and drapes and cleaned them. She spot-cleaned the walls, then tackled windows and carpets. Finally, she scrubbed and waxed the floors before moving on to start working in the entrance, hallway, and porch.

If the apartment and building didn't smell spotless by the time she finished, she might have put out some potpourri, rose petals, or fragrant candles to subtly scent the air. Tenants like that, too. They want their apartments to smell clean and fresh when they move in. But today, a fragrant air freshener can do the job.

Low-Cost Improvements

Cleaning and repainting the entire apartment, hallway, and entrance is well worth your investment and is a low-cost way to spruce up your building so it looks good to prospective tenants. But other improvements will help as well.

Will the building look better if you put low-cost vinyl shutters on the windows? Should you plant a few new low-maintenance shrubs—they're not expensive when they're tiny—to replace those you pulled out? Any effort you make at gardening and sprucing up the property will give prospective tenants more reason to want to come inside and look at the apartment.

Get some new, covered trash cans, the large size. They don't cost much and they'll make your disposal area look much cleaner. While you're at it, don't forget to rake the ground around the trash bins; that can get pretty "trashy" as well.

Some other low-cost improvements might not be quite so obvious, but can save you money. Weatherstrip doors and windows to cut down on heat loss. It will reduce your utility bills. Fix or replace hall lights; lay a new carpet when the old one is ripped or looks worn and shabby.

ALERT!

In some communities a landlord may be required to provide an emergency exit to meet local building codes, even if it means constructing an outside stairway that goes from the yard to the second floor.

Other Valuable Improvements

Improving your property will add to its value, not only in the amount of rent you get for the unit, but also in your equity when you decide to sell. Some renovations, such as upgrading a kitchen or bath, are worth making because they are important to tenants. With an upgraded kitchen and bath, you'll be able to collect more for rent, and later they will contribute to the increased resale value of your property.

Kitchens

Kitchen projects have the largest return on investment and do the most to impress prospective tenants. You can put in new or refaced cabinets. Even just painting the old ones will give some cabinets new life. Purchase new or almost-new coordinated appliances—stick to white.

Install a new light fixture in the ceiling. Add a dishwasher or a disposal and lay a new floor.

Don't tear out walls and change floor plans. Prospective tenants won't notice the change and it won't add to the value of your property. Don't purchase top-of-the-line appliances; they're too expensive. Moderately priced kitchen cabinets will be sufficient. Don't spend too much. Forget about installing a trash compactor; you'll never regain what it cost.

Bathrooms

You can improve any bathroom by putting in new, brighter lights, a larger mirror, and more towel rods and clothes hooks. Updating the sink and installing a low-flush toilet—stick to white fixtures to keep it simple—will pay off as well. Can you install a showerhead over the tub? If you do, also put in a new shower curtain rod. (Bathtub and shower doors are not recommended. They often turn into potential maintenance nightmares because of leaks and mildew.)

Look at the bathroom floor. Is new flooring needed? Some tiles and floor coverings are relatively inexpensive and easy to lay, and will improve appearances greatly.

FACT

Carpeting the bathroom is not a good idea. Bathroom carpets are usually cumbersome to clean. And since wet carpeting takes a long time to dry, you're setting yourself up for potential mold and mildew problems.

Separate Utilities

If you can have separate gas, electricity, and water meters installed, you won't have to worry about your tenant's usage. He or she will be responsible for those bills. If utilities can't be separated, however, or you decide it's not worth the hassle or the expense to install separate meters, you have to determine how to distribute some of the cost to your tenant. Estimate what you think the utility bills will be, and establish a rental rate that will cover the expense. In addition, if you know energy costs will be going up, you might want to add in a cushion, for example, if you think heat to the apartment is roughly $10 a month, set the rent $20 to $25 higher per month.

Another way to share the cost of natural gas heating is to go on the gas budget offered by your utility company. You'll pay the same amount each month for gas. Charge your tenant for half the monthly cost. If the gas budget is $50 a month, you'd add $25 to your tenant's rent each month for heat and gas appliances. When gas prices go up drastically, the utility company will let you know about it and then you can adjust the rental rate for the next year. And when you notify your tenant about the increase in rent, you'll be able to say in all honesty that utility prices have gone up and that's why you need to change it.

Amenities Tenants Like

Some tenants will pay more rent or an additional monthly fee for amenities that make their lives simpler and safer. They want parking near their door. They don't like going to a laundry. They love appliances such as dishwashers and disposals that help reduce their chores.

Kitchen Appliances

If you want to attract tenants with higher incomes and charge more for rent, a dishwasher and disposal are absolutely essential. Tenants who grew up in a home that had these appliances want to have them in their own homes, too.

Offstreet Parking

In some neighborhoods parking is at a premium and tenants have trouble finding a close, convenient, and safe place for their car. In inclement weather, they'd rather not haul sacks of groceries from a car parked quite a way from their home. And when they come home late at night, they feel safer if it's just a short walk to their entrance.

Is your yard large enough to designate a parking place for them? If you have a two-car garage, but use only half, can you give your tenant the option of renting the unused space? That's extra money in your pocket. Find out what people are charging for garage rental in your community and that will give you an idea of what you can ask on a monthly basis. In some urban areas landlords also charge a small fee for off-street parking privileges even though there is no garage. Find out what's common in your community.

If you have to buy new appliances, check *Consumer Reports* to find out which low-to-moderate-cost models are the best buys. You don't need expensive appliances, just the most durable, reliable products.

Laundry Included

No one enjoys hauling heavy baskets of dirty clothes to a commercial laundry. Most tenants would welcome laundry privileges. If that works for you, think about the wear and tear on your appliances. Will they be able to handle the extra use or will you have to buy a new washer and dryer? You can depreciate the equipment you purchase when you do your taxes for several years. If you want to provide access to the laundry, you have to decide whether you should get coin-operated appliances or factor the costs into the monthly rent payments.

Don't forget to make a schedule designating certain days each week when your tenant can do the laundry if you're both sharing a common area.

Air Conditioning

Tenants want air-conditioned apartments, a necessity in southern states and much desired in the hot, humid summers further north. But air conditioning generally costs more than heat, especially if it runs nonstop.

If you have separate electricity meters, you don't have to worry about your tenant's electricity bill because your tenant will pay for it. If you cannot add a separate meter, you might want to talk to a representative at your electric company to find out how you can prorate the bill and add your tenant's portion to the monthly rent.

Cable TV

Even if you don't watch much television yourself, you should be aware that to most families, cable TV is just about as essential as heat and electricity. That doesn't mean you have to get a hookup, but if your tenant wants cable and will pay for installation, don't object. When the tenant moves out, service will be terminated, but the line will still be there as an additional attraction for future tenants.

Yard Privileges

Tenants love to sit outdoors on warm summer nights, watch sunsets, and grill their dinner. If your property has a balcony, porch, or patio, think about whether your tenant can use it. If their apartment has an entrance on the other side of the house, can you put in some patio blocks or an inexpensive fence to give them private outdoor space? Again, you'd be adding a low-cost improvement that makes your unit more desirable to tenants.

QUESTION?

Is my tenant allowed to change the locks on the apartment?
If your tenant wants to change a lock or add a deadbolt, he or she should first get your permission, then give you a key for the new lock. It's illegal for tenants to do the work without your consent and you are entitled by law to have a key to the unit.

Getting the Most for Your Dollars

Once you've decided on a list of repairs and renovations to be done, be smart about doing them. Look for the best deals on materials, and if you decide to hire help, be sure you find the right helpers.

Hiring Help

When you don't have time or don't know how to do repairs and maintenance, look for someone who has spent a lifetime doing carpentry, plumbing, or yard work. Retired workers often want to take on small jobs just to supplement their pension. They have experience and won't charge as much as a contractor who has to pay salaries and benefits to employees. But make sure your hired help has liability insurance and worker's comp; otherwise, if there's an accident you may end up paying the bills.

If you aren't acquainted with a retired handyman, next time you shop for project materials at the lumberyard, hardware, or home improvement store ask if the salesperson can recommend someone to do the work. Ask your friends or a neighbor if they know anyone who's experienced and reliable.

Look for Good Deals

Before you do any project, estimate what materials you'll need. Then watch the ads in your newspaper. Home improvement stores and lumberyards often run specials; some of them also offer no-interest loans on your purchases for six months or a year. Then you can pay the bill in installments without worrying about additional charges mounting up. If you have a lot of projects, will your lumberyard give you a discount on your purchases?

Letting a Tenant Do the Work

You might ask a tenant if he or she wants to tackle a painting project. If the answer is yes, however, make it clear that all splatters and spills are the tenant's responsibility to clean up.

FACT

If your tenant volunteers to spruce up the apartment with fresh paint, say yes. But be certain you supply the white or neutral paint you typically use. Otherwise you might end up with purple or black walls that will take gallons of paint to cover up.

Perhaps your tenant is quite good at small jobs and would be happy to tackle simple repairs, such as replacing washers on leaky faucets. All you have to do then is get the supplies and drop them off.

In return for your tenant's time and effort, you might discount the rent for a month or two. Just be sure that anytime you reach an agreement with a tenant about doing painting or work, put it in writing and have it signed and dated.

Security and Safety

You should never tell a tenant that your building and neighborhood are safe. You don't know whether anyone will attempt to break in or accost your tenant. Do everything you can to keep tenants and their guests safe and thwart criminal acts.

Some states and municipalities are not specific about safety measures. They say only that a landlord must provide a clean, safe, and secure unit. Other states and communities have very stringent regulations and codes about providing a safe environment. Apartments have to be inspected and you may have to purchase a license each year.

ALERT!

Find out what security measures you have to take to be in compliance with your local housing code. Get the information from the building or housing department, health department, and fire department.

You must find out exactly what your community requires, then act reasonably to meet local housing codes. If you don't, you'll be violating the statutes and possibly found negligent if any harm comes to your tenant.

You Benefit, Too

Anything that improves a tenant's safety benefits you as well. In a litigious society everyone wants to assign fault for anything that happens. So if you have not fixed a broken lock and a prowler enters the apartment, your tenant might decide that you are liable and seek damages in court.

Your best defense is to prove that you installed good locks on doors and windows, had a well-lighted entrance and yard, and kept shrubs and trees pruned so no one could lurk behind them.

Keep good records, too, about repairs and maintenance so you can show that you regularly inspect the apartment or that you fixed the lock when the tenant notified you that it was broken. With that kind of evidence, a court might determine that you did everything you reasonably could to discourage crime and accidents and therefore are not liable.

Handrails and Other Important Safety Measures

Even if local housing codes don't require it, you may want to consider putting in new handrails on the stairs. (If you have more than four exterior stairs, you may be required by ordinance to install one.) You are not obligated to put a handrail above the tub or nonslip tile on bathroom floors, or to tack down loose carpet ends, but anything you can do to improve safety for your tenants is well worth thinking about and won't cost you much.

Tenant safety includes many things besides security locks and lighting. Among the measures you might consider are:

- burglar alarm
- fire exits
- hood over the stove to contain grease fires
- smoke detectors
- fire extinguishers, especially in kitchen
- back-door, yard, and parking-area lights
- last name only on the doorbell
- peephole in tenant's door
- locks changed between tenants
- water heater temperature set at no more than 120 degrees
- handrails on stairs

You also have to think about hazards around the house. Threadbare carpets and loose carpet ends can cause accidents, especially on stairs. People can trip on buckled floor tiles or holes in the backyard. Take a critical look at your property and assess its needs. Try to imagine situations in which your tenant or a guest could be harmed.

When you buy hardware or fixtures for the unit, don't cut corners by getting whatever's cheapest. Good midgrade products are usually sufficient. (If you can't afford midgrade, buy the best you can afford.) It will always be less expensive to purchase a better quality item, such as locks for doors and windows, than paying for a lawyer and a liability claim.

When you start fixing up your property, think of yourself as the tenant who will be moving in and living in the unit. What safety features would you like to see included? As the landlord, if it isn't cost prohibitive, why not provide it?

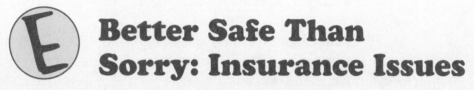

Chapter 6

Better Safe Than Sorry: Insurance Issues

L andlords today need insurance more than at any time in the past. Premiums are at an all-time high, insurers are excluding more from standard policies, and tenants—reflecting the rest of society—file suit much more quickly and sometimes over the smallest things. In this chapter you'll learn how to be more vigilant and involved when selecting an insurance policy and why you should keep track of policy changes and increased premiums.

How Much Do You Need?

One insurance policy will not cover everything. Some property insurance policies exclude floods, earthquakes, and hurricanes. If you live along the coast or in a flood zone, you have to pay a higher premium to include flood and hurricane coverage, or perhaps take out another policy to get it. If you want liability insurance, you'll find it is expensive if you want to be covered for more than $1 million.

Unfortunately, there's no easy answer to the question of how much insurance coverage you need. The insurance world is complex and changing all the time. It's getting more expensive to purchase insurance, and insurance agents can vary significantly in the knowledge and coverage they offer. So the burden falls upon you. Learn as much as you can about insurance companies—what's included in a policy and what's excluded. Investigate several companies and the policies they offer before you purchase anything. Compare prices and search for a qualified, knowledgeable agent who is willing to spend time to find out what you need and the best way to get it for you. When you're a landlord, your risk for claims and liability goes up. You don't want to find out after an accident or fire that your policy isn't what you thought it was.

Your insurance policies will not cover personal property losses incurred by your tenant—your tenant's electronics, clothes, and household goods are excluded. The only insurance available for those items is a renter's policy. Strongly encourage your tenant to get one—better yet, make it a requirement. Also include a hold-harmless agreement in the lease in regard to your tenant's personal property.

Types of Insurance Policies

If you compared any two policies side by side, you might find that although they are similar in some respects, in others they are very different. Your search will go more smoothly if you understand what's available, what you should ask for, and why one feature is more important to you than another.

Property Insurance

If you own a home, you have property insurance on the contents and dwelling. It covers losses to your building and your own personal belongings in case of fire, vandalism, theft, or most acts of God. It probably includes some liability and injury coverage for your guests. It might pay living expenses if you should have to rent an apartment while your damaged home is being repaired.

Homeowner's policies usually also cover owner-occupied dwellings (that have up to four units). If you add an apartment to your home, don't assume it's covered—ask your insurance agent. Find out whether the premium on your house goes up because you now have a tenant. If it does, shop around to find out what other companies and agents have to offer. Don't simply write a check.

FACT

In some states, if you own more than two rental properties you have to buy a landlord protector policy instead of a homeowner's policy. Ask agents about the pros and cons of homeowner's and landlord protector insurance on an owner-occupied or nonowner-occupied dwelling and which is best for you in your state.

When you consider insurance policies, get one that has building ordinance coverage. It will pay enough to meet today's tougher building code standards in case you have to replace or extensively repair your home after a fire or flood. You didn't have to worry about the new codes before because existing older buildings were grandfathered in, meaning that they didn't have to meet the new standards. But that changes when you have to rebuild your home or do extensive repairs. The new standards will be enforced.

Flood Insurance

Losses from floods, earthquakes, and hurricanes may not be included in a homeowner's policy. If you live in a flood zone, on a fault line, or along the Gulf or Atlantic coast, you'd better find out whether the policy includes losses that result from those acts of God. You might be able to have such coverage written into your policy for a higher premium, or you may have to purchase a separate policy to get it.

Mortgage Insurance

If you have a mortgage, your lender probably required you to get mortgage insurance. It covers losses on the property and pays off the balance on the existing mortgage. You don't receive a cent. Some experts say that since few claims are made on mortgage insurance, it is over-priced. Others say it's a protection. If your mortgage company doesn't require it, but you decide to get it anyway, find out from your accountant or tax preparer whether the premium is a deductible business expense.

Title Insurance

Your lender also may require that you obtain title insurance when you purchase property and get a loan. Title insurance guarantees that you have a clear title. It protects you from criminal acts such as forgery, cases of mistaken identity, and any liens on the property that might crop up after closing. Since few claims are made on title insurance, it is a relatively inexpensive policy. Consider purchasing it; it's a bargain and makes common sense.

Liability Insurance

You can laugh at some of the stories in the media about liability claims entering the court system. The awards that plaintiffs receive, however, are no joke. Landlords need more liability coverage today than ever before. But don't panic and try to buy too much. A comprehensive general liability policy that pays a maximum award of $1 million is probably sufficient. Your policy will also pay the cost of legal defense, including lawyer's fees, should a tenant take you to court.

Some landlords say that if you have excessive liability coverage, it only encourages lawyers and some tenants to file suit. If the money is not there, they believe, it discourages frivolous claims by people looking for any money they can get from someone else. It's your decision, but the insurance is expensive. If you worry that you don't have enough liability insurance, instead of paying a higher premium to get more coverage, consider getting a low-cost umbrella policy.

Don't get a homeowner's policy that pays market value on your property and personal belongings. Market value means the insurer will depreciate contents of your dwelling. If the insurer only has to pay the depreciated value, you won't get enough to replace your possessions at today's prices.

Umbrella Insurance

Umbrella insurance covers any award in excess of your maximum on the liability policy. If the maximum is $1 million, you can double that figure with a low-premium umbrella policy. The premiums are low because few claims are made, thus it's the easiest, cheapest way to get more protection. Ask your agent to explain how umbrella policies work.

Your best bet when hiring contract workers or handymen is to ask if they carry their own liability and worker's comp insurance policies. Verify what they say by asking to see their certificates of insurance before they start work. At the same time have them sign a W-9 form for tax purposes. It will save you from having to chase them down later.

Worker's Comp

What? No kidding. Think about this carefully when you consider hiring contract workers or retired skilled professionals. Worker's compensation is very expensive insurance that is not required of small landlords. But if you hire an independent worker who does not have his own policy, and if he is injured on your property, or if the injury is caused by you, you might end up paying all the doctor and medical expenses.

You can carry worker's comp to protect yourself from claims by independent workers, or you can pay more for the repair by hiring a company that has skilled employees and its own insurance coverage. By law companies with employees are required to pay for worker's comp.

What Is the Tenant's Responsibility?

Landlords' insurance policies do not cover the contents of a tenant's unit. Your policies will pay for damage to the apartment and fixtures, but not the tenant's possessions. Nor are you responsible for criminal acts—theft, damage, or break-ins that you couldn't anticipate—and acts of God. So if a tornado takes off the roof and strews contents of the apartment for miles, the tenant has to pay to replace them.

If your water pipes freeze and your tenant's property is subsequently damaged by water, you are not responsible for the losses. If your tenant has to find temporary lodging elsewhere, that, too, falls on him or her.

Careless Smoking

Fires caused by careless smoking are responsible for a lot of property damage, injuries, and deaths. Don't assume it won't happen to you simply because you are renting a smoke-free unit. Property losses caused by a tenant's careless smoking are covered in your homeowner's policy, as are your personal property losses. Your tenant's possessions, however, will be excluded.

Your insurance company will pay for repairs to the walls, floors, fixtures, appliances—anything that belongs to you. After covering your losses, your company will then turn to your tenant's renter's policy for reimbursement.

Renter's Insurance

Encourage your tenants to get a renter's insurance policy so that their personal possessions can be replaced if they are damaged or stolen. Premiums are low and the policy reduces their loss for criminal acts and acts of God. It usually covers losses from their cars and even pays legal fees if they should be sued.

You may want to require that your tenant has renter's insurance. If your insurer has to pay for damage caused by your tenant's carelessness, your own premiums very likely will be increased or the policy will be dropped, especially if you've had a lot of claims in the last few years.

FACT

Start thinking about insurance well before you want a policy to start or be renewed. Experts recommend that you begin the process three to six months ahead of time. That gives you time to talk to several agents and compare policies from large and small companies. Get at least three quotes before you settle on one.

What Should Your Property Insurance Include?

It's very important that you understand exactly what is covered in property insurance, what exclusions there are, and whether your premium is higher because of where you live. High crime areas usually mean higher premiums. Living along the banks of a river that floods every ten years or so or near a fault line has a bigger price tag, too. Ask your insurance agents for an all-risk policy that covers damage caused by:

sewer backup

fire and smoke

lightning, windstorm, and hail

explosions

riots

vandalism and theft

steam, hot water, and leaking plumbing

frozen pipes

heating or air conditioning
    problems

falling objects

glass breakage

physical loss to building

acts of terrorism

Coverage for Vacant Apartments

Try to find a policy that covers loss of rental income if the unit is vacant as a result of a fire or damage that is covered by the policy. You can get coverage for actual loss of rent for up to a twelve-month period. Loss of rents is standard in landlord protector policies, but might not be if you have a homeowner's policy.

If your unit is empty because you are renovating it, a consequential loss rider will cover rent payments. Get a policy that will cover the "fair rental value" of the unit.

Apartments that are vacant are subject to vandalism and theft. Usually vacant properties can be covered as long as there is active rehabilitation going on. If not, the windows must be boarded up to discourage intruders or else the property will be excluded from your policy. Vandals and thieves like to operate where they won't be interrupted; in vacant property they'll destroy or steal appliances and fixtures such as a sink or toilet. If a vacant unit isn't covered in your policy, find out whether an interim insurance policy or an all-risk insurance policy is a better option for you.

Errors and Omissions

Errors and omissions insurance, common in most policies, protects you when you have a loss and subsequently find out that your agent made a mistake or forgot to include something in your policy. Anyone can make a mistake, but you don't want to find out about it the hard way. This will protect you—but even so, when you get your copy of the policy, *read the fine print* so that you know that it's there.

Other Features to Look For

Inflation guard protects you with automatic increases in your coverage. A demolition endorsement (sometimes called a rider) will cover your property if it has been destroyed to the point that what's left has to be demolished before new construction can take place.

If you keep your property maintained and repaired, find out whether improvements made with your tenant's safety in mind will reduce your premiums. In the insurance industry, it's referred to as "difference in condition" or "conditions of premises."

Don't Get Unnecessary Coverage

There's no reason to go overboard when you purchase insurance. You don't want to pay a high premium for features you don't need, so read the policy carefully. You don't want fine arts coverage if all your art is worth less than $500. A court is unlikely to award tenants in an owner-occupied dwelling millions of dollars in a liability lawsuit. So why pay huge insurance premiums every year for excessive coverage?

If a fire destroys your house, an insurance company will only give you as much as it costs to replace your home and possessions, no matter what the limits on the policy are. So take a realistic look at how much your house is worth. Remember to deduct the land value—it will still be there even if the house is gone. Eliminate coverage you don't need if you can, or go talk to another agent.

It doesn't take an actuary to assess your potential risk. Look at your community, your neighborhood, your dwelling. What's the cost of living? How pricey is real estate? Do you live in an area that's quiet and has a low crime rate? Do you live a block away from the fire and police station? Or is your dwelling ten miles away from emergency services down a narrow country lane without a hydrant in sight? This is what insurance companies look at.

Keeping Premiums Affordable

It's no longer simply death and taxes that are the givens of life. You can add rapidly escalating insurance costs that greatly exceed the yearly increase in cost of living. Do everything you can to keep premiums affordable by taking a few precautionary steps.

Shop Around

Never buy insurance from a friend or relative without knowing what's out there. Do your research on a computer, if you like, but don't buy from a company solely advertising on the Internet. All the well-known insurance companies will have Web sites, but you may also find Web sites, pop-up ads, and spam e-mails from fly-by-night operations. You want a reputable insurance company that will pay your claims. Know who you are dealing with. Find out which insurance companies have the highest quality ratings from *Consumer Reports* and A.M. Best Company, then talk to agents from those companies.

Don't limit yourself only to the large insurance companies that spend a lot of money advertising. An independent agent or insurance broker might find you a better deal at a smaller insurance company.

Select the Right Agent

You want an agent who will give you good service, one who knows about insuring rental properties and can give you good advice about what's available and what you should purchase. Your agent should also be willing to spend time talking to you and call when there's an important change in the industry that affects you personally.

Be a Negotiator

You don't have to take the first offer. Negotiate with several companies; even after you've settled on one, try negotiating some of the features. Can you trade off something you don't need for something that isn't included?

In order to be good at negotiating, be sure you know what you're talking about. Be knowledgeable about the different coverages available. Find out how different companies will underwrite your policy. Find out what categories each company is using to determine the rate. Some will base rates on your claim history over the last three years. Others—and it's becoming more and more common—look at your credit standing. These providers say that credit rating is a good way to predict potential losses, and that the lower the score, the more the company will end up paying out. Premiums, therefore, are based on the credit score—people with good credit pay less than people with poor credit. If credit scores are what's important with the company you choose, find out what criteria they use to determine the credit score and how much weight they give it in determining your premium. It may vary greatly from company to company.

Practice Preventive Maintenance and Repairs

Insurance carriers love collecting premiums from low-risk clients. You can put yourself into that category by doing preventive maintenance and repairs religiously. It not only reduces your liability for negligence claims by your tenant, but also will have a positive effect on your bottom line for insurance.

Put a sticky note on your maintenance and repair schedule that asks "Insurance benefit?" It will remind you to think about insurance any time you do work on or around the house. It's certainly worth a call to your insurance agent to find out.

Insurance premiums are a deductible business expense, but why pay top dollar in the first place? Do everything you can to reduce your risks so you can keep your premiums as low as possible.

Give Insurers Detailed Information

You want to let insurance companies know what you have done to reduce your risk for insurance claims. You can't benefit from the dollar savings on the cost of premiums unless you toot your own horn. Let your agent know when you put on a new roof, upgrade the furnace, or replace old water pipes and frayed electrical wiring. Tell them about your security measures, such as providing fire extinguishers, putting in deadbolt locks, inspecting locks and doors. Let them know that you regularly inspect the building for security as well as routine maintenance.

Let them know if you have yearly furnace inspections or have had the fire department or gas company inspect your property for potential hazards and trouble spots. Give the agent a copy of the resulting reports.

If you've installed security alarms or live in a low-crime area, let them know. Tell them if your dwelling is in a flood plain. It's best to be honest up front instead of calling about water damage after the basement floods.

Keep Track of Premium Increases

Never purchase a policy, stick it in a drawer, and forget about it. You want to keep track of how much coverage you have, when the policy is up for renewal, and what the premium is.

You can expect premiums to go up each year. It's the nature of business and a fact of life when you live in a litigious society. But there are increases—and *increases*. If yours falls into the latter category, it's time to shop around again.

Carry Umbrella Insurance

You don't have to pay top-price premiums on costly insurance policies. If you can afford a policy that has a liability limit of $1 million, don't worry about getting liability coverage of $2 million. The premium might break your bank. Get an umbrella policy instead. Since it only goes into effect after your insurance company pays the first million—which hardly ever happens—premiums are much less expensive.

ALERT!

If you've ever had two insurance companies battle one another about who will cover what and how much, you know what a headache that can be for the policyholder. But if you get both policies from the same carrier, there will be no hassles and your head won't hurt.

Forget the Small Stuff

The days of calling your insurance company to pay for fixing a broken window are long gone. Insurance companies don't look at the total payout in a year or five years. They track how often they were called. So it's not worth the risk to phone them about the small stuff. If, for example, after you pay the deductible on your policy, you stand to gain less than $500, it's not smart to let the insurance company know about the loss. You can't predict whether you'll have a claim for thousands of dollars within the next three years. If you do have that second claim, expect the surcharge on your policy to go up fifty- to- one- hundred percent—that is, if your policy isn't cancelled.

Increase Your Deductibles

To reduce premiums, always increase your deductible. If the insurance company knows it will not be getting claims on the first $500 or $1,000—whatever you decide you can handle out-of-pocket or from the money set aside in your maintenance and repair account—premiums will be lower. Insurance agents advise making the deductible $1,000 on a home valued at $100,000 or above.

Look into Taking Multiple Policies

Sometimes it's cheaper to put all your eggs in one basket. Find out if the insurance company will lower the cost of premiums if it gets all of your business. Homeowner's, liability, umbrella, and car insurance might make an attractive package.

It's certainly worth your time to shop around and find out from different insurers just how much savings there will be. Just make sure you always compare apples to apples. Also find out whether you would have any additional benefits or risks for taking out multiple policies with the same insurer.

Have your property professionally inspected before you get or renew insurance. If an inspector from the gas company, electric company, or fire department finds anything that is hazardous or unsafe, you'll get recommendations about how to fix it or eliminate the threat. Insurance companies like low-risk property the best.

Don't duplicate coverage in any of your policies. That might lead to squabbles between insurers about who actually is responsible for what while you're left waiting to make repairs.

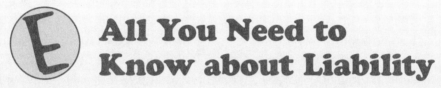

Chapter 7

All You Need to Know about Liability

Accident = Court = Fortune: Today that seems to be how most people think. Someone else is always to blame and should pay for it. You may rue the loss of personal responsibility that affects society, but that won't protect you if you decide to become a landlord. Don't let fears of lawsuits put you off. In this chapter you'll learn about liability insurance, why it's necessary, what you should carry, and ways to protect yourself.

Is Liability Insurance Necessary?

You can be assured there's no consensus on requirements for liability coverage. Most experts say you should be insured for as much as you can afford. Others say if you carry too much, you're a sitting duck waiting for a tenant with an aggressive lawyer—they believe having insurance encourages lawyers to go after "deep pockets." That refers to persons or entities even remotely connected to an accident or claim. The expectation is that they will be willing to settle out of court to avoid a costly court case and unpredictable outcome. If a number of people settle and pay several thousand dollars each, it can add up to a lot of money for the "injured party"—and, of course, the lawyer, too.

What Does It Cover?

Liability insurance covers tenants and their guests when they are injured on the landlord's property. It pays for the cost of your defense and the damages awarded. It does not, however, include problems and criminal acts created by tenants or their guests.

FACT

Your liability policy does not cover business associates or clients of tenants if they have leases stating that they are not supposed to use the apartment for business purposes. If they do and a client is injured, medical expenses would have to be recovered from the tenant's rental insurance.

Conditions of the rental property are taken into consideration in liability lawsuits. If a landlord fails to maintain and repair the property and, as a result, a tenant or guest is injured, the landlord can be judged guilty of negligence. The court has to decide whether the landlord acted reasonably and prudently in caring for the property or did not act as the law expects and was unreasonably careless. Liability claims can also arise from:

- Violations of health and safety laws, including environmental hazards
- Failure to keep premises habitable

- Reckless or intentional acts
- Sexual harassment
- Assault
- Trespassing or repeatedly invading a tenant's privacy
- Libel, slander, or falsely accusing a tenant of crime
- Discrimination
- Wrongful eviction

Choosing a Policy

Look for comprehensive general risk liability insurance with no more than a $1 million cap on awards, or perhaps commercial liability insurance. You don't want to pay high premiums for more coverage. But if you'd like additional protection, get an umbrella policy (see Chapter 6). It only goes into effect if damages awarded in court go over your liability policy's limits. Umbrella policies are a safety net that's rarely used, so premiums are low.

When talking to insurance agents, ask if local and state courts award punitive damages to plaintiffs. If so, you may need insurance that will cover them.

Take Steps to Reduce Risk

Inspect your property regularly and be constantly on the lookout for hazards. If you see something that might cause harm, fix it promptly. Maintaining your property will reduce the potential for accidents to happen.

Keep your property safe and secure. You can't stop crime, but if you did everything you reasonably could to prevent it, the court most likely will decide that you are not at fault if a crime does occur.

Track changes or new rules in state and local health, safety, and building codes. Read legal advertisements after city, planning, and zoning commission meetings. (By law they must be published in a local newspaper.) Then you'll know what's being considered and how it was resolved.

If you know of anything on your property, such as steep stairs, that might contribute to an accident, tell your tenant about it. You might not be able to do anything about the stairs that are too deep or too steep, but if your tenant is warned, then he or she can be extra cautious when using them. Check the handrail on those steps regularly to make sure it doesn't come loose.

Ask your tenant to inform you about any potential trouble spots that might cause an accident. Tell your tenant you want to maintain a safe environment and, without help, you might not spot a problem until you do the next maintenance inspection. If you get a report, fix the problem right away.

Put deadbolt locks on exterior doors and good locks on windows; in most states this is mandatory. Ask your tenants to let you know immediately if the locks don't work properly. Install smoke detectors and fire extinguishers as well.

Watch for hazards to children, a category of dangers known as attractive nuisances. If you're throwing out a refrigerator or other large appliance, remove the door or tape it shut with several rows of strapping tape. Get rid of frayed or exposed wires and standing water on your property. They can be a threat to a child and your tenant's safety and security. Don't let tenants put up a trampoline or swimming pool if your yard doesn't have a fence.

ALERT!

One essential safety measure for you is to never, ever have an uninsured contractor work on your dwelling. If you hire someone to do work, supervise it. Be sure the worker locks up tools and cleans up afterward to eliminate hazards that might lead to accidents.

Keeping Costs Down

Landlords get taken to court for just about everything—personal injuries, discrimination complaints, wrongful eviction, invasion of privacy, crime that occurred on the property, and failure to maintain the premises. And plaintiffs no longer necessarily have to prove that the landlord was negligent.

Liability awards can be costly, so it's no wonder insurers get skittish about writing policies for people with repeated claims and court appearances. If you can, bypass your insurance company as much as possible; it will help keep premiums affordable and prevent your policy from being cancelled. Settle small claims yourself. If someone is injured and it's not serious, get medical help and pay the bill. Don't involve your insurance company unless the injury is serious.

Falls and Injuries

When tenants or uninsured independent contractors working on the property fall and are injured, landlords can be held liable. The injured person can sue for medical bills, pain and physical suffering, emotional damage, permanent disability, emotional distress, and loss of career, education, earnings, family, and experience opportunities. Landlords can also be sued for property damage that occurs because of faulty, unsafe premises, as well as for punitive damages.

Don't try settling with difficult tenants. Your insurance company will not reimburse your expense and you very likely will still face a liability claim. Save your money for then.

What to Do after an Accident

For minor injuries, immediately get medical treatment for the injured party, then call your insurance agent to report the accident. Get statements from witnesses and try to assess whether you were at fault.

When the accident is not serious or property damage is minor, ask your tenant or the worker what would be fair reimbursement. Paying the medical bill or replacing the property might be sufficient to keep him or her happy. If you can reach a settlement, get a signed statement that the tenant or worker has been fully compensated.

Leases Cannot Absolve Your Liability

Never try to avoid a liability claim by inserting a paragraph in a lease or rental agreement that says you are not liable if a tenant is hurt on your property because of your negligence. You can't take away a tenant's right to sue if the apartment and building are unsafe or uninhabitable and an accident occurs. Take care of your property.

Tenant Carelessness

Determining a landlord's responsibility when a tenant is hurt as a result of his or her own carelessness varies from state to state. Thirteen states say a tenant can collect damages from landlords even if the accident was ninety-nine percent the tenant's fault. They are: Alaska, Arizona, California, Florida, Kentucky, Louisiana, Maine, Missouri, Mississippi, New Mexico, New York, Rhode Island, and Washington.

In a majority of states, the court has to determine the tenant's fault at fifty percent or less for a landlord to be held responsible. In Arkansas and Colorado, the only time a tenant can collect is if he or she is less at fault than the landlord. Most lawsuits based on carelessness, however, are settled before they get to court, no matter who was at fault.

Natural Disasters

When you're talking to insurance agents you need to find out what natural disasters are included or excluded in the policy. Depending on where you live, you may want to get coverage for such things as snow load on roofs, windstorms, mudslides, earthquakes, floods, and hurricanes. If they're not included, ask if they can be added to the policy as a rider and what it would cost, or if a separate policy has to be written.

FACT

When insurers experience heavy claims for weather-related damage, they try to entirely exclude coverage for future occurrences from new or renewed policies, or include it only if you pay a higher premium, get a rider, or have a high deductible.

Environmental Hazards

The list of environmental hazards is growing. Now you have to think about mold, in addition to asbestos, lead, radon gas, and carbon monoxide. Your house may be risk-free, but you should still find out if your policy protects you if a tenant gets ill. You need to know what is excluded and assess whether protecting yourself is worth what it will cost to get coverage.

Asbestos

Asbestos, once commonly used as a fire-retarding insulation, can cause cancer. It is presumed to be present in any home built before 1981. It was used for floor tiles and wrapped around heat ducts and pipes to limit heat loss. Your house may have brittle asbestos shingles for siding.

Asbestos is not a health threat until it's disturbed and minute asbestos particles become airborne. Nevertheless, you can be held liable for a breach of habitability if your tenant becomes ill and it's determined that asbestos caused it.

If you suspect your home contains asbestos, tell your tenant or prospective tenants that it's present, but that it's not likely to cause danger. If you later have to disturb the asbestos for maintenance or repairs, warn your tenant well before you start working. And if you hire someone to do the job, be sure to notify the worker as well.

You can hire removal specialists to eliminate the asbestos hazard, but it's not cheap. Many property owners prefer to paint or encapsulate (wrap) the asbestos on pipes and ducts. If you paint, periodically inspect the paint to see that it's not chipping or peeling; if it is, touch up the area with more paint. You can get a copy of regulations for handling asbestos from the Occupational Safety and Health Administration (OSHA).

Lead

When a child ingests lead by chewing on lead-based paint or eating soil contaminated with lead, it can cause serious health problems and even brain damage. Courts have awarded families huge amounts of money to take care of the child's lifetime treatment, education, and loss of earnings.

Any building constructed before 1978 is presumed to contain lead either in lead-based paint or in the solder used to seal joints on copper pipes. Forty-two states and the federal government have residential lead-based paint hazard reduction legislation. The federal government and many states also require landlords to disclose lead-based paint hazards to new tenants before the lease takes effect. The landlord has to give new tenants a copy of the Environmental Protection Agency booklet "Protect Your Family from Lead in Your Home." Be sure you comply with the requirements.

ALERT!

Testers, in the guise of prospective tenants, are looking at apartments to find out whether landlords are handing out the required lead disclosure statements. Keep a supply in your house and car so you always have them available. Then you won't get caught by a tester and have to explain why he or she didn't get one.

Insurance companies, now footing the bill for damages awarded in liability lawsuits, may soon make testing for lead mandatory before they issue a policy. If testing does become mandatory or if you want to know for certain that your building is lead-free, have an inspection made by a state-certified tester.

To protect yourself from lawsuits, routinely inspect your property for deteriorated paint and vacuum up dust and small chips that might contain lead. Then repaint the area. Also show tenants how to identify potential risks and monitor the unit for trouble spots.

Radon

Radon, a radioactive gas that occurs when houses are built on rock or soil containing uranium deposits, can cause lung cancer. Radon also occurs in water from private wells. The gas gets trapped in well-insulated, unventilated houses, particularly those in colder climates.

The Environmental Protection Agency says about six million homes have high levels of radon gas. The gas can be dispersed simply by opening windows for ventilation.

QUESTION?

Are there regulations about radon that I should be aware of?
Only two states currently have programs pertaining to radon gas—New Jersey and Florida. New Jersey established an information and outreach program. In Florida builders now must meet a radon-resistant construction code for new units.

Carbon Monoxide

Carbon monoxide can be an insidious threat in a home because you can't smell it or see it. It's caused by blocked chimneys and pilot lights on gas stoves, clothes dryers, and water heaters. Oil furnaces, fireplaces, wood stoves, and gas and charcoal grills can also cause carbon monoxide to form.

When you do routine maintenance, remove the dust that builds up on common household appliances and the dust and lint from dryer flues. Make sure gas pilot lights burn with a clear blue flame. Don't allow gas or charcoal grills to be used indoors. Specify that you only permit the use of electric space heaters and tell tenants never to turn on the oven to heat the apartment.

Keep rooms well ventilated if you can. Look into getting a monitor that gives out an audible warning signal if carbon monoxide is detected. Decide whether you want to buy one. You might be able to get one from your utility company. Check their Web site.

Built-up carbon monoxide causes dizziness, nausea, confusion, tiredness, unconsciousness, brain damage, and death. You don't want to risk it.

Mold

More than thirty-five states now let insurance companies exclude mold from liability policies. You should find out whether that includes your state, particularly if you live in a humid climate where many types of mold grow. Not all are toxic, yet people are sometimes getting sick because of the mold that is present.

Mold occurs when floods soak drywall and house framing and when pipes leak or water enters a house through a window or roof. Insurance companies may pay for mold cleanup and repairs if it occurred accidentally.

FACT

Landlords who don't maintain the condition of their property will have their policies cancelled by their insurer. Then the only way they can get insured is to go to a high-risk insurer who will charge them a fortune for coverage. You don't want to do that!

Mold grows most readily in tight, well-insulated buildings. It can also occur if a house is not thoroughly cleaned or a bathroom isn't vented, or even if plants are overwatered.

So far the only state that has addressed residential mold is California; it issued permissible standards and exposure levels in the Toxic Mold Protection Act of 2001. California also requires disclosure of known sources. The New York City Department of Health has guidelines on mold for landlords, and San Francisco allows tenants to sue if a landlord doesn't clean it up. (See Chapter 4.)

Landlords are not held liable for mold caused by a careless tenant. But you want to tell tenants how to prevent mold by keeping kitchens and bathrooms clean and well ventilated and not overwatering plants. Also ask your tenant to report the first signs of mold so you can get rid of it. Your best line of defense is to treat mold as soon as it appears. Install storm or double-pane windows and an exhaust fan in the bathroom. Dehumidify areas where mold forms.

Do You Need Terrorism Coverage?

Currently terrorism coverage is included in homeowner's policies, but no one can predict if that still will be true five years from now. Small owner-occupied dwellings, and residential housing in general, are not considered a high risk. But the insurance industry—hard hit with claims after the September 11 attacks and the anthrax scares—someday might want to exclude terrorism from all insurance policies. Some experts believe that in the near future liability premiums for building owners may escalate. Insurers are also expanding an existing exception on policies so that anthrax and bioterrorist substances are not covered. Talk to your agent about your risk and keep tabs on the insurance industry and any legislation that might affect you.

ALERT!

The U.S.A. Patriot Act requires landlords to cooperate with the FBI if they are conducting a terrorism investigation that involves a tenant *if* so ordered by a U.S. magistrate. The Patriot Act protects landlords from being sued by tenants if they "furnish information, facilities, or technical assistance in accordance with a court order or request for emergency assistance under this Act." The most important thing to remember is *do not tell anyone about the investigation*. Keep it to yourself! For more information go to the FBI Web site at *www.fbi.gov/contact/fo/fo.htm*.

Theft or Violent Crimes

When tenants steal from you or from other tenants, or assault or abuse anyone on your property, your best defense is eviction. Do it as quickly as possible, before this behavior becomes a recurring problem.

If your tenant is assaulted or abused by a guest or anyone on your property, your best defense is to show the court that you did everything possible to provide a safe and secure home for your tenant.

Tenants' safety should always be your primary concern, but even when it is, you can't guarantee a crime-free environment. If someone is determined to break in, it will happen. If an assault occurs, sometimes no security measures could have prevented it.

Look at your property critically. Can you find any areas where tenants might be vulnerable to crime? If so, what can you do about it that will help reduce the risk? Not only can you help keep them safer, if you've done everything you reasonably can to provide a secure home, a court is not likely to find you liable if a crime does occur.

In determining a landlord's liability, courts want to know:

- Whether you control the area where the crime occurred
- How likely it was that a crime would occur
- How likely it was that any crime occurring would be serious
- How difficult or expensive it would be to reduce the risk of a crime occurring
- Whether you failed to take reasonable steps to keep your tenant safe

Lower Your Risk

No matter how secure you think your property is, be careful about what you say in ads or verbally promise tenants. Don't put anything in the lease that says your property is "safe."

ALERT!

Strict security laws in Texas put landlords at risk for liability claims if they do not comply with mandated safety requirements and someone is injured on the property. Be sure you know the laws in your state.

Get safety inspections. They may be offered by utility companies, insurers, or even the fire department during a community safety campaign. Some neighborhood associations have a person trained in security who will come to your home and assess your property. Get all the help that you can. If a tenant complains about security, whatever the time of day or night you get the call, get onto it right away.

Carry sufficient liability insurance. Find out what the other landlords in your area recommend. Ask your property owners association for advice, as well as your insurance agent and lawyer, if you have one.

Change all locks after a tenant moves out. Lock up duplicate keys and limit access to master keys. Always trim low-hanging shrubs and trees that are close to the house. Don't give anyone an opportunity to hide behind them. Educate your tenant about crime and safety measures that can be taken. Encourage tenants to report suspicious activities on or near your property. And tell your tenant about any criminal activities that happen in your neighborhood.

You can install burglar alarms that send emergency signals to a security service. If you do get one, the company also may have advice about ways you can make your property safer. Don't forget to let your insurance company know you've safeguarded your house by getting an alarm; it might reduce your premium a little.

If your tenant uses the garage and an electric door opener, tell him or her to keep an eye on the rearview mirror until the door is all the way down. The openers work slowly so that no one gets injured when the door descends; your tenant needs to make sure no one enters the garage before the door is closed.

If you allow pets, have a policy in place about what kind of dogs you allow. Many insurers will not cover certain breeds such as Rottweilers, German shepherds, and pit bulls. Make sure your tenant has only the number of pets permitted in your lease or rental agreement.

Must You Worry about Personal Disputes?

You aren't your tenant's keeper, so arguments should not be a concern unless they occur often or turn violent. If you are disturbed by an argument, ask your tenant to be quiet and considerate. If the arguments don't stop or if you hear someone being knocked around or battered, you might have to terminate your tenant's lease.

Your Tenant's Insurance Responsibility

Some renter's insurance covers losses when a tenant is robbed or mugged, when checks and credit cards are stolen and forged, or when there's theft from a locked car. They might also include personal liability when the tenant or a guest is hurt or their personal property is damaged by a third party.

Renter's insurance covers physical damage to the apartment caused by your tenant, a guest, or a third party. It will cover negligence or improper use of plumbing, windows, appliances, and anything else provided in the apartment. If a fire caused by a tenant's careless smoking damages your property or injures someone, your tenant is responsible for damages.

Tenants with renter's insurance are less likely to sue their landlords for losses. Since the monthly premium is low (usually ranging from $10 to $25), encourage your tenant to get it. You can keep mum on how it benefits you.

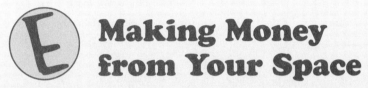

Chapter 8

Making Money from Your Space

The foundation of your landlording business is what you get for rent each month, but there are other ways to make money, too. You get long-term gains as you increase the equity in your home and as it appreciates, and the tax benefits of depreciation and writing off the interest on your mortgage. In this chapter you'll learn how to determine rent, how to calculate your return on investment, and how to take advantage of the tax benefits of owning rental property.

How Much Should You Charge?

You may already know how much money you'd like to get for renting the apartment. But is it realistic? You need to find out, because if you ask too much, people looking for an apartment will pass you by and go to landlords with more competitively priced units. If you don't charge enough, people may flock to your door in a rush to become your tenant—but you won't make enough money to pay expenses, let alone make a small monthly profit.

FACT

A rule of thumb landlords in some regions of the country use to calculate rent is the one percent factor. If your property is worth $100,000, it should rent for at least one percent of the purchase price: $1,000 per month for a break-even cash flow. This formula, however, may not work where property values are very high. If you live on either coast or in a major metropolitan area, you'll be better off basing rent on what comparable, similarly sized apartments cost.

Instead of arbitrarily picking a number and calling it "rent," plan on doing your homework, including market research. Find out what competitors in your area are charging for comparable duplexes or owner-occupied buildings. Find out if there's a glut of empty units on the market and whether rents are stable or showing signs of going up.

Consider Your Situation

One expert estimates that twenty percent of each month's rent goes toward paying taxes, sixty-five percent toward the mortgage and other monthly bills, and twelve percent toward repairs and maintenance. What's left—three percent—is the monthly "profit" on a unit. Others put the return a little higher—at about six percent. And yet another group will say they don't expect to realize a profit until they sell their rental property. That may be especially true if your tenants are renting a single-family home.

If you are a retiree, chances are you've already paid off your mortgage. So as long as you didn't go overboard by taking out a huge home improvement loan to convert your home into a two-unit, you should get enough rent each month to help you stretch your retirement income. That means your pension and savings will go further.

If you're just buying a new home and got a good deal on an inexpensive fixer-upper in a neighborhood that's being revitalized, the rent you collect undoubtedly will help you pay the mortgage. Your profit will be mostly on paper as you build equity and the dwelling appreciates.

Landlords in both of these situations will be able to deduct the cost of repairs and maintenance—which, of course, will be higher for a fixer-upper than those on a single-family residence owned by a retiree—on their tax returns. You'll be able to depreciate your building and the cost of capital improvements, and you'll benefit from income tax write-offs.

If you purchased a duplex that doesn't need major repairs, it can be valuable even though you don't realize a profit on the rent—your tenant will help pay the mortgage and you'll be able to take advantage of the tax benefits while you build equity in the dwelling. And as you improve the property using the no-cost and low-cost suggestions in Chapter 5, your property's value will appreciate, especially if it's in a good location.

Analyze the Market

So how do you figure out how much to charge for rent? First you have to find out what other landlords in your area are asking for rent. Start out by looking at "For Rent" ads in the newspaper or on the Internet. Find listings for units that sound similar to yours and make note of the rent. If prices aren't included, call, pretending you're looking for an apartment. You don't have to actually see it, just ask a few questions on the phone.

Next, talk to someone with a professional interest in property. Make a call to the owner or employees at a local property management company, a real estate office that advertises apartment listings, an apartment-finding service, or a professional association for landlords. They'll have sound information about what rental rates are for properties similar to yours.

Talk to landlords, too. You might not want to ask a neighbor with an owner-occupied home just like yours—after all, you're competitors. But landlords with fourplexes or six-unit buildings will have a good handle on the entire market. They'll know what sort of rent owner-occupied dwellings can support and whether property values are stable or increasing. Ask them where they think the rates will level off. They might not be exactly right, but they'll be close enough to give you an idea of what you're working with.

Find a mentor, someone who's been in the business a long time and is willing to help you learn the ropes. Get together periodically for a working lunch. You can probably list it as a deductible business expense on your income tax return, along with seminars and workshops you attend. Check with your tax preparer.

FACT

When figuring out how much to charge for rent, put yourself in a tenant's shoes. How much would you be willing to pay to live in this unit? Is it a Cadillac or a Chevy? If you're selling a Chevy, don't ask Cadillac prices—or vice versa.

Forecast Market Trends

To have a viable business, keep current on market prices. Look at the ads at least once a week. Watch what's happening at the apartment complexes. If they are offering a month's free rent, you can be certain there are too many vacancies and the competition for renters is hot. If the complexes are raising rent, then the market has swung in favor of landlords. You can probably ask a little more.

Keep in mind, however, that you have a totally different product than an apartment in a large multifamily community. Your duplex or house may have a nice backyard, which is a lot more attractive to some renters than a third-floor unit in a big building.

You especially want to track comparables on a regular basis. Those are the owner-occupied dwellings in your area. Look for vacancy signs and watch the newspaper ads. Are the owners still asking the same amount of rent that you are? If so, you should be fine for a couple of months. Don't slack off, however. Check out prices at least once a month.

What's the Cost of Living?

Another gauge of what's happening is the cost of living. Has the Consumer Price Index (CPI) gone up? If so, how much? When you see prices rise on other goods and services, it can indicate that rental rates will soon be following, if they haven't already. If your tenant has a yearly lease, you're locked into the rent until the lease expires. But make plans to raise it when the lease is renewed. (See Chapter 14 for more information on renewing leases.)

Don't ever give your apartment away. When your rent isn't high enough to cover expenses, including property taxes and insurance rates—which creep up every year—you're not making good business decisions.

Calculate Return on Investment (ROI)

The money you put into your property is your investment. It's money that you have to pay back to the lender or else it's your own savings that you want to replace. You want to do that with your profit from the rent. But will the rent you decided on give you a profit?

Follow these steps to determine your cash flow:

1. Look at a year's worth of bills for utilities, water, sewer, garbage collection, and any other ongoing expenses. Add them up. They are your annual operating expenses.
2. Now figure out how much you'll pay for a year on your insurance, property taxes, and mortgage (or home improvement loan).
3. Factor in five to ten percent of the rent for repairs that you might have to make in the next year. Use the higher percentage for property that the previous owner didn't keep up.
4. Now add five percent more to cover possible vacancies. If a tenant leaves, your unit will be empty while you search for someone new.

5. Add up the totals. That gives you a good estimate of what your total expenses will be for the coming year.

6. Take the annual rent amount you have come up with based on market research, and subtract from it the expense total from step 5. That gives you the amount of income the rent will generate—or, as landlords call it, your net operating income.

Keep in mind, however, that most fledgling businesses don't have a positive cash flow in the early years. Can you afford to put more of your own money into the building until it starts paying for itself? Some landlords say that it takes five to seven years to realize a profit.

From your calculations, you will be able to determine the minimum amount of rent to charge. Now figure out what you need to establish as a rental rate that will allow you to set some money aside each month for some of the more expensive items that you want to get for the apartment—perhaps a new refrigerator, a dishwasher, or a new furnace. After that you can determine the return on your investment—your profit.

To calculate the ROI, use this formula:

Net operating income (see the steps above) × 100 = percent return on your investment

Percent return on investment ÷ Purchase price of investment = ROI.

FACT

If you haven't saved last year's receipts for your home, use your checkbook register or the invoices and receipts from a previous year to calculate how much it costs to run your home. If you are buying a duplex, look at the owner's books, records, and receipts for the property. They might not be an accurate gauge of what you will have to spend in the coming year, but they'll serve as a starting point.

What to Do If a Unit Stays Empty

If you borrowed money, you have to meet mortgage or land contract payments each month, whether or not your unit is vacant. If your tenant pays $1,000 a month, a two-month vacancy can kill you. Even at $500 a month, the cost of vacancies rapidly escalates. So what can you do to keep losses to a minimum? Some landlords just ride it out; others say they'd rather collect less as long as there is a tenant renting the unit.

Is the Unit Overpriced?

You've been running a For Rent ad for over a week and gotten only a few phone calls. No one wants to make an appointment. That should tell you that you're asking too much; callers know they can find a better deal elsewhere. Renters are a cost-conscious group. They would rather have a little disposable income after they've paid rent each month than give their money away to a landlord.

Try reducing your asking price by $25 and running a new ad; if that doesn't work, reduce it again. Not getting as much rent as you'd like might make things a little tight, but it's better to have an occupied unit bringing in money regularly than a vacancy draining your budget.

For example, when the economy is good, you might be able to get a rental rate of $600 a month, but if that's too steep for the current market, you drop the asking price, first by going down $25; if there are no takers, you reduce it another $25. Recognize that in the end you may be collecting only $500 a month in rent just so someone occupies the apartment. Don't gulp! Do the math. If you have a tenant renting at $500 a month, in a two-month period you'll gain $1,000. Your loss will be only $200. But if you're stubborn about sticking to your original asking price, in two months you're down $1,200. Which is the better business decision?

What about the Security Deposit?

You can reduce the security deposit amount, too, but it's not a wise decision. Security deposits are usually about two months' rent in most states. Going any lower is risky, especially if you should get a problem tenant. You'd be surprised at how quickly that money will evaporate if a problem tenant trashes the apartment, causes extensive damage, or gets behind in rent.

For the same reasons it's not a good business practice to say a security deposit includes the last month's rent, and in some states it is not legal to do so. If you do include the last month's rent, the tenant won't pay you for that last month. Then if the apartment is trashed or the tenant owes back rent, you'll have to use the courts to recover what's owed. You want to collect as much money as possible in the security deposit just in case you have problems. (See Chapter 14 for more on security deposits.)

New tenants have to come up with the equivalent of three months of rent to move in: the first month's rent, plus another two (in most states) to cover the security deposit. Legally the deposit belongs to the tenant unless he or she owes you money for rent or repairs.

Depreciate Building and Contents

One way to make money on your property is to depreciate the building and some of the contents. Calculating wear and tear on your property is a strategy to reduce the amount you owe in taxes. It saves you money indirectly, but shouldn't be overlooked. To keep on the right side of Uncle Sam, however, you have to follow the rules exactly.

Don't confuse depreciation and deductible business expenses. Depreciation occurs over a period of years. Currently the items you can depreciate for wear and tear are:

- Computers and other capital investments (improvements)—5 years
- Appliances, carpets, window coverings—7 years
- Landscaping, paving, outdoor lighting—15 years
- Residential buildings—27.5 years

Tax laws change frequently, however, and to be safe when using depreciation, you should check with an accountant.

A business expense, such as having a plumber rout a badly clogged drain, can be deducted from your taxable income on your next annual income tax return. You pay the plumber in one year and then claim all of the expense when you do taxes for that year.

Your Property Will Appreciate

Don't forget to look at the big picture when you go into landlording. Any improvements you make will increase the value of your property. As the value goes up, so does the amount you will realize when you decide to sell it. If you chose well by buying an inexpensive duplex in an up-and-coming neighborhood, property values are sure to escalate even more. It's a long-term investment that's sure to pay off.

The improvements you make on a fixer-upper can appreciate your property values as well unless you went overboard and purchased top-of-the-line products. Gold-plated faucets and custom-made cabinets are fine for a mansion; your tenant will be happy with less. You won't be able to recover the cost for these expensive products by increasing the rent unless your property is in an exclusive, high-rent district. Prospective tenants will compare the cost of similar apartments in your neighborhood and choose one that's competitively priced, clean, and attractive. And if you decide to sell, prospective buyers will not pay a premium for your property simply because the kitchen cabinets and bathroom fixtures are top grade. Choose wisely.

Sticking with the Budget

Establishing a budget is not easy when you're trying to improve rental property. Once you have your budget for improvement in place, work on a time-and-material basis. In other words, whenever you have a little cash, purchase what you need for one job only, and if possible, do the work yourself in order to save money.

You'll have to be vigilant about not going overboard. Don't take on more work at a time than you can handle financially. Break big jobs down into small components so they'll be more affordable—and give yourself enough time to do the work yourself.

You may have improved your income and net worth when you went into landlording, but don't go crazy and splurge on yourself—if you don't already have a membership in the country club, don't use landlording as an excuse to join. Don't rush out to buy the expensive car of your dreams or caviar for dinner every night.

ALERT!

Don't forget that you can't use all of your resources. You'll still have to have money available for the repairs that crop up from time to time. And there will be times when the unit is vacant and no rent is coming in while you search for a new tenant.

Remember that most new businesses don't see real profits when they're first starting up. New businesses require a lot of work and effort on the part of the owner and it usually takes a couple of years before there is enough difference in your income level to make lifestyle changes. Try not to be impatient. Do what you have to do to build up your business, set some money aside for emergency expenses, and keep at it.

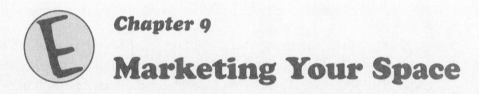

Chapter 9

Marketing Your Space

You've selected an apartment and done the necessary work to prepare it, and now you are eager to get someone moved in. First you have to start advertising the space. In this chapter you'll learn what you can say in ads, and what you should not say so that you can avoid discrimination complaints. You'll also learn different ways to advertise your unit that can help you find a tenant quickly.

For Rent

What do you have to think about when it comes to marketing your property? Can you just place an ad in the newspaper or stick a sign in the yard? The answer is yes; in fact, many landlords rely on the local newspaper and/or yard signs. But there are also other options—you have to decide what is the best means for reaching the people you'd like to have as tenants.

Before you do anything, you should review Title VIII of the Civil Rights Act of 1968 (The Fair Housing Act) and your state and local fair housing codes. The 1968 Act, amended in 1988, states that no person shall be subjected to discrimination in the sale, rental, or financing of residential dwellings on the basis of race, color, religion, sex, handicap, family status, or national origin.

The 1968 federal Civil Rights Act and 1988 amendments also make it illegal to discriminate against families with children and the 1990 Americans with Disabilities Act prohibits discriminating against those who are disabled. (Chapter 4 discusses these laws in more detail.)

Without a clear understanding of what you can and cannot say when writing an advertisement or showing your property to prospective tenants, you might inadvertently say or do something that can imply discrimination. The last thing you want is to have someone file a discrimination complaint with local or state authorities.

What You Can't Say

When you're ready to advertise your apartment, review and understand the federal, state, and local fair housing laws. You don't want to be inadvertently discriminatory with the wording of your classified ad. Even pictures or illustrations in ads can imply discrimination if they don't picture both minority and majority groups, both sexes, and different types of families.

Words You Should Avoid

It's important that your ads not contain words, phrases, or symbols that might indicate you have discriminatory preferences or limitations. You should also be cautious about words that imply discrimination. While many landlords understand that they cannot discriminate based on categories of people, they fail to think about how some words are perceived. So if you use a word implying discrimination—even if your intent was not to discriminate—you could face a discrimination complaint. And landlords rarely win. Examples of words to avoid are:

restricted	integrated
exclusive	traditional
private	adults only

Eliminate All Religious References

Never use a particular church or synagogue when you describe where your unit is located, because that, too, might imply unintended discriminatory preferences, limitations, or exclusions. If you have any doubt about how to word your ad, check with a lawyer before you call the newspaper.

What You Should Say

You can be as descriptive as you want in your classified ad when you are describing the apartment, the rent, and the amenities that are included. You can legally restrict or welcome pets or specify "nonsmokers only." You can talk about the location—without referring to a church—and give an address.

You can say when the unit will be available for move-in and whether references and/or a credit check are required. And don't forget to include a phone number where you can be reached. If you want to restrict viewing and calling, say so in your ad or let after-hours calls go to an answering machine. If you're out of town frequently, you might want to list an alternative number and have someone take calls for you.

ALERT!

Don't say that your unit has amenities that aren't available. Whether you describe it verbally or in print, your tenant then can demand that you provide that feature, even if you subsequently decided it was too expensive or not feasible to put in.

To make your unit stand apart from other advertisements, describe special features. You can say the apartment is:

- affordable
- deluxe
- quiet
- cozy
- desirable
- peaceful
- spacious
- newly remodeled
- historic
- convenient to public transit
- rustic setting
- adjacent to shopping
- established neighborhood

In other words, think in terms of what you are offering, not the tenant you'd like to offer it to. If you can make your apartment sound attractive, prospects will call.

Newspaper Ads

Seven days a week the classified section of your local newspaper is full of For Rent ads. If you look at them regularly, you'll notice that the Sunday paper seems to have more listings than any other day. As you read through the ads, you'll also notice that some landlords list their property for one day only, others run the ad three times, and occasionally you'll see an ad for a full week. You'll notice ads of different lengths, some more specific than others. Obviously there are choices to make when placing an ad. Consider the following points to come up with a newspaper ad that will attract the tenants you want.

Cost Is a Factor

A major decision is how much you will spend. Newspapers rely on classified ads as a profit zone. So when someone—like you—has something to sell, the charges can mount up quickly. Cost will be affected by how many times you want the ad to run and how many words you will use.

FACT

One reason there are more ads in the Sunday classified section of your newspaper is that landlords and other advertisers realize circulation goes up on Sundays, simply because people have more time to spend reading the newspaper.

At one newspaper in a medium-sized city, if you ran your ad for only one weekday, you would pay $21; that same ad on Sunday would cost $24. However, discounts are applied if your ad runs for more than one day in the newspaper. Thus a basic ad in some cities—fifteen words and three lines—would cost about $100 for a full week of insertions. (If you rent the unit before the end of the week, you can cancel the ad, but you probably won't get a refund.)

You might want to call the classified department before you place an ad. Ask about their rates. Is it more expensive to run the ad in the Sunday paper? If it is, how much? It's likely to be only a couple of dollars higher, and it has the potential to reach more readers. Once you have the pricing information you need, thank the customer service rep and hang up. Then figure out exactly what you want to say and what you can leave out to reduce the cost of placing the ad.

Which Paper?

In addition to the major daily newspaper in your area, you may have a weekly newspaper in your community. If the weekly is distributed in a wide circulation area, consider advertising there. Generally the rates for classified ads in a weekly newspaper are lower than what the daily newspaper charges, although it may be a mere couple of dollars' difference.

Other newspapers to consider are the alternative publications in your community, student newspapers at nearby colleges and universities, and shoppers. (Shoppers are the tabloid newspapers dropped off each week on your doorstep. Unless you're looking for a used car or furniture, or an apartment to rent, you may not even glance at the paper before you throw it out.) Running ads in any of these publications is likely to be less expensive than the daily.

Look through the classified listings before you write your first advertisement. It will give you ideas for what to say about your property and how to say it, including common abbreviations for amenities.

How Specific Should You Be?

The less you say in your newspaper ad, the more people are likely to call asking about it. But then you may be inundated with calls. Do you want the phone to ring off the hook, day and night, only to have them hang up once you've told them what the rent is, where the apartment is located, how many bedrooms it has, or whether utilities are included? Do you want to take these calls and weed out unqualified buyers yourself? Do you know what say to the callers? (If you don't, Chapter 10 will help you with this.)

On the other hand, if you say too much in the ad, will that eliminate prospects who have decided not to spend that much on rent? Some landlords believe that if the callers actually see and like a higher-priced apartment, they are willing to pay more. These landlords want a chance to sell the apartment on the phone, then show it to prospects who have been hooked.

Basic information in an ad that is not too wordy should include:

- Location (especially important in larger cities)
- Number of bedrooms
- Rental cost
- Deposit required (if any)
- Utilities included
- Unique features or amenities
- Your phone number

Don't be too specific about the location. Describe the area in general terms, such as Downtown, near Northside, Southeast, the name of suburb or rural area. When you give a specific address, you run the risk of having people ringing your doorbell without calling first for an appointment.

With a few select adjectives and nouns you can convey a lot of information, even in short ads. Here are some samples of brief classified ads:

Northeast—Clean, quiet area, laundry, porches, yard. $795/mo., plus utilities. (111) 222-1313.

Northwest—East Street, Very nice 3 bdrm, $600/mo., plus gas, electric. (111) 222-1313.

Southwest—3 bdrm upper, $575; 24-hr. recorded message (111)222-1313.

Here are some sample ads that give slightly more information:

Southeast—Nice 1 bdrm, air, disposal, laundry, free heat, cats ok, $475, (111) 222-1313 or (111) 222-1315.

North—lower, large 2-bdrm, remodeled, off-street parking, washer/dryer hookup, large backyard, $575 plus utilities, cats welcome. $400 deposit. Call (111) 222-1313.

Southeast—Carter City, near CC elementary, high school, 3 bdrm, full bath, backyard with deck, appliances, washer/dryer. Most pets ok. $1150 plus utilities/deposit, (111) 222-1313.

Other Ways to Advertise

You don't have to spend a lot of money on classified advertising if your unit is in a desirable neighborhood or near colleges and hospitals. In areas near a campus, For Rent signs sprout like mushrooms at the end of semesters and mostly disappear by the end of summer when students come back for the fall term. Yard signs are not the only vehicle for low-cost advertising, however. You can advertise in newsletters, on bulletin boards, and on the Web.

Yard Signs

You can purchase durable, custom-printed For Rent signs at many of the sign shops listed in your yellow pages. Depending on the size of the sign and materials used, prices can run from $35 up for one color on a white or one-color background. In addition to looking professional, it's a good investment because one sign will last for years, meaning you won't need to get a new one every time a tenant moves out.

Among the choices of materials available are corrugated plastic signs with wire (think political yard signs), aluminum with an iron frame (much like the ones used by real estate offices), and corrugated plastic jacket signs. The typical yard size is 18 x 24 inches, but some landlords prefer the larger 23 x 30 inch corrugated jacket signs to increase visibility.

When you custom-order a sign, it's best simply to have it say "For Rent" and list your phone number. You want to attract the attention of passing motorists and want them to see and remember the phone number so they can jot it down. Any other information would be distracting from these two important messages.

Newsletters

If you have a homeowners association in your area, find out if they put out a newsletter. Some homeowners associations also publish a monthly list of apartments available in their area and circulate it upon request. Although the list may not be distributed widely, it is especially effective in reaching people who want to move into a particularly desirable area or historic district.

Residents who are proud of their neighborhood often tell friends about units that are available, so they may spread the word for you even if the list or newsletter doesn't make it to as many people as you would like. Don't forget your place of worship. Will they include a brief advertisement in the newsletter or bulletin?

If you have two or more units, don't fail to let your other tenants know when you will have a vacancy in one of your properties. Word-of-mouth advertising doesn't cost you a dime.

Bulletin Boards

You'll find just about anything available for rent or purchase on the bulletin boards at your local grocery stores, hospitals, work sites, and other public places. Considering how many people post advertisements on sheets of paper, cards, and even paper plates with their phone numbers on numerous tear-off tabs along the edge, these no-cost ads must work.

Give it a try. Remember, however, that your notice may disappear after a week or two since the store or organization likely wants to make room for others who want to advertise. Check the posting policy.

If you have a computer, you can design an 8 x 11 inch flyer to tack onto the local bulletin board. A flyer gives you more space to go into detail and you could even reproduce a picture of the unit or a floor plan. Don't forget to include your phone number!

Apartment Rental Magazines

Many communities now have magazine-sized publications that list available apartments. Produced on newsprint, these publications typically are found in or outside large supermarkets. If your community has one, it will list a phone number for those who are interested in placing ads in the next edition.

Campus Housing Office

If you live in a community where a college is located, you can register your apartment at the student housing department. Students typically check there first when they come to the campus. It won't cost anything to list your apartment. Most colleges and universities now also maintain Web sites with convenient housing information.

Using the Internet

Consider creating a Web page to advertise your unit. Apartment seekers are increasingly turning to the Internet to find a suitable home and management companies that maintain multiunit complexes are taking advantage of it by having their own Web sites. It's a good, inexpensive way to reach prospective tenants, especially people moving into a new area. In addition to listing prices and all of the amenities, the managers of these multiunit buildings include detailed floor plans, exterior shots of the building, balcony, parking area, landscaping, and the entrance and foyer. You'll also find interior photos of the kitchen, bathroom, living room, dining area, bedrooms, and sometimes even large walk-in closets. Visit these sites and get ideas for advertising your own unit.

Does your community have a Web page advertising availability of apartments? One historic district maintains a Web page upon which members can showcase their units. They descriptively and attractively detail all the best features of their apartments. You'll find square footage, descriptions of the yards and the views, and proximity to local stores, colleges, hospitals, and public transportation. Find out if homeowners in your community do something similar to advertise availability of apartments, or if they are interested in starting something.

FACT

You can check out online listings for your community by going to a search engine such as *www.google.com*. In the search box type in "apartments" and the name of your city and state. Then spend some time looking through the various sites and listings available.

You don't have to live in a historic district or use a neighborhood association's Web site. If you're handy with a computer, design your own Web page. If you're not an expert, take advantage of the Web-page design services offered by many Internet providers. Several providers offer no-cost Web sites and design elements and often have an expert to walk you through the process. There may be restrictions on size and number of photos you can include, but with their help you can get on the Web too!

Another way to advertise on the Internet is to list your unit with Web sites set up expressly for that purpose. They advertise apartments free of charge, but you should expect to pay a small commission if you find a tenant by using the Web site. Before you actually list with a Web site such as *www.rent.com*, *www.homestore.com*, or a community-based page such as *www.bostonapartments.com*, be sure to ask how much you will be charged if they connect you with a tenant who signs your lease.

Rental Agencies

You can hire a real estate management firm or a real estate agency to advertise and show your apartment and screen prospective tenants, but it will not be cost effective unless you're working a full-time job. Look under Real Estate Management and Real Estate Rental Services in your yellow pages. A management company can also handle month-to-month maintenance issues. The service is particularly helpful if you are unable to maintain the property yourself or spend time away from your building.

ALERT!

Anytime you ask anyone to help you with your property—whether agency, management firm, or skilled professional—ask for credentials. You want to hire only those firms and individuals that are reputable and insured.

The agent who finds a tenant for your unit generally is paid a commission of a month's rent or the security deposit. Then if the firm also manages your property—and that would be standard with a management company—you also pay either a flat fee per month or ten percent of the total rent the property grosses. In other words, if your unit rents for $650 per month, your monthly fee for management services would be $65.

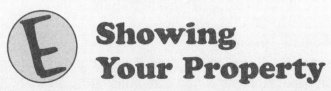

Chapter 10

Showing Your Property

You've fixed up the apartment, painted the walls, cleaned the rugs and floors, washed windows, scrubbed the tub and sinks, spruced up the entry, and put out your yard sign. In this chapter you'll learn what else has to be considered before you take people through, what to say when prospective tenants phone, how to avoid discrimination complaints, and what you need to know about rental applications.

Getting the Unit Ready

Before you show your apartment you should install new locks, make sure appliances are in good working order, fix or replace leaky faucets and missing or broken hardware on kitchen cabinets and doors, repair frayed wiring, and get rid of insect infestations. Call city hall or your local fire department to find out where smoke detectors should be installed in rental units and what kind should be used. Does the water heater still work? What about the furnace?

Don't forget to take care of the outside as well. If the grass is too long, mow it. Pick up papers that have blown into the yard, remove trash, and rake up the area where the trash bins are located to tidy it up.

FACT

Smart landlords will provide smoke detectors even if they are not required by local ordinances. Your responsibility is to provide a safe environment for your tenants. You benefit, too. If there's a smoke detector in the unit, your insurance premium might be reduced.

Before you take anyone through the apartment, inspect it one more time. You want to make sure that none of the faucets started leaking, that water isn't running in the toilet tank, and that the stove and refrigerator are still in good working order.

Try never to show the unit until it is completely ready. Most people are left with a negative impression if it's seen before it is painted and cleaned.

When Prospective Tenants Phone

You're likely to have your first contact with prospective tenants over the phone. Don't forget that they are your potential customers. They expect you to be pleasant, courteous, and businesslike. Your goal in talking to them is to convince them that they want your apartment. Make it sound attractive by talking about special features so that they'll make an appointment to see it. You can ask what they're looking for and how many bedrooms they need. But never ask any personal questions such as how old someone is or their marital status.

Talk about the Property

When you answer the phone, instead of asking questions, talk about the apartment. Tell callers how much rent and security deposit you require. Describe the number of bedrooms and bathrooms, whether or not utilities are provided, and when the unit will be available for them to move in. Tell them what appliances are provided; if you include a washer and dryer, let them know whether this equipment is coin-operated.

Describe Special Amenities

Be descriptive but truthful about amenities. You want to "sell" your apartment so that potential tenants will want to see it. Does it have a fireplace, hardwood floors, spacious rooms, walk-in closets, a balcony, or a patio? Is there a cable hookup? Is there off-street parking or a garage that the tenant can use? These special features appeal to tenants and may set your unit in a category apart from other apartments available at the time—if your property offers any of these things, be sure to mention them.

ALERT!

Be aware that sometimes you may be showing your apartment to testers. They work in pairs—usually a minority and a Caucasian—to see if landlords are adhering to federal, state, and local fair housing codes. Testers won't identify themselves, and you won't know they were there unless they report a violation on your part.

What's in the Area?

Talk about the nearest public schools—both grade and high schools—and the school district you're in. Tell the caller about shopping in the area, whether public transportation is available, the proximity of parks, a lake, or a river. Some landlords can talk about a spectacular view or a countrylike setting even though the apartment is located in town. Be sure to promote any of these that apply to you.

Tell Them What You Need

Let callers know what criteria you'll use in deciding on a tenant. For instance, will you do a credit check? Will you require the employment history of all prospects? Let them know. Tell them if you routinely talk to previous landlords and employers as references.

By listing your criteria for evaluating prospective tenants, you can turn the conversation into a prescreening process conducted solely by the caller. Those whose background won't stand up to scrutiny very likely will thank you and hang up. After they opt themselves out, you are free to concentrate on more likely candidates.

Treat Each Caller Equally

Before your ad appears, jot down a list of your apartment's features. That way you'll have a "script" to run through when you answer phone calls. The list will help you keep the conversation on track so that you don't inadvertently ask any questions that might be misconstrued by the caller as being prejudicial. A list will also help you recall every detail you want to include that will help "sell" your apartment. As soon as you hang up, write down who called, what time they called, when they will view your unit, and what both of you said. Be sure to include the date you talked to them.

If you have to leave an outgoing message on an answering machine asking callers to leave their name and telephone number, play it back. How do you sound? Would you want to leave a message for this landlord?

Show the apartment to everyone who wants to see it. Never arbitrarily rule out prospects based upon information you get in a telephone call. All of your decisions in the process of selecting a tenant must be objective. If they aren't, you might face a discrimination complaint.

Walking Them Through the Apartment

When you show the apartment, you want to treat each viewer equally. Don't offer one couple a cup of coffee, then not offer it to anyone else. It might imply preferential treatment toward the first viewers. If any of those who subsequently saw the apartment should later compare notes with the first couple, they might conclude that since they weren't offered coffee, you were biased against them. Then they might file a discrimination complaint.

It might be beneficial to hold an "open house" on a particular day—weekends are the best. This will better ensure a uniform selling approach and save time for you. In addition, prospective renters aware of competition for the property are more willing to make quick decisions.

Never talk about what you would like to do to the apartment. You may change your mind later, discovering that it's too expensive, not feasible, or just too much work. But if that was one of the features that sold the apartment to your new tenant, you may be expected to honor your word. A tenant can hold you to a verbal statement as well as any feature you listed in the for-rent ad and later didn't deliver.

Don't assure prospects that the apartment is "very safe" or "very secure" because you've put in the very best locks you can get. If someone breaks in later, despite the locks, you could be held liable.

Avoiding Discrimination Complaints

Just as when advertising your apartment or discussing it over the phone, you must avoid overt and implied discrimination when showing the apartment. Never mention sex, race, color, national origin, religion, disabilities, age, or sexual orientation. And don't ask about the prospect's marital or family status. You may be exempt from federal Fair Housing Act requirements if you have only one unit to rent, but you still have to follow local and state laws and most likely don't want to do anything that might provoke a fair housing complaint. (See Chapter 4 for more information about exemptions for small property owners.)

ALERT!

In addition to the federal antidiscrimination acts, most states have legislation prohibiting landlords from discrimination when they rent apartments. Many local communities also have nondiscrimination clauses in their housing codes.

Even if your idea of a "perfect tenant" is an older person or couple, you cannot use that as criteria when you select a tenant. Only housing specifically designated by the city as a retirement community or senior housing can legally be rented to "seniors only." These codes often are more stringent than the state and federal requirements. Check them out first.

So what if a family with six kids wants to rent your apartment? If the unit only has two bedrooms, you can turn that family down, based on the two-persons-per-bedroom, plus one, occupancy guidelines established by HUD. (See Chapter 4.)

Who Said What? Write It Down

As you walk prospects through your unit, you can get a lot of information from them that is not legally prohibited. You can find out what they're looking for in an apartment and ask them other things pertaining to their jobs, pets, and rental history. After they've left, summarize their visit on the back of their rental application. Note all pertinent information, including things you discussed and any additional comments they made, and be sure to write down the date and time they came through.

Questions you can legitimately ask, without worrying about discrimination complaints, are:

- What are you looking for in an apartment?
- When do you need it?
- How many people will live there?
- What special features would you like?
- Why do you want to move?
- Is there anything wrong with your current apartment?

- What do you do for a living?
- Do you have a pet? What kind?
- Are you of legal age to sign a lease?

Anyone who's old enough—eighteen and above—to sign a lease must be considered as a potential tenant. It's the only way to avoid age-based discrimination complaints. If you later decide to reject their application, base your decision on financial, credit, or other verifiable legal reasons. (Prospects younger than eighteen can also be considered if they have an adult cosign the lease. The decision on whether to rent to them is yours.)

Rental Applications

Rental applications, filled out when you take people through your unit, provide you with information that will help you decide who will be your future tenant. In addition to the basics—name, address, telephone number—the application asks for such things as a current address and employer, and who will reside in the apartment.

Experts recommend using a standard rental application form, rather than making one up. With a standard form you get the same information from everyone, which makes it easier to make comparisons. By sticking to the questions in a rental agreement, you also are less likely to ask personal questions that might inadvertently imply that you are biased.

Have each adult who will be living in the unit fill out a rental application. If all the parties are working, you can combine their earnings to find out whether they can afford the rent you're asking.

Rental applications are an essential element in the selection process. The information provided by prospects can help you select the best possible tenants. It gives you solid, objective information that allows you to compare candidates and make your decisions.

Rental applications typically ask applicants for the following information:

- Personal details: date of birth, social security number, driver's license number, model and color of car, and license plate number
- Names of others who will live in the unit
- Rental history: former addresses, names and phone numbers of prior landlords
- Current employment and employment history: title or position held, supervisor's name and phone number
- Gross income
- Credit and financial details: banks, savings and checking account numbers, credit cards
- Monthly credit payments
- Whether applicant has had bankruptcies, lawsuits, evictions, or criminal convictions
- Number and type of pets, if your lease allows them
- References and emergency contacts: their names, addresses, and phone numbers

Review Applications Immediately

After the forms are filled out, take time to go over them while the applicants are still there. Verify their social security and driver's license numbers by looking at their card and driver's license. The social security number, current employment and employer, and emergency contacts are the information you need if you ever have to collect unpaid rent from a tenant who leaves before the lease is up. Make sure they've answered every question you've asked.

Above all, make sure the applications are signed. It gives you authorization to verify the information they've provided and to do a credit check.

Release Forms

Some landlords also ask prospects to sign a separate release form authorizing the landlord to verify information with an employer, credit bureau, bank, or savings institution. Banks in particular are reluctant to say anything without a release, and even when you provide it, most will only tell you whether or not that person has an account with the bank.

What do I do if someone doesn't fill out the whole application?
You can make it your standard policy to automatically reject an incomplete application without going any further. Of course, don't make any exceptions to this standard.

Narrowing Down the List

When you decide you have enough applications, you can stop showing the unit and start checking the information supplied by the applicants. First weed out applications from those who have not answered all your questions. Then look at the financial and employment backgrounds of the rest and eliminate those that have few or no resources or a spotty work history.

When you've narrowed the field—perhaps to three to five prospects—you're ready to move on to the next steps in finding the perfect tenant. You will check their credit, verify their employment history and their current employment, and look at whatever else you've decided is important to you. (See Chapter 11.)

Sometimes you'll get calls from a person or family who needs an apartment immediately. Don't rush into accepting any tenant. Take your time. Always go through all the rental applications and winnow them down step by step using the criteria you've established.

Don't Throw Applications Away

Experts recommend that you keep a file for each applicant for at least a year. Several years would be better. The file should include the applicant's rental application, your notes on conversations with the applicant, credit checks you've conducted, and any information you got from banks, employers, and references.

Every time you reject an applicant, write down the reasons why you came to that decision. It's easier to take a few minutes documenting the rationale for your decision than trying to recall the process months later. Those written, dated notes also build your case should you ever be taken to court.

Never eliminate every applicant in a protected category. For example, keep one single parent with children or one group of college students as prospects. If you don't consider any of those applicants who are in a protected group, you risk implying that you're prejudiced against single parents or students.

It can't be said often enough: Be absolutely certain you make all your decisions about eliminating applicants on facts that will stand up in court, not for personal or subjective reasons or just plain dislike.

You may sense that an applicant would be a headache as a tenant, but that's not a good enough reason for rejection. You have to substantiate that gut feeling with proof that they are unable to keep a job, that they don't pay their bills on time (or at all), or that previous landlords have had trouble with them. You will learn more about selecting and rejecting tenants in Chapter 11.

Chapter 11

Finding the
Perfect Tenants

Choosing a tenant. No job in your new role as a landlord will be more significant. And no matter how carefully you select tenants, you'll have no guarantees that you made the right decision. But there are things you can do to tip the balance in your favor. This chapter will explain how to check credit, background, and references in order to make an informed decision and protect yourself from discrimination charges.

What Do Tenants Want?

People looking at your apartment want rent to be reasonable. They take its location into account and they look at the overall design of the unit. They are particularly interested in the size of the apartment and the layout of the kitchen. After that they'll consider whether you can provide a quiet, safe environment.

Tenants want a landlord who is courteous, friendly, professional, and businesslike. They want their landlord to be responsive when repairs are needed and unobtrusive the rest of the time. They'd also like to have a landlord who shows some interest in them, yet allows them to have their privacy.

Tenants are entitled to live in a safe, sanitary, structurally sound apartment that has heat, hot water, and plumbing and appliances that work. The doors should lock, and the building should be free of insects and rodents. In other words, you should be offering a unit that's quiet, secure, and habitable. Do your part to provide these things, and you will attract applicants.

Interviewing Applicants

As a landlord, you have every right to ask a prospective tenant certain things. For example, you're entitled to know whether a prospective tenant is able to pay the rent you're asking, and to pay it on time every month. But there are also some things you should not ask. Learn the difference between appropriate and inappropriate questions before you speak with anyone who is interested in renting your space.

What You Can Ask

You can ask prospective tenants what they're looking for in an apartment, when they need it, and why they want to move. You can ask whether anything is wrong with their current apartment, what they do for a living, and whether they are of legal age to sign a lease.

You can ask if they've ever declared bankruptcy or been evicted. You can ask if they've ever been convicted of a crime. (Phrase this carefully—you may not ask if they've been arrested.) It's all right to check their credit and work history, and talk to previous employers to find out how much they made. You can even ask about outstanding debts—money they owe on a car loan or for credit cards.

ALERT!

Never ask prospective tenants if they've ever been arrested. An arrest is not the same thing as having been convicted of a crime. In the United States, people are presumed innocent until a judge or jury decides otherwise. Therefore, it is illegal to deny housing to anyone because they have been arrested.

What You Can't Ask

To avoid discrimination complaints, don't refer to anyone's sex, race, color, national origin, religion, or—even if they are obvious—disabilities. Don't ask about an applicant's age, sexual orientation, or family status (single, divorced, children). Never say you "prefer" mature tenants.

Treat all prospects equally. If you don't, that could imply discrimination and disgruntled applicants could file a complaint under local ordinances or state laws. Likewise, never arbitrarily raise the amount of rent you're charging or the security deposit you require for some prospects and not others. And don't make rent concessions for one person because you feel sorry for him or her. Everyone who comes to see the apartment is entitled to the same terms. Never tell someone that the unit has been rented when that's not true.

Applicants with Section 8 Federal Housing Assistance

The Section 8 Tenant Based Assistance: Housing Choice Voucher Program is managed by the Department of Housing and Urban Development (HUD). Section 8 housing assistance allows tenants to live in an apartment of their choosing. This program is totally separate from subsidized housing projects where hundreds of low-income residents live in numerous units all located within a specific area.

When government assistance is for an entire housing project, the money goes to the landlord or manager for all the tenants living in the apartments. If one family moves out, the money that covered that family covers the next family that moves in.

The focus is completely different with federal rental assistance. There the government funding is tied to the tenant. If he or she moves, the subsidy goes with the tenant for a new home.

If you do decide to take on tenants who have rental assistance, you know you'll get a check every month that will cover a substantial portion of the rent. The balance is paid by the tenant, who has to qualify financially for the federal program. The tenant is also responsible for paying the security deposit.

Benefits and Disadvantages of Section 8

Current law states that you don't have to participate in Section 8. It has been a matter of choice, although that may be changing because of housing shortages for low-income families. Thus legislators may decide to require that landlords accept tenants qualifying for Section 8. The main advantages of Section 8 to you as a landlord are:

- Fair market rental for your unit
- Regular payments from the government
- Tenants who don't want to lose their assistance and will avoid doing anything to jeopardize it
- Government money that continues for a while if the tenant has to be evicted

There are some disadvantages to joining the Section 8 program, too. These include:

- A contract with housing authorities that commits you to the program for at least a year

- More paperwork to fill out and regulations to be aware of
- Tenants who might not be as responsible as those who have higher incomes

If you accept a Section 8 tenant, spell out in the lease what portion of the monthly cost is to be received from the federal government and what portion is the tenant's responsibility. Use the words "housing assistance payment" in describing the government portion. The Housing Assistance Payments Contract (HAP contract) specifically states that the money is not to be considered rent—it is a housing assistance payment. Use those exact words when you fill out your paperwork and receipts.

FACT

Landlords in New Jersey must accept Section 8 vouchers if their tenants become eligible for the program. Connecticut landlords are required to accept vouchers from new and existing tenants. If you live in either state you can get more information from your local HUD office.

Screening Tenants

Don't assume applicants with Section 8 approval have been screened by the housing agency, because they haven't—except for their income. They will not have the income level you would ordinarily require of prospective tenants. But it is still important for you to prequalify them as you would anyone else applying to be a tenant. Check the credit history, employment history, previous landlords, references, and anything else important to you.

Evicting Section 8 Tenants

Section 8 tenants are no different than other tenants when it comes to evicting them. If you made a mistake and have a problem tenant, you can get rid of him or her for the same reasons you would anyone else: for nonpayment of rent, not abiding by the lease agreement, illegal activities, or damage to the unit.

The major difference is that while the eviction process is taking place, you will still receive a housing assistance check from the government. It will come to you, and you can cash it, even though your tenant is not paying rent. So this eviction process will cost you a little less than other evictions. (See Chapter 20 for more on evictions.)

Getting Fair Market Value

The housing assistance agency may think you are asking too much for your unit and offer you less. You can try to convince the agency that the rent that you are asking is the fair market value of duplexes or owner-occupied housing in your area. Be prepared to prove it. Get comparable information for similar units in your area, point out the features that make your unit better, use pictures of your property and the data you collected when you first decided how much to charge for the apartment.

Applicants with No Social Security Number

If a prospective tenant does not have a social security card, you will not be violating the fair housing laws if you refuse to rent to the applicant. Some landlords routinely turn them away. But once you make the decision not to accept applicants in this situation, don't reverse it later even if you meet a particular individual you think would make a good tenant. You want to be consistent at all times.

Applicants without social security cards are usually recent immigrants or foreign students in the United States. They can be very good tenants. If you'd like to consider them, there are other ways you can get the information you need.

Your first option is to use a state or federally issued identification card that has their photo on it instead of the social security card. This can be a passport, visa, green card, or driver's license. If you insist on identification issued by the state or federal government, you can be fairly certain it's not a fake.

You may also want to check to see if the applicant has a criminal history. The only identification you need for a criminal check is the person's name and birth date. You should be aware, however, that there's always a chance that two people with the same name share the same birthday.

FACT

To avoid fair housing complaints, make it your standard policy to do criminal histories on all candidates who sign the rental application but don't have a social security card. Never base your decision to check into criminal backgrounds on one individual's appearance. Either do it for everyone or don't do it at all.

As a final safety measure, get as much information as possible. Take down the applicant's full name (double-check any unfamiliar spelling or capitalization), birthplace, country of citizenship, and the names, addresses, and telephone numbers of two contacts in their home country. Write down their alien registration number, the type of visa they have, and the visa's expiration date. (If their visa has expired, they may be in the process of getting another one.) Ask how long they've been in the country, what their previous addresses were, and what their immigration status is. Write down the number of any driver's license they hold.

Verifying Rental Applications

As you go through rental applications, think like a sleuth. Verify listed employers and places of employment against the phone book. Do the company names, addresses, and phone numbers match? If you can't find a business in the phone book, find out why it's not there. If the applicant says the company went out of business, go to the library and look for listings in old phone books. Libraries usually keep them in the reference section.

If an applicant provides pay stubs, verify the social security number on the stub with what was written down on the application. Be wary of prolonged periods of unemployment or gaps in an applicant's employment history that may indicate the applicant doesn't hold jobs or doesn't want to list some of the workplaces.

If you discover that the applicant provided false information on the rental application, reject him or her as a tenant. (False information on a lease or rental agreement gives you grounds for evicting the tenant if he or she has already moved in.)

Keep a chart or file of local, state, and federal antidiscrimination laws at your fingertips as you go through applications. Don't forget about the Americans with Disability Act. Your policy may be "no pets," but if a prospect is blind and has a guide dog, for instance, you'd be violating that person's rights if you refused to rent the apartment because of the dog.

Background Checks and References

You can learn a lot about prospective tenants by talking to the people they've listed as job references, personal references, and former landlords. Along with a credit report, this information will help you to determine which of the candidates is the right one for your apartment.

Always double-check. Use the telephone book to determine whether the people listed actually live in your community and if the telephone numbers are correct. You want to know how truthful applicants were in filling out the form. (Keep in mind, however, that more and more people rely solely on cell phones or have an unlisted number.)

Employment History

Your goal is to find out whether the applicant has enough income to rent your apartment. Does the income reported on the application concur with what the employer tells you? Verify dates with former employers as well. Ask when the applicant started working there and whether he or she still is employed. This information is available in the Personnel or Human Resources departments of most companies and businesses. Don't forget to write down the name and title of the person who gave you the information and the date and time you called.

Sometimes applicants ask friends to field calls from prospective landlords. Use your intuition. Listen to how the "employer" answers questions. When he or she picked up the phone, did you hear the name of the company they allegedly work for? Were responses businesslike or not quite right? What did you hear in the background? If something doesn't ring true, you have reason to question the validity of the information you're getting. Make a note of it.

Some companies will not release information unless they get authorization from their employee. You can mail or fax them a copy of a consent to background check form signed by the applicant when he or she filled out the rental application. (See Appendix B for a sample consent form.) Some books say you can forward a signed copy of the rental application instead of a consent form, but if you do that, be sure to black out confidential information like the prospect's credit card numbers and information about bank accounts.

Anytime you suspect that you're not talking to a bona fide employer, you might double-check the business listings in the phone book. If the "company" is located outside your calling area, call information for that city and ask for the company's telephone number.

Previous Landlords

Talking to an applicant's previous landlords will tell you a lot about the applicant you're considering. If they didn't have problems with the tenant, you probably won't either. The information you need is:

- When the tenant moved in and moved out
- Whether the tenant was prompt in paying rent
- Whether the tenant was considerate of neighbors
- Whether the tenant had pets (and whether the pets caused problems)
- Whether the tenant gave the required notice
- Whether the unit was left in good condition
- Whether the security deposit was used to repair damage

Before you hang up, ask if the landlord has anything to add and if he or she would rent to that tenant again. This answer to this question may be more revealing than anything else the former landlord said.

References

Checking references can be tricky. Nothing bars an applicant from listing close friends or relatives. You want to know how long the reference has known the applicant. Ask "Would you recommend this person as a prospective tenant?" Then follow it up with "Why?" Take notes on their replies and, again, use your intuition. Did that person sound truthful?

FACT

Always take notes: write down the name of the applicant and what unit he or she wants to rent if you have more than one. Get the names and titles of people you talk to. Make a file for each applicant that contains the rental application and credit report. Don't throw anything away.

Banks

When you see shaky credit reports, you may want to check with the bank(s) listed to find out whether the applicant actually has an account there. Banks only verify that a person does have an account with them, and you will be expected to provide a signed release before they give you even that scant information.

Court Records

It's possible to get information about your applicants from court records. Bankruptcies are usually listed on credit reports, but you can also get information through the state court. Landlord-tenant records and lawsuits pertaining to collections or eviction will be held at your local district courthouse. You can expect to pay a fee whenever you check court records. If you do this, however, don't check only one individual. Look for records on everyone you're considering.

How to Do a Credit Check

After narrowing the field of applicants based upon the information in rental applications, you are now ready to do credit checks. Why is this step necessary? Simply because a credit report gives you a good indication of how responsible each prospect is when it comes to handling money. But while you are looking at their credit reports, keep in mind that credit bureaus make mistakes and some reports may contain inaccuracies.

Credit reports will tell you if a person pays rent and bills on time, was evicted (this information may not be available in some states), is involved in a lawsuit, and whether he or she has a credit history.

What's Involved in a Credit Check

Credit ratings are based on an individual's credit-paying history, the amount of money owed, the length of his or her credit history, new credit, and types of credit used. The report will give you specific information about the applicant's bank loans, credit card accounts, real estate loan payments, student loans, bankruptcies, and accounts in collection.

The data is given a numerical score ranging from 300 to 850. The higher the score, the more likely an individual is to pay bills in full and on time. Most people have a score in the 700 range. The following chart will help you interpret the score an applicant receives:

Credit Score	Delinquency Rate
800–850	1%
750–799	2%
700–749	5%
650–699	15%
600–649	31%
550–599	51%
500–549	71%
300–499	87%

Getting an Applicant's Credit Report

You can join one of three national credit-checking agencies by paying an annual fee. They also charge for each credit check, approximately

$50, and there's a small additional amount if you want the applicant's credit score. You'll get the information quickly, within minutes or a few hours. The three national agencies are Equifax Credit Information Systems, Experian (formerly TRW Information Services), and TransUnion. (See Appendix A for contact information.)

A cheaper way to get a credit history is by joining a credit union or the rental property owners association in your area. They also will charge a fee, but much less than the national services. You can also check credit histories online for a small fee, typically under $20. One service is Rental Housing On Line (RHOI).

You can also call banks, stores issuing credit cards, and finance companies individually (they'll be listed on the rental application) and find out whether your applicant has paid the bills on time each month. Information about bankruptcies is public record and available at your local courthouse.

If you reject an applicant based on his or her credit history, you should inform the applicant of the criteria you used for your decision, according to the Fair Credit Reporting Act (FCRA). The Federal Trade Commission (FTC) says that a rejection letter should state where you got the credit information and give the reporting agency's name, address, and phone number.

Tell the applicant what information you received, that he or she has the right to obtain a free credit report from that agency within sixty days, and that the applicant has the right to dispute the information in the report if it's inaccurate or incomplete.

ALERT!

If you eliminate a prospective tenant based upon a credit report, federal law requires you to give that person the name and address of the credit agency upon which you based your decision. That way he or she has an opportunity to contest what may be inaccurate data.

Charging Fees for Credit Checks

Some states now allow landlords to charge a prospective tenant a reasonable fee to cover the cost of getting a credit report, so the money doesn't come out of the landlord's pocket. Find out if your state will allow you to charge tenants and whether there is a limit on how much you can charge.

If you decide to charge a fee, you should let your prospects know that paying it does not guarantee that they will get the unit. Also tell them that selecting a tenant is a process of elimination and only the finalists will have their credit checked, therefore the fee may be refundable. Be sure they understand that fees paid by the finalists are not refundable. Tell them you will mail the uncashed checks to those who don't make it to the final round. Put your policy in writing on the rental application and also explain it to applicants when they fill the form out.

What If They All Have Bad Credit?

You want to select a tenant who does not have a lot of debt and who habitually pays bills on time. If your choices are limited, however, because everyone who looked at the apartment has only a fair or poor credit rating, then be sure to talk to previous landlords. Ask if the tenant regularly paid rent in full and on time. Ask how much rent the tenant paid. Does it match what the applicant wrote down?

When credit ratings are fair or poor, you should also verify what they've said about having a savings and checking account.

You can require people with poor credit histories to have a cosigner whose credit record is better. You can also require a cosigner if the applicant is too young to have built up a credit history.

If you select a tenant with poor credit, be sure to get as much of a security deposit as your state law permits. In Michigan, for example, the maximum security deposit is one-and-a-half times a month's rent—so if rent is $500 per month, then the security deposit cannot be greater than $750.

The last thing you should consider in looking at credit reports is whether the applicant is doing something to improve his or her credit rating. Since the information provided goes back seven-to-ten years, you can easily see whether the applicant is trying to improve the rating by paying off old debts. Take such things into account when making your decision about the best tenant for your unit.

Credit check fees are not a way for you to make extra money. Only cash the checks of people you are seriously considering as tenants because you will need only those credit reports. If you don't want to mail checks back to the others, you can do a preliminary elimination of applicants based on whether the people earn enough money to afford the rent. Then phone the others and ask them to come back and pay the credit check fee.

Report Results to Applicant

Applicants who are rejected because of their credit reports must be notified of your decision by letter. The letter should state why they were eliminated and what the basis was for your decision. You must also send a letter to an applicant if you conditionally accept him or her as tenant. Conditional acceptance means that you want a third party to guarantee the lease before you approve it. These notifications are requirements of the Fair Credit Reporting Act (FCRA).

Valid Reasons to Reject Applicants

You can protect yourself from discrimination complaints filed by applicants you've turned away by adhering strictly to facts—information you've collected from credit agencies, banks, previous landlords, former employers, and current employer.

Set Up Evaluation Guidelines

You can protect yourself further if you have guidelines for evaluating tenants in place from the beginning of your search process. Decide ahead of time what criteria are most important to you. Give them a numerical order. What will you look at first—what reasonable standard do you require? For those who past the first test, what will come second? Third?

If you check each application and credit history according to that pre-established order as you weed out candidates, you're all set. And you won't have to worry about whether you made a sound decision or have broken any fair housing rules. The following criteria are all valid reasons to turn down an applicant when used as part of a standard set of guidelines.

Poor Credit Record or Insufficient Income

If your applicant's credit history indicates frequent nonpayment of rent or if, based on information submitted, the rent is too high for the reported income, you can turn down an applicant.

FACT

Typically rent payments should be about a third of a person's gross monthly income. Keep in mind, however, that some prospects may be getting rent subsidies from state or federal sources. If they are, the amount they get has to be factored into your calculations. You cannot discriminate with regard to the source of a tenant's income.

Poor Prior-Landlord References

If previous landlords say the applicant's rent payment often came in late or that the apartment was left in poor shape, you can refuse to rent to that person.

Evictions and Civil Lawsuits

If an eviction is noted on the credit report and the landlord won the lawsuit, you can turn that person away. (If, however, the tenant prevailed, you should make your decision using other criteria.) If you have any doubt about whether your decision would be considered valid, consult a lawyer before notifying the applicant.

Criminal Records

You can refuse to rent to anyone who has been convicted of a criminal offense (with the exception of a drug use conviction). In some locations you may find convictions listed on an applicant's credit report.

An applicant with a prior drug use conviction is protected by the Fair Housing Amendments Act because the use of drugs is considered a disability. You cannot reject the applicant for previously using drugs. But you don't have to rent your apartment to anyone who has been convicted of manufacturing or selling drugs; you can legally refuse to take them on as tenants.

Incomplete or Inaccurate Rental Application

You can reject anyone who has not answered all the questions on your rental application. Likewise if you discover that someone gave you false or inaccurate information, you can reject that person, too.

Unable to Meet Terms of Lease

You don't have to consider anyone who is unable to pay the required security deposit or to rent the apartment for the length of the lease. If you have a one-year lease and they only want the apartment for nine months, it's legal to say "No."

If a couple, married or not, wants to rent an apartment, you must use both of their incomes in determining whether they can afford your rent. If you don't, you risk a discrimination complaint about marital status or sex.

Pets or Smokers

You can refuse to rent to smokers or people with pets if your space for rent is designated "nonsmoking" or "no pets." However, if an animal is trained to assist someone who is blind, deaf, or mentally or physically disabled, it must be allowed.

Always Write Down Why

When you reject an applicant, note the reasons for your decision. Put them on the back of the rental application. Then file it and other appropriate documentation. Don't throw any of this information away. You may need it later if a discrimination complaint is filed. The application also might come in handy later if that person tries to rent another apartment from you.

Chapter 12

Providing a "Perfect" Home

Renting an apartment is a two-way obligation. While your tenant has to take care of your property, not do anything illegal while living there, and keep it in a sanitary condition, state laws and local housing codes say you must keep the apartment clean, safe, and habitable. In this chapter you'll learn more about the "assumed standard of habitability" and what you can do to provide the home your tenants want.

Cleanliness Counts with Tenants You Want

It's move-in day! The apartment looks almost new—it has been fixed up, painted, and cleaned so well that everything looks spotless and smells fresh. The plumbing works, hot and cold water run through the taps, and there's electricity and heat.

The building is structurally sound; the entrance, stairs, yard, and porch are clean and uncluttered with trash. There are no rodent or insect infestations and the garbage area is tidy and won't attract them.

Your tenant expects you to keep the property that way. But state and local officials make it a requirement. If there are any housing violations that affect the health and safety of tenants and their guests, public officials can impose fines. In extreme cases of neglect, they can shut down your building.

State housing laws and local building codes place a burden on landlords to repair and maintain their property so that tenants are not exposed to hazardous or unhealthy conditions. You should want that, too, because anything less might lead to a liability suit.

If you discover anything in the apartment that might be unsafe, fix it immediately. Keep stairs safe by nailing down loose boards and replacing broken treads. Fix frayed wiring and cords. Repair leaky faucets. Exterminate insects and rodents as soon as you know there's a problem and waterproof wet areas to discourage mold and mildew from forming.

FACT

Also let your tenant know that if he or she puts food away right after a meal, keeps counters clean, rinses out bottles and cans, and takes out trash regularly instead of letting it collect in the kitchen, most bug and rodent problems can be avoided.

Make Them Feel Secure

Tenants are entitled to a safe, secure environment, and housing codes were enacted to ensure that landlords provide it. Landlords must do everything they can, in a reasonable manner, to prevent accidents and crime. "Reasonable" means that landlords don't have to spend a fortune or go way beyond their means to make their building safe.

Look for Nuisances

Any malfunction or problem that is dangerous to life or harmful to health can be considered a nuisance if you do not promptly fix it. These can range from having blocked sewage lines to not providing enough heat. (If you set the thermostat at a minimum of seventy degrees Fahrenheit in cold weather, you should not have a problem.) Landlords who have created a nuisance can be cited by local housing officials and subject to penalties.

The potential for health hazards goes up when trash collects in a dirty area, a building is infested with bugs and mice, or a clogged or cracked toilet is not fixed. Roofs that leak and windows that are broken make an apartment uninhabitable. Frayed electrical wiring can cause a fire and people can be hurt or die if furniture is blocking a door or window that could be used as an emergency exit. You should already have dealt with such nuisances before your tenants arrive, but ask them to monitor for anything that comes up after they've been there for a while.

So-called "attractive nuisances" on the property include abandoned vehicles, appliances, and other equipment that might attract curious children who want to climb into them and play. Open wells and shafts also attract children and can potentially cause harm. Safety codes require that you get rid of such nuisances. If you don't, your risk for a liability claim goes up.

You can't repair something that you don't know about. Ask your tenant to tell you immediately if he or she knows of any situation that might be harmful to adults and/or children. Then ask again several months later. You want your tenant to know that you are a concerned landlord who wants to provide a building that is safe for tenants and guests.

If you allow drug dealing to take place on or near your property, it can endanger others. It is illegal for a tenant to use, sell, manufacture, or distribute drugs. If your tenant is the problem, you should immediately start the eviction process.

Fire Extinguishers Increase Security

Buy fire extinguishers for your unit. Since stovetop grease fires are a common occurrence, place one extinguisher near the stove. When you're buying an extinguisher, however, keep in mind that those filled with pressurized water will only make a grease fire worse. Look for an extinguisher that specifically stops a grease fire from spreading.

Why should you spend the money? You have two good reasons: First, it's your own home that will be threatened if a fire occurs. Second, you can't collect rent if the unit is empty. Your tenant will move out while you're repairing the fire-damaged apartment and might not come back.

Listen to Your Tenant

If a tenant thinks something is broken or not working the way it should, get the full story, then check into it. Tenants can tell if a stair rail is loose or door and window locks are broken. Once a tenant is living in the apartment, he or she will serve as your best resource for identifying problems early, before they develop into something more costly.

Go even further than just listening to your tenant. Encourage your tenant to report anything that doesn't seem right. He or she will appreciate your thoughtfulness and think you are the best landlord around.

How hot is the water coming from your water heater? If it's too hot, your tenants run the risk of being scalded. It's easy enough to set the heater at 120 degrees Fahrenheit. Then they'll still be able to take hot showers and wash dishes and clothes without harm to anyone.

A Quiet and Restful Space

Providing a habitable dwelling means that your tenants are entitled to quiet and peaceful enjoyment of the unit. You don't have to spend a dime to take a few extra measures that will allow them to relax and have peace of mind. And again, you, too, will benefit from your efforts. Not only will you be able to attract good tenants, but you'll have peace and quiet, too.

Use Tact to Handle Complaints

Is there a noise ordinance in your community? If so, you'll find "noise" covers many things—loud neighbors, barking dogs, souped-up motorcycles revving up and down the street, and amplified music pulsing out of open car windows.

It takes diplomacy, tact, and good will to handle noise intrusions so that the matter doesn't escalate to a full-scale war with your neighbors. If a neighbor often disturbs your tenants with loud music, you should talk to the offender and try to get it resolved. Otherwise when the lease expires, your tenant will simply move out and into an apartment in a quieter neighborhood.

Do Your Part

Respond to a tenant's noise complaints and work with neighbors to eliminate problems with rowdy teens or uncontrolled pets. Everyone will benefit when you succeed. Even if your tenant or neighbor is upset, you should stay cool yourself and be diplomatic.

You can be quiet, too. Don't mow the lawn too early in morning or late at night. If your tenant works odd hours, find out when the lawn mower and snow blower will be least disturbing. If your tenant is the one making the noise, don't be afraid to bring this up as well, as long as you are diplomatic about it. You and your tenant both should respect the quiet hours you agreed to in the lease. After a long day at work or at home, everyone wants to sit back and relax.

FACT

Never be a nuisance. Tenants are entitled to privacy and quiet. They don't want a landlord who hovers over them or gets in their way. You want to be personable, not personal or nosy.

Notify Tenants of Work Schedules

If you know that the city will be working in your neighborhood, let your tenant know when it is scheduled to start and end. You especially want to notify your tenant if the work will be noisy. Reasonable tenants will understand that you are just informing them of the schedule—you didn't set it up. If trash pickup in your neighborhood is at 6 a.m., your tenant will just have to grin and bear the noise. It doesn't last long.

Also tell tenants if you're getting a new roof, taking out concrete and pouring a new drive, having siding installed, or doing other major work to the property. They shouldn't get too upset if the commotion is short-lived.

Schedule Periodic Upkeep and Maintenance

After your tenant moves in, housecleaning is his or her chore. But you still have to care for the property, including the yard, entry, and hall. When something breaks or needs repairs—and it wasn't caused by your tenant—you have to fix it. You are responsible for fixing any breakage or malfunctions caused by normal wear and tear of your property.

If your tenant or a guest breaks something, such as a window or door, he or she has to repair or replace it. Responsibility for repairs shifts to the tenant when it's not the landlord's fault or the result of wearing out. For liability reasons, however, it's best for landlords to fix the window or door, then charge the tenant for the repair bill.

Try to schedule time for routine maintenance of your property about every six months. To keep track of what's necessary and what you've already done, you can use a semiannual and annual maintenance schedule. (See Chapter 18 for more on keeping maintenance records.)

Anytime the tenant has a complaint, be responsive. Unless it's obviously an emergency (in which case you need to act immediately), let your tenant know when you'll be in to fix the problem. Then keep your word. Tenants trust reliable landlords; if you say you're going to do something, do it.

Don't let trash and garbage spill over or pile up outside the trash cans. In addition to attracting rodents and bugs, it looks "trashy" and that might reduce the value of your home.

No matter how busy you are, never delay doing one repair job until you have several others to do. That will only frustrate your tenant and tarnish your image. If it happens too often, he or she may seek another place to live at the end of the lease.

Broken windows, doors, and loose shutters also detract value from your property. Take care of them right away. Keep an eye on the roof, too. If you can afford it, reroof when it starts looking bad to prevent the inevitable leaks that will damage ceilings and walls. A new roof also increases the value of your property, and your insurance company will be happy you've replaced it. Tell your agent about all of your improvements. Some of them might reduce your premium a few dollars.

Don't Forget the Grass and Snow

First impressions count. And the first thing people see when looking at your home is the exterior of the building and your yard. Don't neglect either. Your tenant wants to live in a house that's cared for, and if it is, you'll be able to get more for rent.

In addition to mowing and weeding the lawn regularly, you should pick up trash that blows into the yard. Rake leaves. If you live where it snows a lot, you can give your tenant responsibility for shoveling his or her sidewalk or driveway. But make sure you have a written agreement that the tenant will take care of removing snow and ice.

Keep some sand or salt handy for those winters when ice builds up on the sidewalk. If someone slips, falls, and files a liability claim, but you regularly put salt down, you'll be able to say you did everything reasonably possible to protect your tenant and guests.

The Importance of Keeping Tenants Happy

If you ever feel like the constant maintenance of your property is a waste of time and energy, remind yourself why you're doing it. Just about anyone in business will tell you that it's cheaper to keep customers than it is to find new ones. When tenants renew their lease, you profit—both in time and money. If a tenant renews, you don't have to clean, paint, and get the unit ready for someone else. You don't have to advertise, take phone calls, show the apartment, or do credit checks on prospects. Obviously, keeping a good tenant should be your goal.

QUESTION?

Is there anything extra I can do to make my property more appealing?
If you can provide a deck or patio for your tenant to use, do it. It's a nice touch that tenants appreciate almost as much as off-street parking. These special touches can make the unit more than just another apartment for them. It will be their home.

How Can You Keep Them?

The process of keeping tenants starts soon after a tenant moves in. Build a relationship and be responsive, but always remember that you're in business. You should act professionally at all times. When you see your tenant, be friendly and courteous. Be cheerful, even if you're having a bad day. Listen to your tenant! Show interest in what he or she has to say.

In addition to responding to maintenance requests in a timely manner, call your tenant occasionally to find out if everything's okay. Always let tenants know how much you appreciate their paying rent on time each month or otherwise acting as good tenants. If a tenant shovels a sidewalk when you're tied up or lets you know in advance that he or she is having a party—promising that it won't go past midnight—say thank you. Let your tenant know that you appreciate these courtesies.

Effective supervisors, managers, and bosses know that complimentary words show appreciation and build loyalty in their employees. You don't oversee a huge department or dozens of employees, but you still can adopt the best business practices from people who know what to do and who are liked and respected by other employees. Chapter 21 will give you more tips on keeping good tenants.

Chapter 13

Move-in Procedures to Safeguard Your Space

Two people see exactly the same thing, yet afterward their descriptions can be entirely different. In a landlord-tenant relationship, that can lead to major disputes about exactly when damage occurred— prior to the tenant moving in or while he or she lived there. In this chapter you'll learn how a tenant's checklist and move-in letter can protect both of you.

What Are Tenant's Checklists?

An inventory and condition of premises checklist—commonly called a tenant's checklist—documents the condition of the apartment at the time the tenant moves in. The checklist should be filled out and signed by both you and your tenant after the lease is signed and you inspect the property together. When both of you note that a floor, wall, or closet door was in good condition prior to the tenancy, and you then notice damage when the tenant moves out, you know it was your tenant's fault.

Since the checklist has both your signatures, it indicates that you both agreed that the unit was originally in good shape and that your tenant agreed to keep the property that way. This means a tenant has little room for dispute when you withhold some of the security deposit to make repairs or clean up excessively dirty areas after he or she moves out.

You can see examples of many of the forms landlords use in Appendix B of this book. You can find other forms at professional landlords associations or on the Internet. You can also purchase software such as ProBiz 500 Legal Documents at bookstores and stores selling computer supplies. To be on the safe side, once you decide to go into landlording, obtain copies of forms specific to your state, to make certain that they conform with landlord-tenant regulations in your state or community.

How to Use Tenant's Checklists

A tenant's checklist typically contains an itemized inventory of the whole apartment, room by room. It lists everything—the condition of the walls, windows, drapes, lights, electrical outlets, floors or carpeting, towel rods, and clothes hooks. It may even include ice cube trays and whether the refrigerator and other appliances are in good working condition.

Checklists for Move-in and Move-out

Often landlords will use one checklist to indicate the condition of the apartment when the tenant moves in, and another for when he or she moves out. It's important that before your tenant moves in, you both agree that the apartment and the furnishings are in good condition, so a move-in checklist is completed. At the end of the tenancy when the move-in checklist (signed by both of you) is compared to a move-out checklist, you can determine whether any damage occurred during the tenancy that goes beyond normal wear and tear from use.

Look at several types of sample forms and decide which checklist might work best for you (Appendix B includes one version of move-in and move-out checklists). Some are extremely detailed, itemizing everything from light switches to light bulbs. Others let the landlord decide what's important. You go through the rooms and fill in contents that you want to keep track of.

All checklists provide room for the tenant to make comments about what needs to be fixed or cleaned and there should be space for each of you to initial every item that is satisfactory. The last part of the checklist is filled out by the landlord when the tenant moves out. After comparing the move-in list to the move-out list, you will write down the estimated cost of any repairs or replacements necessitated by the tenant's use, then add them up. The total tells you how much you can retain of the security deposit to get the apartment back into satisfactory shape.

Be very careful not to make mistakes when you fill out the checklist. If you try to withhold money to repair something that was not the tenant's fault, your tenant can use the checklist as proof that he or she did not damage the property and is entitled to receive the full amount of the security deposit.

ALERT!

Eleven states now require landlords to give tenants a detailed statement about the condition of the property before tenants move in—Arizona, Georgia, Hawaii, Kentucky, Maryland, Massachusetts, Michigan, Montana, North Dakota, Virginia, and Washington. Then tenants have the right to inspect the premises and dispute any statements with which they disagree.

Some landlords simply hand a checklist to their tenants and ask them to fill it out and return it. That can cause problems later if the landlord wasn't there to agree or disagree about what was listed as unsatisfactory. You can have more clout in disputes if you inspect the property together, because it will be easier to substantiate your position.

The Inspection Process

As you go through the apartment together during the inspection, you each check off items that you judge to be in satisfactory shape. If something on the list is missing or needs to be repaired, write down specifically what is missing or the details of the damage. For example, is the bedroom shade torn or is there a twelve-inch red stain on the living room carpet?

It's important to be very specific when describing damage. Never simply say that an item "needs fixing." Instead, say a light switch doesn't work, that there's a bulb out in the fixture, that the hall area is scuffed and dirty, or that the door has a two-inch scratch about halfway down. Write down that there's a mildew problem in the shower or tub, evidence of pests or rodents, or a one-inch hole in the wall above the light switch in the master bedroom. Be extremely specific about the fire extinguisher and smoke detector; say they were working during the inspection and have your tenant confirm it by initialing the sentence. That proves you're doing everything you can to ensure your tenant's safety and that the tenant agreed, which will work in your favor should he or she later attempt to file a liability claim.

You and your tenant should both sign and date all copies of the checklist. You keep the original and give your tenant a carbon or photo copy. If you purchase inventory checklists from a professional organization, you'll very likely get documents that have carbonless multipart forms and thus avoid possible alterations.

After the inspection you should fix and clean anything noted on the inventory to be in unsatisfactory condition. If you and the tenant both agree there is work that should be done, you have two options. You can delay signing and dating the checklist until you've completed the work, or you can take the signed document back to your tenant afterward for another signature or initials to indicate that the problem has been satisfactorily repaired. As you make repairs, write down the date you completed the task.

When your tenant checks and signs the tenant's checklist, he or she tacitly agrees that the premises, currently in satisfactory condition, will be left that way. In other words, the tenant is promising to take care of the apartment so that when he or she moves out the landlord will find the only deterioration of the unit was caused by normal wear and tear.

Take Pictures During Inspection

As you and your tenant walk through the apartment, it helps to take pictures of preexisting damage and wear and tear. Consider purchasing a Polaroid camera, then as each picture develops you and your tenant can sign and date it on the back.

Be sure your pictures show the most-damaged areas. Try to get your tenant in one or more of the pictures to verify that he or she looked at the apartment on that date. Some tenants won't want their pictures taken. You can still substantiate the date if you buy that day's newspaper and display the front page headline in the picture. Since the applicant will sign and date the checklist, the newspaper will prove you were both present on that day.

After the tenant moves out, you should also take pictures of damage that occurred during his or her occupancy. Then you have evidence to present if your tenant decides to go to court to recover the security deposit.

How Do Checklists Protect You?

When your tenant signs the checklist, he or she is saying that the apartment was in good shape at move-in. Then if you find something broken or missing when the lease expires, you have documentation that this was not the case when you initially rented the apartment. A checklist should help you avoid arguments with your tenant and the possibility of court action. It also substantiates your justification for withholding some of the security deposit to make repairs and clean the unit.

Protection for the Landlord

Meticulously kept records are a landlord's best defense against any tenant complaints. When property damage occurs and there is no documentation, complaints easily deteriorate into a "he said, she said" contest. No one is able to prove when the damage actually occurred.

FACT

Some landlords devote one paragraph of the checklist to smoke detectors and read it to the tenant during the inspection. It should state that you told the tenant where detectors are located, how they work, and how to take care of them. Have the tenant sign or initial the paragraph when you're finished.

Tenants typically don't complain unless you fail to fix something that was unsatisfactory or you withhold some or all of the security deposit for a repair. Then they might go to small claims court to recover their money. You have a better chance of convincing the judge that your position is justified if you show the court the signed checklist. In the few minutes allotted for your defense, you can also show the judge the before-and-after-pictures you took. That evidence will put you on solid ground for a decision in your favor.

Protection for the Tenant

The checklist also protects your tenant. It establishes proof of preexisting damage and wear and tear. When damage noted during the inspection is not repaired by the landlord as promised, tenants can use the checklist to demonstrate why they are withholding rent or breaking their lease. It shows that they rented an apartment that needed a lot of repairs and that the landlord wasn't responsible enough to fix them.

Avoiding Potential Problems

A big advantage of inspecting the property together is that you can settle any potential disputes right on the spot. If your tenant wants something fixed and you agree that the repair request is reasonable, it's on record; he or she can use the checklist to ensure that you follow through with repairs. If damage is slight, you can both check off the column that says it's satisfactory. The important thing is that you both agree.

Handling Move-in Complaints

Be prepared for complaints the tenants may have on moving day. Here are some common complaints and suggested ways of handling them:

- **"The apartment is dirty."** Not if you cleaned it thoroughly a few days before and have vacuumed and dusted counters and windowsills. But if you've unwittingly rented to a demanding tenant, ask where the problem is and go over it again.
- **"I don't like the paint job."** If you painted the bedroom blue, they may want it green or pink. Avoid this complaint by avoiding colors. If you always decorate the apartment in neutrals—white or off-white—you should never have a problem. Or is the tenant complaining about some paint spills and spatters? If so, you'll want to clean them up.
- **"My oven doesn't work."** Even if it worked when you last checked it, there could be a problem. Check it out immediately. If you find something wrong, fix it right away. Tell the tenant exactly when the work will take place.
- **"I saw a mouse."** Whether it's a mouse or bugs, tell your tenant you'll take care of a pest problem right away and that should be the end of the complaint. Get an exterminator and have the company come back a week or so after the first appointment to make sure everything's fine.
- **"The plumbing is leaking."** Is it minor or major? If the faucet is dripping, fix it within a day or two, but if the toilet is overflowing, it obviously needs immediate attention.
- **"My key doesn't work."** Maybe you goofed and gave the tenant the wrong key. Keep an extra set handy so you can give the new set to the tenant in exchange for the ones you originally handed over.

You can avoid complaints about keys that don't work or work only with difficulty. Before you turn over the apartment, check the locks with the tenant's keys to see that they can be smoothly closed and opened before you give them to the tenant. Sometimes keys wear out and then it gets harder and harder to lock and unlock doors. Giving your tenant a new set should take care of the problem.

Move-in Letters

Some landlords give tenants a move-in letter that restates the terms of the lease and has other information about the apartment. The move-in letter can tell tenants what procedures to follow when they move out and explain how they can get their security deposit back. This is one way to put basic information about taking care of the apartment and grounds in writing—things that are not included in the lease or rental agreement.

Basic Information and Procedures

You can list basic information such as your telephone number and an alternate or emergency number (such as a cell phone) for times when you can't be reached at home. Tell your tenant how to report problems with plumbing, for example. The letter is a good place to say that you would like to be notified immediately any time your tenant spots what could become a health or safety hazard so that you can take care of the problem before anyone gets hurt. Let them know what the best way to notify you is.

Spell out any special instructions for using the garbage disposal or laundry area. You might want to reiterate procedures for moving out at the end of the lease or what they need to do if they want a roommate to move into the apartment.

The letter can also remind your tenant that you will inspect the apartment once or twice a year for routine maintenance and safety. Describe the notification procedure you will use to come into the unit for repairs and maintenance.

Remind the tenant that you must be notified about phone number changes and that you must be notified if he or she wants to change a lock. You can restate what's in the lease, that you must be given one of the new keys.

FACT

As a courtesy, some landlords give new tenants the forms used to apply for utility hookups and phone service. You can include change of address cards, a map of the community if the tenant is new to the area, and a list of the local hospitals, schools, and stores.

Renter's Insurance

You should also remind your tenant that it is a good idea to carry renter's insurance because your policies do not cover the tenant's personal belongings. Rental insurance covers acts of God—damage to personal property caused by such things as a windstorm, hail, or tornado. It also covers property damaged by a fire or if a water pipe freezes and bursts. (See Chapter 6 and 7 for more on insurance and liability.)

Trash and Recycling Programs

The move-in letter is a good place to give your tenant details about the garbage collection services in your area—what day the truck will come and where to leave the cans for pickup. If there is a recycling program in your community, let your tenant know about it. Tell them what materials are recycled, how they are collected—some cities have special recycling containers—and whether or not the recycled items will be picked up on the same day as the trash.

Moving Out

Move-in letters also contain information about moving out of the apartment. Restate that you require thirty days' notice of moving out, whether the tenant has a rental agreement or intends to move out after the lease expires. Also tell your tenant that you will inspect the apartment for overall cleanliness and damage before you return all or part of the security deposit and that returning the security deposit is also contingent upon whether the tenant owes back rent.

If your tenant wants to be with you while you inspect the apartment before he or she moves out, go through it together as you did before move-in. It could eliminate hassles about using the security deposit for repairs. But warn your tenant that you will be looking at how clean the unit is, as well as for damage.

In your letter, list the items that you will be looking at for cleanliness—counters, cabinets, closets, the oven and refrigerator, and so on. Most tenants want their money back and if they know what is expected, they'll make sure it gets done.

Move-out procedures also should include a reminder that tenants need to call the phone, cable, and utility companies to turn off services so they will be billed only for what they have used.

Chapter 14

Rental Agreements and Leases

You'll hear the terms "rental agreement" and "lease" used interchangeably. Although they are both agreements arranged between you and your tenant before you hand over the keys, and they both specify details about rent, occupancy, house rules, and other conditions, they are really two different things. In this chapter you'll learn the difference between leases and rental agreements, what they should include, and how to renew a lease.

What's the Difference?

Rental agreements are not the same thing as a lease although sometimes the terms are used interchangeably. One gives you flexibility; the other is a binding agreement between two parties for a fixed term. You might decide ahead of time that you prefer one over the other. But you'd be better off to keep documents for both on hand and decide when you're investigating prospective tenants which one you want to offer. Landlords do not have to give every tenant a one-year lease. You can offer a lease for three or six months, or use a month-to-month rental agreement instead of a lease.

What's a Rental Agreement?

Think of a rental agreement as a month-to-month contract between a landlord and tenant. It gives both parties flexibility to make changes or get out of the agreement after giving the other party thirty days' notice.

Also known as a "periodic contract," a rental agreement spells out the landlord's and the tenant's duties and obligations. It includes the landlord's rules and expectations and informs the tenant about such things as trash disposal, changing locks, and storage and may include an attachment that has additional provisions and rules for tenants. Both parties should sign and date this attachment, as well as the rental agreement itself.

What's a Lease?

A lease—usually written for one year, although it can be shorter—is a binding legal contract between two parties. As with rental agreements, attachments may be also provided, usually containing additional provisions and general house rules. Again, such an attachment must be signed by both parties to be valid.

During the period of the lease rent is fixed, rules cannot be changed by the landlord, and the only way to get rid of a tenant is by evicting him or her. Tenants can only be evicted for serious situations, including nonpayment of rent, violations of lease terms, damage to property, or illegal activities. Consult a lawyer if you're not sure whether you have legal grounds to evict a tenant.

ALERT!

There are also restrictions on the wording of a lease. Landlords cannot give tenants a lease that waives their right to privacy and quiet enjoyment of their home, waives the landlord's liability for damage and injuries to the tenant, or waives the tenant's legal rights to sue or have a jury trial.

Pros and Cons of Rental Agreements

Rental agreements establish a month-to-month (or week-to-week) tenancy; tenants can stay in your apartment for as long as neither of you want the relationship terminated. Despite the uncertainty of how long your tenant will live there, the agreement should be in writing because it also sets forth your expectations and rules.

Landlords have much more flexibility with rental agreements than with a lease. They can get rid of problem tenants without going through the hassle of an eviction. They can raise the rent if expenses go up or a variable or balloon mortgage with higher payments kicks in. And they can change rules in the agreement. The only requirement is that the tenant get thirty days' notice before having to vacate or before changed terms go into effect.

The only reason you might not want to use a rental agreement is that it can establish a revolving door. In other words, you might have tenants moving in and, a short time later, moving out. Of course, they, too, are required to give you thirty days' notice that they are leaving. You have to decide whether you want to risk having to prepare for and find suitable tenants over and over again.

Pros and Cons of Leases

Leases may be written for any length of time, but will typically run a year. During that time neither tenants nor landlords have flexibility to change anything written into the document or any attachments to the lease signed by both parties. The lease locks in the length of time a tenant will be residing in the apartment, rules that have to be followed, and how much rent has to be paid.

FACT

A long-term lease encourages tenants to stay, but, of course, it's not absolute. If your tenant decides to break the lease and move, there's little a landlord can do about it except to try to recover rent for the remaining months.

Tenants are locked into their responsibilities and obligations. They agreed to stay a year and if they move sooner, they have to continue making rent payments until a new tenant moves in. (Landlords are not allowed to collect double rent.) Tenants can break a lease without being obligated to pay the remaining rent, however, if they go into the military or a nursing home.

However, the downside is that you're also locked into the agreement you made. If your lease allows the tenant to have a dog and you later regret it, you can't do anything about it unless the dog damages your property or creates a noise nuisance. When the year is up, in most states the lease ends automatically. Then you can raise rent, change parts of the lease, or change your tenant.

Benefits of Six-Month Leases

Sometimes landlords issue leases for less than a year. A six-month lease has all the benefits of a lease, but since it expires twice a year, landlords are free to make changes and raise the rent more frequently.

If you expect your expenses to increase dramatically or if rental rates in your area are unstable but on their way up, you might want to give your tenant a short-term lease. Then you can make an adjustment before you issue anyone a new lease. A short-term or six-month lease is also a good idea if you plan to start renovating or remodeling your property in a few months.

If the people who answered your ad seem to be less than the ideal tenants you had hoped to get or if the unit has been vacant for too long and you need the monthly rent payments, you don't want to be locked into the binding one-year contract that is typical for a lease.

If you are thinking of selling your property, this is another case where you may want a short-term lease. If you find a buyer, the new landlord won't have to wait long before the lease expires and he can decide whether to keep the tenant, find a new one, or work on the apartment before putting it up for rent.

With a rental agreement all you have to do to have a tenant move out is to give them thirty days' notice to quit. You don't have to say why, but try to link your decision to the provisions in the rental agreement—they can be the same as those in a one-year lease—so that you don't have to worry about breaking a fair housing law.

When to Make Rental Concessions

When there are too many vacant apartments in your area, a large apartment complex may be able to offer new tenants a rent-free month. They have so many units that it's easier for them to absorb the cost. But it's not feasible for landlords with only one tenant.

You can, however, give a new tenant a couple of rent-free days if he or she wants to move in just before the end of the month in a competitive market. It might tip the prospect's decision toward you. (In normal circumstances if a tenant moves in before the end of the month, most landlords prorate rent for a few days, then collect a full month's rent for the new month.)

When a tenant does small repair jobs in your dwelling, takes care of the yard, or shovels snow, you can reimburse him or her with a rent reduction the following month. The best way to handle reimbursement is to collect full rent every month and, after your tenant does the work, rebate the amount specified in the written agreement you prearranged with your tenant. That puts you, not your tenant, in control of deciding whether you owe him or her money.

Lease and Rental Agreement Basics

Your lease or rental agreement and the security deposit you require must comply with your state and local laws. The document cannot contain language that attempts to take away any of your tenant's legal rights—to file complaints, sue for liability or injury, or get the security deposit back promptly if the unit is left in good condition.

How much the tenant pays for the security deposit is usually limited by the state and local government. Some communities require you to pay interest on your tenant's money.

ALERT!

Agreements that you'll give a rent rebate for work performed should always be a separate document signed by both parties. It should never be included in the lease. If it is, your tenant might take it for granted that rent is automatically $25 less even for those months when no work was performed.

Preprinted Leases and Rental Agreements

Many landlords like to use preprinted forms available through professional associations and several online companies. You might find a multipurpose document that can be used for either a lease or rental agreement—you cross out the wording that doesn't apply—or you might get two separate forms. They have been prepared by experts and give you the security of knowing that the lease or rental agreement is legal.

When you use a preprinted form, you fill in the blanks. Start out by writing in the complete address of the unit and your full name, address, and phone number. You can cross out parts that don't apply and substitute or add whatever you choose. (Make sure that both you and the tenant initial all changes made by hand.) If you make changes, however, be wary of adding anything illegal to the form. If in doubt, check with your local landlord association or with your attorney. Some of the forms available have been prepared by attorneys and are specifically targeted to individual states.

Getting Signatures

You should prepare two copies of the lease or rental agreement and any attachments, one for you and one for your tenant(s). All copies should be signed by you and by all adults who will be living in the unit, including the tenant's spouse or roommate(s). It's a good idea to check their signatures against the signatures on their driver's licenses.

FACT

It's better to use a preprinted lease or rental agreement and cross out paragraphs that don't pertain to what you are offering in your unit than it is to write your own document from scratch. Without legal training or years of experience as a landlord, you might inadvertently use language that a court might interpret as being prejudicial or unenforceable.

Make sure that you and your tenant(s) have initialed any changes made in the lease, as well as specific clauses that say that your tenant was informed verbally, as well as in writing, about certain provisions. You don't want a tenant to say later, "I didn't know—you never told me."

If you make many changes and things are difficult to read, it's a good idea to replace it with a new lease or rental agreement. Make sure all copies of this new version of the document are signed by you and your tenant(s).

Get Everyone's Name

The lease or rental agreement should contain the full names of everyone eighteen and older who will occupy the unit. It should state the date the lease or rental agreement begins, when the tenants must start paying rent, and the date on which it ends—usually the last day of the month. If no dates are specified, it's considered that you have given the tenant a month-to-month agreement.

QUESTION?

How old does a tenant need to be to sign a lease?
Anyone eighteen and older can sign a lease or rental agreement. If your prospective tenants are under legal age, you should require that they bring in a cosigner. If you later find out that a tenant lied about his or her age and signed the document, it is invalid.

Clauses about Rent and Fees

Your lease or rental agreement should include exact information about rent, the security deposit, and other fees that the tenant is responsible for. You should include not only amounts, but also details about when and how fees should be paid.

Rent Due Dates

A lease spells out the total amount of money that must be paid for the year and how much of it is due each month (a twelfth of the total). It should say that rent must be paid promptly and is due on a certain day each month. A rental agreement will specify what money is due each month and when it is due.

Both should clearly state when rent will be considered late, if there is a grace period, and what late payment fees you charge. Also include a clause if you decide that you will also charge a fee for any bounced checks. Late fees and bounced check charges should never be negotiable and that should also be clearly stated in writing.

ALERT!

Never negotiate or waive fees for late payments or bounced checks. Even if you feel sorry for your tenant, you're setting a precedent if you decide to waive fees. It could give your tenant reason to believe you'll do it again.

Security Deposits

A lease or rental agreement specifies how much security deposit is required, how much was paid when the document was signed, and how the money will be used by the landlord. It also should state whether the last month's rent is included in the security deposit. Doing so, however, is not recommended by most experts because if a tenant doesn't pay the last month's rent, you might not have enough money left in the deposit to cover repairs and cleaning for an exceptionally dirty apartment.

Special Fees

There should be a clause or rider in the lease or rental agreement that spells out additional fees to be paid for such things as garage privileges, pets, or a waterbed.

You can include a provision that your tenant will be held responsible for paying all of your costs should it be necessary to hire an attorney and go to court for eviction proceedings.

Clauses about Policies

It is important to have a section that spells out your policies about the rules of the house. Leases and rental agreements can say that tenants are responsible for sewer and drain blockages that they cause. You can include general rules about parties, quiet hours, parking, garbage, pets, waterbeds, changing locks, and attaching pictures or anything else to the walls.

List appliances and utilities that you provide with the unit and what utilities have to be paid separately by the tenant. If your tenant wants to use his or her own appliances, the lease or rental agreement should contain a sentence saying that the tenant owns the refrigerator, stove, or washer and dryer.

The document should state that tenants cannot make alterations to your property without getting your permission, and that tenants are prohibited from doing any repairs that cost more than $10. Also include a statement that tenants cannot run a business in the unit without the landlord's approval.

What about Visitors and Guests?

Let tenants know that guests can stay in the apartment, but that if they are there longer than two weeks, they will be considered to be tenants. By law, you can legally increase the rent if someone moves into the apartment.

Think Twice about Restrictions

Some landlords believe that not allowing tenants to have pets and waterbeds is too restrictive and creates more problems for the landlord than it does the tenant. After all, you turn away, sight unseen, potentially good tenants who like waterbeds or pets. Another thing to take into account is that when there are a lot of vacant apartments in the community, allowing a pet might tip the prospect's choice of rentals in your favor.

Generally, damage from pets or waterbeds is very unlikely. That's why many landlords will, instead, stipulate what kind of pets are acceptable and charge tenants who have pets a separate pet deposit or a monthly fee on top of the rent.

Never give a tenant keys to the apartment or allow any possessions to be stored there until you have been fully paid the first month's rent. If you write a receipt for a partial payment, do not say that the money is for rent. Say it is "on account." Then when you receive the balance, write a second receipt that states the rent is paid for the month and year.

Clauses for Protection

Devote a paragraph to the lead disclosure statement that you read to the tenant before the lease or rental agreement was signed, and to the fact that your tenant got a copy of the EPA pamphlet "Protect Your Family from Lead in Your Home." Tenants should sign or initial the paragraph to confirm that you notified them verbally and in writing that lead might be present on the property and have given them information on what they can do to protect their children.

Entering the Unit for Repairs

Don't forget to include information about your right to enter the apartment—after notifying the tenant—for maintenance and repairs, in emergencies, and to show the apartment to prospective tenants. In your lease or rental agreement, describe the notification procedure you will use and say that the only time you will enter the apartment without first notifying the tenant is if there is an emergency and no one is at home.

Consent to Enter Form

To protect themselves, many landlords issue a lease or rental agreement that includes a waiver, signed by the tenant, giving their consent for landlords to enter in emergency situations. Others also ask tenants to sign a one-page waiver statement, in addition to the lease.

States that have statutes covering access by an owner—about half—generally say that a landlord must give a tenant between twenty-four and forty-eight hours' notice before accessing the unit. Some say that notice must be given in writing and must specifically indicate when access is desired. If your state is one of those that does not have a statute, you can inform the tenant verbally that you want to enter. Just be sure to allow a full day or two to elapse before you go in.

FACT

When your tenant gives notice, you have the right to show the apartment before he or she moves out. In signing the lease, your tenant agreed to let you conduct your business and that includes showing the apartment to prospective tenants while the space is still occupied. You should ask your tenant what times would be most convenient for the showing.

You can legally enter without permission when there is an emergency. Emergencies include smoke coming out of a window, water flowing underneath the door or leaking through a ceiling below the unit, or if you hear screams and no one answers your knock. Always knock first if you hear someone screaming. If no one responds, call the police. Then after you've notified authorities, you can use your key to enter the apartment.

If there's an emergency and you have to enter the apartment when the tenant is not at home, write a note explaining why you had to enter and specify the date and time you went in.

Insurance Clause

Your insurance does not cover your tenant's personal property. Make sure the lease contains that information. Read it out loud and have your new tenant initial the clause. Encourage the tenant to take out renter's insurance because that covers personal losses and liability.

Security Deposit Policy

An ideal tenant always pays rent when it's due and cleans thoroughly before vacating the apartment so that after he or she is gone, you find only signs of normal wear and tear. But not all tenants are like that, and that's why landlords collect security deposits. They use the money to reimburse themselves for money owed by the tenant for unpaid rent, cleaning filthy apartments, and repairing damaged property.

Laws covering security deposits vary from state to state. Nine states have exemptions that pertain to small landlords: Alaska, Arkansas, Georgia, Illinois, Maine, New Hampshire, New Jersey, New York, and Tennessee. So you should find out what state—and perhaps local—laws you must follow.

Some states and communities specify that landlords must place security deposits in a separate account. Some states also say that landlords must tell tenants where their money is being held. Others stipulate that the money earn interest while you hold it.

You can find out how much you can collect as a security deposit, when it must be returned, whether it needs to be placed in a separate account, and if you have to pay interest on the money by checking the landlord-tenant laws for your state at your library or a law library. Also check with the city housing authorities.

How much you can ask for a security deposit is also regulated in some locations. Typically a security deposit may not be more than two months' rent, but in some states it may be restricted to forty-five instead of sixty days. Other factors considered might be whether the tenant is a senior citizen, whether the apartment is furnished, whether the unit is rented on a month-to-month agreement, or whether the lease allows tenants to have pets.

You should look at local ordinances, too. They may include limits on security deposits and specify when the deposit has to be returned to the tenant—usually within fourteen to thirty days. Some local laws also require landlords to pay interest on the money while it's being held. A few landlords will do so anyway because they think it's the best way to handle the money.

Put It in Writing

Your lease or rental agreement should clearly state that a security deposit is the tenant's money and that they can get it back if they clean the apartment thoroughly before moving out, have not damaged the property, and don't owe back rent. Most tenants will want to get their money back so will try to make sure they have the unit in good shape, especially if you provide them with a specific list of things that should be cleaned.

When Tenants Come Up Short

If your tenant has trouble giving you the full security deposit before moving in, you can collect it in installments. Be sure you put the installment agreement in writing and have it signed. You can also consider having the tenant take out renter's insurance in lieu of paying the full security deposit.

Another option is to have your tenant give you half the first month's rent, plus the full security deposit, in return for a written agreement to hold the dwelling. This agreement states that you will hold the unit off the market for the approved tenant for a specified time, with the understanding that you will then receive the balance owed. The form should also specify what you will do with the money paid initially if the tenant pays the balance and notifies you that he or she intends to move. You should also say what will happen to the down payment if the tenant does not come up with the rest of the money.

How much of a security deposit should I ask for?
Your security deposit should be the highest amount allowable in your state or community. That will give you the most protection in case you have problem tenants.

Last Month's Rent Not Included

Saying that a security deposit includes the last month's rent is a mistake, according to most experts. If you set it up this way, when your tenant intends to move out you will not receive the last month's rent. Then if the apartment is filthy or there is damage, you'll have to pay for repairs and cleaning out of your pocket. You'd have to go to court to recover those costs.

Renewing (or Not Renewing) Leases

In most states after a one-year lease expires, the tenancy reverts to a month-to-month rental agreement unless you issue a new one-year lease and it is signed by you and your tenant. After a successful tenancy, few landlords or tenants worry about having a new one-year lease. But there are a few exceptions—in some states the lease automatically renews into a second one-year lease.

When You Want Your Tenant Out

If you do not want your tenant to stay longer than the period specified in the lease, you should notify your tenant at least thirty days before the lease expires that the lease will not be renewed. Or you can give the tenant a Notice to Quit, effective when the lease expires.

If you really want the tenant out, don't take any money from your tenant for extending the lease a few extra days beyond the expiration date. In most states a lease automatically converts into a month-to-month rental agreement after it expires if the tenant stays on. If you accept money and later want to formally evict the tenant, the payment might be construed as your having given consent to the rental agreement under the terms of the old lease. Then you'll have to give the tenant another thirty-day Notice to Quit.

When You Want to Change the Lease

Give your tenant sixty days' notice if you want to increase the rent or change some of the rules when the lease expires. All that's required is thirty days, but the extra month gives your tenant time to think about how the changes will affect him or her. There will be time for your tenant to look at other apartments and compare features and prices, to plan a move and give you plenty of notice, to negotiate with you, or to decide to go along with the changes and just stay put.

When You Want Your Tenant to Stay

Two or three months before the lease expires, phone your tenant to find out if he or she intends to renew. If you'd like to raise the rent, this is the time to say so. But generally landlords who have good tenants will keep increases minimal so the tenant won't leave. When you start looking for another tenant to sign a lease, that's the time to implement a major increase in rent.

Not less than thirty days before the lease expires, send your tenant a letter inviting him or her to renew and indicate that the rent will be increased when the new lease goes into effect. This ensures there will be no misunderstandings with regard to dates and amounts.

Chapter 15

Collecting and Increasing Rent

If you can't ask for money—relentlessly sometimes—you shouldn't be a landlord. Your survival depends on collecting rent. It's the most important thing you will do each month, and sometimes the hardest. It calls for business smarts and people skills, especially if your tenant has financial problems. When a difficult tenant makes you angry, you can't show it. In this chapter you'll get tips about collecting rent, learn what to do about late payments and bounced checks, and the best way to handle rent increases.

Collecting Rent

Now that you know how much rent to charge, you have to spell it out in your lease or rental agreement. (If you don't know what to charge, go back and read Chapter 8.) Your tenant has to know how much rent is due each month, when it has to be paid, and what the penalties are for paying late.

When Is It Due?

Most people expect to pay a full month's rent on the first of the month. That's true for residents in nineteen states: Alabama, Arkansas, Connecticut, Delaware, Florida, Hawaii, Iowa, Kansas, Kentucky, Montana, Nebraska, Nevada, New Mexico, Oklahoma, Oregon, Rhode Island, South Carolina, Tennessee, and Virginia.

Five states (California, Indiana, New York, North Dakota, and South Dakota) stipulate that rent is due on the last day of the preceding month.

All the other states leave it up to the landlord. If you live in one of these states, you can start your month any time you choose. Thus if a new tenant wants to occupy the apartment a week or two after the start of the month, you have two options. You can collect partial (prorated) rent for each day that's left and a full rent payment when the new month begins, or you can start the month on move-in day, say the fifteenth. Then the next rent payment will be due thirty days later. Most landlords, however, find it easier for them and their tenants to always make rent due on the first of each month.

Make sure your lease or rental agreement covers all the bases when it comes to rent payment. Rent sometimes falls due on a weekend or holiday. Let your tenant know whether you still want to be paid on that day or prefer to get the money on the next business day. When will rent be considered late and when will you assess late-payment fees? Decide ahead of time what your policy will be and put it in writing.

Don't Take Cash

Ask your tenant to write a check or pay you with a money order instead of cash. There's less likelihood of error when you don't have to count money. Bookkeeping is easier, and on the way to the bank you'll be less of a target for thieves. Plan to collect the rent in person or ask your tenant to deliver it to you. And don't give your tenant a discount for paying rent early. On the receipt write "Payment in full for _____ (*month/year*)."

If your tenant owes you money for a previous month's rent, the payment should be applied to that outstanding balance first. Use whatever is left over as a partial payment on the current month's rent.

When Tenants May Withhold Rent

If there is a written agreement stating that the tenant can pay for some repairs, then he or she can legally reduce the next month's rent by that amount.

A tenant can also legally withhold the monthly rent payment when there is a substantial flaw in the apartment that hasn't been fixed by the landlord. To do so, however, the tenant must set up an escrow account in a bank and deposit the full amount of the rent there each month until the landlord has repaired the apartment. In other words, the monthly rent must be paid by the tenant, but it will not be turned over to the landlord until he or she fulfills the obligation to keep the unit in good repair.

Late Payments

While some landlords want to give tenants a grace period—a time during which they'll accept rent without penalty—most experts think it makes better business sense to impose a late payment penalty a day or two later. Some also charge their tenants an additional small fee for each day rent is late.

FACT

If you decide to give your tenant a grace period, it's best not to go beyond three to five days. Then if your tenant still hasn't paid, add a late-payment penalty to what they owe, and the day after it was due, start the eviction process by giving your tenant a Pay Rent or Quit notice or Unconditional Quit notice. (Five states specify exactly how long you must wait before sending out either notice; they are Connecticut, Delaware, Maine, Oregon and Rhode Island.)

When Good Tenants Are Late

If you have a long-term tenant who has paid on time consistently, you can make an exception for a late payment—if you want to and if you don't violate fair housing laws by establishing preferential treatment. It's not a good business practice, however. Watch your step!

Landlords who allow a one- or two-week delay do so figuring that anyone can have a temporary financial setback or make errors in a checkbook. A good tenant very likely will notify you before rent is due that it will be a little late. You can work out a catch-up payment schedule and move the due date back a week or two. Put it in writing, however, and it should be signed by both of you.

ESSENTIAL

Catch-up payments are more of a risk with a new tenant since a record for prompt payment has not been established. When it's a new tenant, you'd be better off charging the late-payment penalty and starting eviction proceedings. If you decide to give your tenant a little leeway, don't make it longer than one week.

Keep track of your tenant's catch-up payments. If they meet the updated due date on time, you have nothing to worry about. If not, your only option is to hand out a Pay Rent or Quit notice with specific dates for leaving. Don't procrastinate too long. Start the termination process.

Determining Late Charges

Your late payment penalty should be high enough that tenants want to avoid it, but not too high. Some tenants who believe that the late fee is too high might contest it in court. If the court agrees with them, your penalty will be unenforceable.

Some states have laws that prevent landlords from setting extremely high, unreasonable late-payment penalties. In rent-controlled areas there may be regulations on how much you can charge.

Fourteen states restrict the late payment penalties to about four to five percent of each month's rent. By staying in the range of four to six percent, you shouldn't run into any problems. States that have restrictions are:

Arizona	Nevada
California	New Jersey
Connecticut	New Mexico
Delaware	North Carolina
Maine	Oklahoma
Maryland	Oregon
Massachusetts	Tennessee

Daily fees also can be added for each day rent is late. They, too, should not be coercive. Three to five dollars a day would be reasonable.

ALERT!

If you impose a late-payment penalty on rent, never waive it. It weakens your standing with your tenant and sets a bad precedent. If you waive it one month, your tenant will assume you'll waive it again.

Include Late Fees in Lease

Your lease should say that you will charge a late payment penalty at x dollars a day with the total not to exceed $xx.xx. Let your tenant know exactly when the penalty is imposed, whether it's one day or more after rent is late. If you also have a daily fee for each day missed, put that in writing, too. Include a statement that penalties are not negotiable. Highlight the paragraph in the lease and read it to your tenant; then both initial it.

You may question why initials are so important, but when they're next to important items in your lease, like late fees, they serve as proof that the tenant knew beforehand that the fees would be imposed and therefore, it might make the tenant less likely to try to take you to court.

How to Handle Late Payments

The day after rent is due talk to your tenant or give him or her a reminder letter saying that rent was due on the previous day and that now, in addition to rent, the late fees spelled out in the lease or rental agreement also must be paid.

At the same time, file a five-day (or seven-day) notice to Pay Rent or Quit. It notifies your tenant that he or she will be evicted if rent is not paid in a specified number of days. (The time allotted may vary from state to state and communities may also have eviction regulations.) Then one full day after the deadline you can start filing papers in court to evict your tenant.

Most states allow landlords to give a tenant a Pay Rent or Quit notice after rent is one day late. Connecticut, Delaware, Maine, Oregon, and Rhode Island have rules about how many days a landlord has to wait. Handing out a notice does not invalidate the late payment penalties that the tenant owes.

If you've given your tenant the notice and, subsequently, are paid the full amount owed, the notice to Pay Rent or Quit is automatically can-celled. Be aware that if your tenant pays only a portion of the amount owed and if you accept that partial payment, this also means the current Pay Rent or Quit notice is cancelled. So if your tenant does not come up with the balance of the money, you have to issue another notice and start the process all over again.

Don't give your tenant too many chances. After rent is late a second time, even if it's six months later, it's better to give a tenant with a lease an

Unconditional Quit notice. Tenants on a month-to-month lease should get a thirty-day Notice to Quit. (See Chapter 20 for more details on the eviction process.)

FACT

Some communities have rules about evicting tenants for nonpayment of rent. They'll specify when rent is due and when it is to be considered late. Find out what your community's regulations are and periodically check that they haven't been changed by local officials.

If you have the name of your tenant's employer and your tenant's social security number, you can garnish wages, income tax returns, or savings accounts to collect back rent. (See Chapter 19 for more on this.)

Should You Accept Credit Cards?

Credit card payments may make sense for landlords who have several rental properties or a large complex. But you have to pay a fee to the credit card company on the money they send you. The fee might eat into your profit and that's not good if you are right at the break-even point on income and expenses.

But if the credit card payment seems to be the only way you'll collect rent and you need the money to cover bills, accepting a credit card might be worth your while. You'll have to look into it and decide whether it has merit for you.

Bounced Checks

Nowadays bounced checks affect everybody. The bank collects a hefty fee from the person who wrote the check and another from the person who tried to cash it.

You have every right to impose your own fee for bounced checks. But it has to be reasonable. Use banks as your guideline and don't go any higher. So, if the banks in your area are getting $28 to $30 for each returned check, you can ask for just as much without having a problem.

Partial Payments

Accepting partial payments is not a good business practice. But you can make exceptions. If you do, you want your tenant to know you're doing it reluctantly and only once.

When you write a receipt for a partial payment, write down the balance due "On Account." Never, never say on that first receipt that the money applies to a particular rental period. You will write down the rental period covered by the payment on the second receipt after you get the rest of your money. This is important because some tenants have gone into court claiming that they "lost" the second receipt and the judges have ruled in their favor, delaying the eviction process.

Likewise, if your tenant owes more than one month's rent, when you do receive some money, it should be applied to the oldest debt, never to the current month. If you give your tenant a receipt for the current month while back rent is owed, you are establishing a receipt record that has gaps in it. Then if you go to court to evict your tenant, he or she can say the receipts for the missing months were lost or misplaced. The judge might decide to accept the tenant's word and not rule for an eviction. Don't take a chance on the outcome.

In general you are taking a chance if you accept partial payments. But if your tenant's situation seems to be temporary and he or she has a good record of paying on time, you might want to give your tenant another week. Just be sure to get a written repayment schedule—a one-week extension in most cases—and have it signed by both of you.

Accepting a partial payment cancels the current Pay Rent or Quit notice. So when you get the money, immediately hand your tenant another notice to Pay Rent or Quit. That way you won't get hung up by the exacting time-table that delays the eviction process. Those delays could cause you to lose even more rent if you do end up having to terminate the tenant.

How to Handle Rent Increases

Raising the rent is easy if you gave your tenant a month-to-month rental agreement; all it takes in most states is a thirty-day notice. If your tenant doesn't like it, he or she can find a new apartment and move out at the end of the thirty days.

It takes longer to raise rent and more sensitivity on your part if your tenant has a lease. The lease is a legal contract and both tenant and land-lord are locked into what it specifies until it expires.

Why Increase Rent?

One of the primary reasons for raising rent is the increased cost of running your business. Taxes and utilities go up and maintenance and repairs can get more expensive. Price increases will affect you even if you do your own work because the cost of parts and materials goes up. And when you want to make a capital improvement or replace an appliance that's on its last legs, you'll very likely find prices have gone up on those as well.

If the rent on your apartment has been stable for quite some time, you may want to raise it just to stay competitive with similar owner-occupied units. If you've substantially increased the value of your property and the apartment by making significant improvements, that, too, calls for raising the rent.

When's the Best Time?

With a lease, you can raise rent only once a year—when the lease expires. Or you can raise it when a tenant moves out. With the ideal, long-term tenant, however, most landlords try to keep the status quo unless their costs have escalated to the point that they can no longer go without collecting more money.

How much notice do I need to give the tenant if I decide to raise the rent?
Some states say you must give forty-five to sixty days' notice to raise the rent when your tenant has a month-to-month rental agreement. Check the laws in your state. In areas with rent controls the increase may be linked to the Consumer Price Index (CPI) or an annual percentage rate.

Breaking the News

With a longtime tenant it's best to be honest. Tell your tenant you hate to raise the rent but have to do it because gas and electricity prices have gone way up, your taxes are higher, the improvements you made last summer have to be paid off, and now the city's raising rates for garbage collection.

If you can, deliver information about rent increases personally. That way you can explain how much thought you put into the process and why you decided it's essential. Stress the fact that you want to provide the best environment you can for tenants. If your tenant seems upset, say that you've already cut costs as much as you can and this is the only option you have left to meet expenses. Your tenant will calm down if it doesn't seem as if you're price-gouging or being greedy. In general, rent increases should be about four to six percent. Some landlords on the high side would go up to ten percent. Let the market in your area be your guide.

If you keep good records on income and expenses, you can figure out whether the rent you're collecting is high enough to pay the bills and still give you a profit. Go over those figures at least once a year.

When you talk to your tenant, emphasize that you haven't had an increase for quite a while—tell long-term tenants exactly when that was—and explain that you can no longer ignore increasing the rent. Your tenant might not like the increase, but after thinking about the cost of moving to another place and finding out that similar apartments are in the same price range, most likely he or she will stay put.

You can also soften the blow by giving the tenant a higher estimate of the rent increase than you think will be necessary, so that once you've determined the actual amount you need to raise the rent, the tenant will be happily surprised by an amount that is lower than the one you quoted at first. Try to avoid the opposite scenario, which would leave you with an upset tenant asked to pay more than you originally estimated.

Tenants are savvy. They know it takes more money to run a household nowadays and that you're essentially paying expenses on two of them. If what you ask sounds reasonable, they will be, too.

Some landlords prefer not to use increments of five or ten dollars when they raise rent. They think it shows more concern for the tenant and more thought into how much rent is actually needed when it goes up, for example, by $32.50.

Avoid the Appearance of Retaliating

If your tenant made a complaint or you've recently had a dispute, don't turn around and raise rent three or six months later. If you do that it might look like you're still harboring bad feelings and doing it in retaliation. Many states specifically prohibit raising rent within a time period established by state law. Consult your lawyer or professional organization if you have questions about when and how to proceed without your tenant filing a legal complaint.

Postponing the Increase

When you are contemplating raising rent, you should also consider what it will cost you to advertise, screen, and prepare for a new tenant should yours decide to move because of the increase. If the increase you're thinking of is about as much as the expense of finding a new tenant, it might be better to postpone the increase until your current tenant moves out for other reasons.

Yearly Increases

Instead of periodically raising the rent, you might want to try annual increases that reflect the increase in the cost of living. Boosting rent by one or two percent a year shouldn't upset a tenant, especially if it has been written into the lease. Whichever way you go, you're not locked into that decision. You can always change your policy for increasing rent as soon as the current tenant moves out and you draw up a new agreement.

Chapter 16

Maintenance, Repairs, and Emergencies

Any homeowner knows that you can't ignore your property. If you do, everything starts to fall apart. Rain seeps under old roof shingles and damages the ceiling. Appliances break down and furnaces wear out. Faucets drip, wires fray, and wood rots. It's the same with rental property— you have to repair and maintain it. In this chapter you'll learn the difference between maintenance, repairs, and emergencies, your rights in emergencies, how to schedule repair work with your tenant, and how to find the right help.

What's the Difference?

Understanding the difference between repairs, maintenance, and emergencies is essential for landlords. Tasks in each category have completely different time frames for being taken care of. In general, think of repairs as fixing things that break and maintenance as routinely keeping up the property. Emergencies, obviously, are situations that need immediate attention. In an emergency, you also have a different set of rules about entering your tenant's home without permission when he or she isn't there.

Repairs

According to the dictionary, to repair means "to restore by replacing a part or putting together what's torn or broken." There are innumerable things around the house that need repair—dripping faucets, leaking and plugged toilets, cracked or broken windows, malfunctioning furnaces and water heaters, refrigerators that won't stay cold, handrails that pull free of the wall, and dry, cracked putty that falls off window frames. Spend a few minutes thinking about it and you'll have a list of repairs around the house that fills several pages.

If your tenant or a guest breaks something in the apartment, such as a window, it is the tenant's responsibility to pay for the cost of the repair. You are responsible for repairs that occur when parts get old through normal wear and tear or haven't been maintained properly.

Most repairs are not urgent. You can let a faucet drip for a day or a week or even longer if you don't mind an increase in your water bill. It might get worse if you ignore it and it will certainly cost more because of increased usage; but you can fix the leak when the time is right for you.

There's a difference between a leak in your home and your tenant's home, however. Tenants don't like procrastination, especially if it's a recurring trait in their landlords. So when he or she asks you to repair something, and you don't do it in a reasonable length of time, the tenant might decide you are unresponsive and uncaring. If you have a habit of putting off repairs, that might persuade your tenant to find a new apartment when the lease expires.

Minor repairs include fixing such things as:

- Doorknobs and locks on windows and doors
- Shelves in closets and cabinets
- Shower curtain rods, towel bars, and hooks
- Faucets that leak
- Clogged pipes and drains
- Burnt-out light fixtures and bulbs
- Ripped screens, shades, and blinds
- Broken windows
- Broken tiles and torn linoleum
- Doors and windows that stick
- Furnace and air conditioner working inadequately

Even though most repairs are not urgent, some should be undertaken within a day or two after they've been reported to you. For example, if a handrail comes loose and you delay fixing it and then if your tenant or a guest falls down the stairs and is injured, you are liable for neglecting to repair your property. Likewise, if a furnace breaks down, it should be repaired within twenty-four hours if it's cold outdoors. Otherwise you're failing to keep the apartment habitable.

Maintenance

To maintain means "to keep in an existing state of repair, efficiency, or validity," according to the dictionary. Think of maintenance as the upkeep of your property.

Some of the tasks associated with maintenance are painting the unit between tenants, making sure appliances and utilities are working as they should, and replacing blinds or shades when they are getting too worn or won't function properly.

Sometimes maintenance means replacing a refrigerator or stove or faucet that is so old that you no longer can get parts or so worn that whatever you fix will soon break down again. Anytime the cost to repair exceeds or comes close to what it will take to buy a brand-new product, it is wiser to purchase the replacement.

ALERT!

If you don't keep your unit in good repair, your tenant can call local health or housing officials to complain. If they come in to inspect the property and find you at fault, the local building inspector can impose fines for neglected repairs or shut down unsafe dwellings.

Set Up a Maintenance Schedule

The best way to keep track of routine maintenance is to set up a schedule for the apartment. It should include the dates that you inspected the property, what you looked at, and what repairs you performed.

Keep track of when you purchased appliances and fixtures. Make note of any problems or potential problems you spot during your semiannual and annual inspections. With good recordkeeping, you'll know how much money you spent originally on something, how much it's costing you to keep it functioning, and how soon it's likely to need replacing. Then you can set aside money each month in an escrow account and save for the purchase. It gives you better control of your income and expenses. You can also ask your tenant to do semiannual maintenance inspections. (Chapter 18 will give you more information on keeping records of inspections and maintenance.)

What Should You Look For?

Periodically check appliances to see how they are working. Examine light fixtures, the furnace, and the air conditioner, if there is one. Look at all of the faucets to see if there are any water leaks or damage. Is there water around the base of the toilet? Sometimes toilets need to be reseated.

Do the doors and windows open easily? What about the locks; are they working properly? If locks are in good working order and you inspect them regularly—logging those inspections in your maintenance schedule—it reduces your risk for liability claims. You can prove to the court that you have done everything you reasonably can to see to the safety of your tenants.

FACT

Ward off possible accusations of theft by giving your tenant written notice at least twenty-four hours before you want to enter the apartment. That gives the tenant time to put valuables away.

Respect Your Tenant's Schedule

Your tenant's space is private and you have no right to go in without an invitation or permission. You wouldn't want your tenant or a neighbor to enter your house without your consent, either. So whenever you want to maintain or repair the unit, you should talk to your tenant and schedule a time that's convenient for him or her.

When you hire someone to do plumbing or any other skilled job, however, you don't always have that flexibility. When you call for service, pick a day that's convenient for you and the worker, then hope the worker will actually be there "before noon" or "between one and five" as promised. What's convenient for your tenant is not always an option. In most cases, however, that is not a problem. Tenants don't mind someone coming in when they're gone, since they want the work completed probably even more than you do.

If the work is not urgent, however, try to schedule someone to do the repairs a few days after you call. Then you can notify your tenant that you will be entering the apartment in two days for repairs. It will give your tenant enough time to rearrange the furniture or put valuable objects away. If you've hired someone to do the job, stay in the apartment until it's finished. Make sure the work area is cleaned up and that no tools are left behind.

Unless it's an emergency, never schedule your own repair work without giving your tenant at least twenty-four hours' notice that you will be entering the apartment. Routine maintenance is never an emergency. It should always be at the convenience of your tenant.

Is It Really an Emergency?

Inevitably you'll have tenants who see things in black and white. If something goes wrong, they'll think it's an emergency that needs to be fixed *right away*. Living under the same roof might even exacerbate the demands because your tenant might reason, "All you have to do is come next door."

Bells clang, lights flash: those are the consequence of emergencies. When something specified in your state and local building code goes wrong—anything that threatens the health and safety of your tenant—you most likely have an emergency.

You have a bona fide emergency when:

- Smoke and flames come out of windows and beneath doors.
- Water flows from under your tenant's door or drips down the walls from an upstairs apartment.
- You hear screams.
- There's a natural disaster such as a tornado or an earthquake.
- Gas lines rupture.

Less dramatic, but also requiring immediate attention, are:

- Frozen water pipes
- A dead furnace during a cold spell
- Electrical wires shorting out
- A cracked toilet bowl
- Bug and rodent infestations
- Broken locks on the door or windows

Any condition that threatens the health and/or safety of your tenant can be described as an emergency. As a landlord, your obligation is to take action and fix it right away, if not sooner. Otherwise your tenant is not obligated to remain in your apartment no matter how much time is left on the lease.

Your tenant or neighbors can call health or housing officials about code violations. The authorities will inspect the property, issue repair orders, and, very likely, charge you an inspection fee. If you don't do the repairs within their time frame, they can fine you for violating housing and health codes. And if you continue to ignore them, in extreme cases, the authorities might even shut down your building. It won't matter to them at all if you are living in the other part of an owner-occupied dwelling.

Your Rights in Emergencies

Although under normal circumstances you have no right to enter your tenant's apartment without permission, the law makes an exception when it looks like there's an emergency and your tenant is not at home.

Legally you can enter the apartment if you see smoke pouring out of a window or water flowing underneath the tenant's door or through the ceiling, or if you hear screams and no one answers your knock. When no one responds to your knock, however, you must first call the police, then use your key to enter the apartment.

If you ever have to go into your tenant's space while he or she is absent, it is extremely important to leave a note inside explaining why you entered. Write down the date and time you were in your tenant's space, how long you were there, and who, if anyone, came in with you.

FACT

Some landlords have been accused of stealing their tenant's property after they entered without express consent. Be careful not to disturb anything while you are in there. And if you hire someone to do any repairs, supervise the work. It will protect both you and the worker.

Keep a copy of your note in the tenant's file, along with copies of any receipts or bills for labor and parts associated with the entry. This documentation is important if the tenant should decide to sue you for trespass or invasion of privacy. Also log the entry into your record book.

Calling In the Pros

Even if you do most of the repairs and maintenance in your building, there will be times that you have to call an expert. The job may be beyond your expertise or require extensive work by a licensed professional who has all the right tools and, perhaps, a helper. And even though you may know how to do the work, there will be times when you're simply too busy to do it.

Finding the Right Contractors

Looking for a plumber or electrician is akin to searching for a needle in a haystack. If you don't have recommendations, you stare at listings in the yellow pages and wonder which person to call—the one that's nearest to your house, the one that promises he has the most experience? How do you find someone who will stand behind the work? And how many people should you call—one, two, or three?

To eliminate some hassles, ask neighbors and friends if they can recommend anyone for the job. Get names and phone numbers. You might also ask at the local home supply store to find out whether they know anyone they'd recommend.

Researching Contractors

Most experts recommend that you get three names or companies, especially if your project is going to cost a lot of money. After you have three names, look them up in the phone book to find out what they say in their ads—how much experience they have, how long they've been in business, and whether they are licensed and bonded.

Does the ad display the Better Business Bureau logo? Are they members of the local Home Builders Association or any other professional organization? If so, that should reassure you that the business isn't a fly-by-night operation. Then start calling.

When you call, ask if they are bonded and licensed. You can also ask for a ballpark estimate on what the job might cost—reassure them that you realize it's only an estimate and you know they can't tell you what the job will cost until they see the house. Then they might be less reluctant to name a figure. Get references, too—and call those people up before you have anyone come to the house to bid on the project.

What you spend on repairs during the year is deductible as a business expense on your yearly tax return. If you are making a capital improvement, such as installing a new carpet, that has to be depreciated over a number of years. It is not a deductible business expense.

When you meet contractors in person, look at their credentials. Verify their licenses and don't hesitate to ask for proof of insurance. Then if anything goes wrong or if someone is hurt, their insurance will cover it. If the credentials check out, ask them to bid on the project. Let them know, however, that you'll be getting other bids before you come to a decision.

Take notes on how each bidder plans to do the work, especially if it's something you know little about—perhaps waterproofing a basement or improving drainage in your yard. Your notes are the only way you can figure out afterward who said what and whether you're comparing apples to apples.

When to Get Bids

When you need a plumber to unplug a toilet or an electrician to replace bad sockets, you might want to phone a couple of companies to find out what their fee is to walk into your house—usually covering only the first hour of labor—and the hourly rate beyond that. Parts needed are extra, so you may want to find out what those might cost as well. Or ask a neighbor if they can recommend a company or individual whose rates are reasonable. You don't need bids for small jobs.

However, for big projects, it's very important to shop around carefully and know what you're getting yourself into. Consider what you might go through hiring a roofing contractor. Some roofers put on new roofs that leak. Some leave a mess after pulling off old shingles and won't come back to clean it up. Others may require eighty or ninety percent of the bill to be paid up front. Then they do a lousy job and will not come back to fix it to your satisfaction.

With a new roof costing upward of $5,000 for labor and materials—as compared to a few hundred to hire an electrician or plumber—it's important to verify the credentials of those you hire and to get someone reliable. Don't leave it to chance. Find a reputable company that's insured.

Paying for Maintenance and Repairs

If you can, try establishing a fund dedicated exclusively to maintaining your property. The first year or two of owning a duplex will be tight. You won't have money set aside, yet you may find that everything needs fixing or replacing because the former owner, intending to sell the property, refused to put any money into it.

You can either pay for those repairs out-of-pocket or extend your mortgage to give you a cushion for replacing the big stuff—a roof, furnace, appliances. Try to do as many of the smaller repairs as you can yourself and be diligent about maintaining the property.

Then when you can, try to set aside five to twelve percent of the rent each month in an escrowed account. Use that money only for upkeep and the big-ticket items. Chapter 17 will give you more information on how to take care of repairs when money is tight.

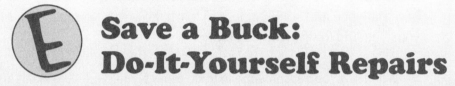

Chapter 17

Save a Buck: Do-It-Yourself Repairs

You'll find amazing new products on the market that make simple home repairs and maintenance much easier today than they were in the past. So even if you think of yourself as not particularly handy, there are many repair jobs you can learn to do yourself. Your confidence will grow when you do the work yourself and you'll save money by not hiring help. In this chapter you'll learn some simple repairs you can tackle, some tools to get, and how to schedule the work with your tenant.

What Can You Handle?

Whether or not you can handle a lot of repairs on your own depends partly on your situation. Some people are all thumbs and resent time spent on household repairs. When they have to do the work, they lose their temper and succeed only in raising their blood pressure. If that describes you, you need a good handyman at your beck and call. If you have patience and a willingness to learn, however, you can do a lot in your building to save yourself a buck.

FACT

Whenever you get someone in to do repairs, you pay for materials and labor—including travel time. They are deductible business expenses when you prepare your income tax return in April, but you need to pay for those repairs up front. Will it have to come out of your pocket or have you set money aside to use exclusively for repairs?

If you are retired, you have more time to do things around the house than when you had a full-time career. But it's still important to assess your interest, curiosity, and the time you're willing to spend before you decide to give it a try. If you're up for it, you might find you enjoy doing simple chores.

If you're just starting out on a career and family, you have less time on your hands to work on these projects—but if you want to save money, you have no choice. Start out by doing things that won't take much time; as your experience grows, tackle the more complicated and time-consuming jobs.

Questions to ask yourself before taking on a home improvement task include:

- Do you want to do the job?
- Do you know how to do it?
- Do you have time for it?
- Who will do the work if you don't?
- What will it cost to hire someone to do the work?
- Can you afford to hire someone to do the work?

Tools and Screws

Nothing is more frustrating than starting a job and then having to stop because you don't have the right tool or the right fastener. Knowledgeable landlords keep a toolbox on hand, as well as an assortment of screws, nails, glue, and cleaning products.

What should you have? Start out with:

- Hammer
- Needle-nose and flat-top pliers
- Putty knife
- Electrical tape and painter's or masking tape
- Razor knife and scraper
- Wire cutter and stripper
- Assortment of wrenches
- Measuring tape and yardstick
- Level
- Paintbrushes
- Electric screwdriver and drill
- Various screwdrivers

Fill baby food jars or small plastic containers with sorted screws and nails. Buy several kinds of glue—for wood and plastic—and a product that holds stripped screws in place.

Simple Repairs You Can Do

Household repairs fall into different categories—some require experience and training, and others can be done by nearly anyone. Save your repair money for the jobs that take more experience, but learn as much as you can about everything else. Deal with anything that can be handled with the tools in your kit. Doing simple jobs yourself will add up to real savings over the long run.

Tackle Plumbing First

Experienced landlords will tell you that tenants most often call about the plumbing. Start your education there. Look at the books and pamphlets stacked near the checkout counter or in the plumbing department at a home improvement store.

Grab all the free pamphlets you can get. Also find one or two well-illustrated books written in clear, precise, understandable language. (You don't want a book that is just as confusing as some of the instructions found in ready-to-assemble products.) Usually these books are not very expensive and will serve as good references. *The Everything® Fix-It Book* (Adams Media, 2004) is a great resource to get you started.

FACT

The Internet also provides many tips on how to do small jobs around the house. Go to your favorite search engine and type in "do-it-yourself home projects." In addition to telling you what products or tools to use for a job, the Web sites likely have illustrations of how to go about it.

Replacing gaskets on leaky faucets, unplugging clogged drains with a plunger or perhaps an auger or "snake," replacing the inner workings of a toilet that's running constantly, or even repairing a wax seal under the toilet are not difficult tasks. When a valuable ring falls into a drain, it's not lost forever; it's waiting to be released from the trap—the U-shaped pipe—under the sink. With the right tools and a little bit of research, you can tackle these chores.

Move On to Locks

Always change your locks between tenants. You'll find that some tenants will make a point of asking whether locks were changed after the last tenant left. You may also have someone who wants you to change the lock in the middle of the tenancy. Hiring a locksmith is not expensive, but why pay anything for a job you can handle on your own?

Buy several similar locks—one brand from one manufacturer. Once the first lock is installed, all you have to do "to change locks" is remove the inside cylinder and exchange it for another. Your tenant will be happy to get a new key and you won't have to do any other work since the rest of the lockset stays the same.

Replace Light Fixtures

You may not want to rewire your house or figure out what's causing lights to flicker and go out. Big jobs like that should be left up to an experienced electrician. But if you need a new light fixture in the hallway or apartment, it isn't a big chore. Read your literature carefully, and turn off the power at its source! Then you needn't worry about handling the job. All you really need to do is detach the two wires that run through the ceiling from the two wires in the old fixture and reattach them again to the new light. Your fix-it book or Web site will explain which two wires go together.

Tighten Screws

Screws work their way loose, and after a number of years it's impossible to get some of them tight again. But you'll find liquid products that will adhere to metal screws and bolts and lock the threaded fastenings so that they will not loosen from vibrations. After setting for twenty minutes to twenty-four hours, these fastenings will be as tight as when they were first put in. Why wasn't this product available years ago?

Painting and Redecorating

Just about anyone can paint walls and woodwork if they can get up and down ladders and reach overhead to paint ceilings. Is that something you want to tackle? If not, you still might be able to save money—ask if your tenant will do it for a rebate on rent. Be sure to get a written agreement. Then supply the paint, plenty of dropcloths and brushes, and supervise the job.

Wallpapering is not difficult. You'll find that the walls and ceiling are not perfectly straight. To get a plumb line, tie a long string onto a screw or nail and insert it into the wall, up near the ceiling. The string will fall straight. Use that line to pencil in straight lines on the wall, then match the edges of wallpaper to them.

FACT

Wood putty, caulking, patching plaster, and similar products can be used to repair and fill small holes and cracks in the walls. Then all they need is to be sanded and repainted. If it's not quite right the first time, take it out, and try again. There are other products that can repair glass, tile, plastic, and vinyl, and fill small holes in metal pipes.

Other Jobs to Tackle

Inside and out you can do many of the odd jobs yourself. Learn how to trim shrubs and trees. Clean leaves and other debris out of gutters and flush water through the downspouts to clear them. You'll be surprised what comes out. Get rid of mold and mildew—on a monthly or bimonthly basis. Clean carpets, but don't use too much detergent. You won't get it all out and the soap residue will only attract more dirt.

When a furnace or water heater goes out and you don't smell gas, check the pilot light before you call for service. You don't want to pay for a $40 to $60 service call just to have it relit. If you do smell gas, however, don't attempt to ignite a pilot light; it might cause an explosion. Instead call the gas company or a professional who responds to emergencies immediately. They'll know what to do.

You can glue down loose tiles, tighten screws on doors and shelves, replace hardware on cabinets, and sand and seal wood floors if they're gouged or marked up. It might take a little time to get the hang of it, but put up curtain rods and blinds. Use a level to keep them straight.

You don't have to hire an expert if the mortar between bricks falls out. Just take out any broken pieces with a putty knife or screwdriver. Then mix up a small batch of new mortar and push it into areas where the old mortar is missing. (Use your thumb if you have to.) You can gradually replace the mortar in sections in your spare time.

Quick Projects That Save Money

It doesn't take a licensed contractor to keep a house in tiptop shape. You just need to do a little regular preventive maintenance or fine-tuning to keep all systems running smoothly. Many of these projects can be done in less than half an hour. You can do them yourself and by getting to them once or twice a year you will reduce your operating costs.

Keep Heating Bills Down

Periodically unscrew the floor and wall heat registers and clean out the ducts with your vacuum cleaner hose. You'll be amazed at the "treasures," dust, and dirt you'll find buried there. Your hose isn't long enough nor your vacuum powerful enough to clean out everything, but every little bit will help move hot and cold air more efficiently. It also will cut down on some of the dust floating throughout the house.

Don't forget to change forced-air furnace filters several times a year. The furnace will run more efficiently and you won't be recirculating the collected dust.

ALERT!

You don't need to have the furnace or air conditioner turned up high when the apartment or your house is vacant. Get a thermostat with a timer that allows you to set the temperature at different levels throughout the day and night. It will reduce your fuel and electricity bills.

If you live in a cold climate and have a window air conditioner unit, you should put heavy canvas over the air conditioner if you leave it in place during the winter months. Otherwise the cold air seeping into the house through the unit will negate the effect of a hard-working furnace.

Next, turn down the water heater. You need hot water, but it doesn't have to be scalding. Reset the thermostat on the water heater. The safest level is 120 degrees Fahrenheit. That will be hot enough to fill a relaxing bath without sending your tenant to the local burn unit.

You can also save money on heating bills simply by watching where you place furniture. If you block cold air returns and heat vents, your furnace will not be able to efficiently heat the house. Remind your tenant, too, not to place heavy, solid pieces of furniture in front of them, because the room will be more comfortable if they're not blocked.

Keep Water Bills Down

It's amazing how much water drips down the drain in twenty-four hours. You don't want to pay for that unused water, so be quick to repair leaking faucets and toilets that run nonstop.

You can also install flow restrictors to cut down on the amount of water used. Ask your hardware store to recommend the best type of water restrictor to use on your showerheads and faucets. You and your tenant will still get plenty of water for washing and less will be wasted.

Use Appliances Wisely

Pull out the refrigerator and look at the air conditioner. You'll find thick dust built up on coils. If you vacuum them twice a year, your appliances will run more efficiently and you'll pay less money for electricity.

Lint and dust often collect in dryer vents, then it takes more energy to dry clothes. Clogged vents also cause fires if the lint should ignite. Often the fire gets a good start and races up between the walls of a house before anyone detects it. Ask your tenant to unclog the vent frequently.

Consider setting up a humidifier in the winter, especially if you have a forced-air furnace. Humidity in the air makes rooms more comfortable. Not only will your tenant feel better, you might be able to keep the thermostat set lower.

Check your light bulbs. You really don't need hundred-watt bulbs in hallways and foyers. If your electricity bill has crept up, put in sixty-watt bulbs or energy-efficient fluorescent bulbs instead. It might save a couple of dollars each month.

Sometimes the best way to cut down on costs is to replace old furnaces, water heaters, air conditioners, refrigerators, and anything else dependent upon power. Products being sold today are better insulated and much more efficient than the older ones in your home and unit.

Scheduling Work with Your Tenant

As mentioned previously, after your tenant moves into the apartment, you cannot enter it without permission. The space is no longer yours; it's your tenant's home. Whether you or a contractor will be doing the work, anytime you need access to the unit for repairs, it's a good idea to give your tenant written notice at least twenty-four hours beforehand and then arrange a convenient time to do the work. Even if your state permits a verbal notice, putting it in writing is documentation for your files.

The notice should include when you plan to enter, how long you will be there, why you are entering, who will do the work, and who will be with you, if anyone. You can also state that the tenant does not have to be present while you're doing the work. Keep a copy of the notice in your tenant's file. (See Chapter 18.)

ALERT!

The lease or rental agreement your tenant signs should have a clause stating that you have a right to enter the apartment to do repairs and maintenance. Show it to tenants when they sign the document.

What If Your Cash Flow Is Still Tight?

You collect rent, then pay the mortgage, interest, insurance, and taxes. You pay bills—advertising, maintenance, small repairs, cleaning supplies, utilities, water, and garbage. If you have an accountant, a lawyer, or a handyman, they have to be paid, too. On some properties there might not be much left as a cushion for emergency repairs and a monthly profit.

Ideally you want to collect enough rent to cover all expenses. So what happens when cash gets tight? If the unit isn't bringing in enough to meet the bills, you have to figure out why and find ways to reduce your expenses.

Read the Bills Carefully

Look closely at your monthly bills. Are they getting too high? Take a good look at what's happening with your heat, electricity, and water bills. Perhaps your tenant is roasting when the furnace turns on and opening one or more windows to get cool, fresh air. If you control the thermostat, ask if there's enough heat or too much.

If your tenant controls a thermostat, ask to check it. Explain that your heat bills have skyrocketed and perhaps the thermostat is defective. Find out if your tenant ever has to open a window to cool down the apartment. Perhaps then your tenant will take the hint and turn down the thermostat, and you won't need to do anything else.

FACT

Check the Web sites of your local utility companies. The sites may include tips for ways to save energy in your home. They also may have a home energy analysis that you can do online. There might also be an online "store" where you can purchase such things as energy-efficient light bulbs.

You might be losing heat through windows and doors. Put in some weather stripping and check it every year before winter sets in. The weather stripping might help you save money that can later be applied to new energy-efficient windows and doors. Heat loss also occurs when buildings are not insulated, and few buildings were insulated before the 1970s. Before you have the house insulated, think carefully about the total cost (including replacement of siding, if necessary) and the length of time it will take you to get a return on this investment.

When you can't figure out why the water bill was so high one month, inspect all the faucets, toilets, and water heaters for leaks. Don't forget to look at the water meter that's in your house. Sometimes it, too, leaks or needs to be replaced. A slow drip from an indoor or outside faucet can add up to quite a few extra gallons that you have to pay for.

Some people, including tenants, rarely turn off the television, lights, or fans, and that raises the monthly cost of electricity. You won't succeed in getting your tenant to change habits, but you can install sixty-watt bulbs or the new energy-efficient bulbs in the entrance, yard, and hallway. They use much less electricity. Perhaps you can also purchase a package of those bulbs as a "gift" for your tenant.

Don't hesitate to ask the utility companies and the city to check your meters. Sometimes they're not working correctly, and if that's the case, you'll get a replacement at no cost.

Are You Charging Enough Rent?

You can raise rent each year when your tenant's lease expires. But don't expect that to solve your problems immediately. If you boost the price of rent too much, you'll probably be looking for a new tenant while the unit sits empty. Plus you'll have to pay for advertising, credit checks, and cleaning and repainting the apartment. Ten percent a year is about the highest you can go on a rent increase if you want to keep your tenant.

ALERT!

Even in an emergency, paying for something by tapping into money saved for taxes is never a good idea. You'll only have to find more money for the taxes. And the security deposit you got from your tenant is off limits. It doesn't belong to you and you might be required by your state to earn interest on the money while you have it.

Look at Your Budget

Are you spending too much on improvements? Apartments don't need expensive refrigerators, cabinets, or bathroom fixtures. Be realistic and frugal.

Carpeting is a recurring expense in an apartment, and in the long run hardwood floors, especially in high-use areas such as living rooms and hallways, are a better buy. Wood floors are attractive and last forever.

Are You Paying Yourself Too Much?

When you start out landlording, never take more "profit" out of the rent than you actually have in order to improve your lifestyle. For the first few years keep detailed records on expenses; know how much you need each month to stay on top of your bills. When you feel confident that you know exactly what it takes to run a small business, then you can start paying yourself.

Use Credit

If you think your shortfall is temporary, pay your bills with a credit card. That will give you an additional thirty days to come up with the cash. But don't pay only the minimum amount due on the card when you get the bill, because of the high interest rate charged by most credit card companies. At credit card rates of twelve percent and higher, you'd soon be in a deep hole on the unpaid balance.

It's best to be conservative when you first start out in business. Each month put a twelfth of what you need for taxes in a savings or money market account so you can also earn a little interest.

Refinance Your Mortgage

If interest rates are low, you can refinance your property if you've owned it for a while. When you refinance, you can get cash to make repairs and pay old bills. Working on repaying a low-interest loan is a lot easier than paying the interest rate on a credit card.

Sell the Property

If you tried all the cost-cutting measures, raised the rent as high as the market will bear, paid the bills with borrowed money, and are still coming up short, it may be time to unload the property. Some investments simply don't work out and it's better to cut your losses. When you sell, you might get enough cash to start over again in another, and perhaps better, location.

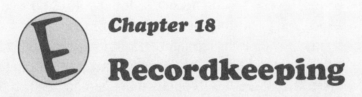

Chapter 18

Recordkeeping

The essence of business is to know what you're doing. You have to understand your cash flow—the difference between your total expenditures and your income. If you don't keep good tenant, maintenance, and repair records, you risk spending more than you're collecting, and you also won't have the documents you need if you're audited or taken to court. In this chapter you'll learn about the records you should keep, how long you should keep them, and what you can do to avoid audits.

Developing Your Recordkeeping System

You may think you got away from recordkeeping by becoming a landlord. Nothing is further from the truth. You need good office skills—organizing, filing, using a computer or typewriter, and bookkeeping—to run your business. Think of it this way: You have to satisfy the bank, the city, the state, the courts, several federal agencies, and the IRS. You also want to know at a glance if your business is in the black or red.

The easiest way to keep things straight and understand exactly how you're doing is to keep good books. You'll have to find the system that works best for your tenant records, property management records, financial records, and maintenance and repair records.

Find a Corner for Your Office

Set up a home office with a filing cabinet, some shelves, a desk, a computer, and a printer. Figure out how you want to keep your books, and get organized right from the start while you're getting the apartment ready for your first tenant. If you delay organizing, you'll soon be buried under a mound of receipts that you need for income tax purposes. The rental applications, credit reports, and other tenant records also will pile up. All of these are essential business documents. If they're stuffed in shoeboxes or crates, whenever you need something you'll waste time hunting for it.

FACT

If you have to purchase a new printer, get one that is a combination printer, fax, and copier. That way you won't have to run out to a print shop or other store every time you have to copy a form.

Develop a Filing System

Some landlords throw unpaid, incoming bills into a folder. They have other folders for bank loan information, insurance records, paid invoices and receipts, tenant records, and all their accumulated rental applications.

That may work for some, and it's a good start to getting organized, but it still means sorting papers and wasting time whenever you need to find something specific.

A folder stuffed with paper doesn't help you analyze and assess your business. In addition to keeping all those records, you need to transfer the information onto a balance sheet or another form to know at a glance how you are doing and whether you have a positive or negative cash flow.

Some landlords like to keep records in a three-ring binder with dividers. Others prefer filing cabinets. When you start out and have only one rental unit, a three-ring binder may be sufficient. If that sounds good to you, buy prepunched paper or a three-pronged paper punch, and some large envelopes or plastic sheet protectors for storing receipts and invoices.

A traditional filing system might give you more flexibility to make changes and additions to the records you keep. If you purchase file folders in five different colors, you can color-code categories. One color should be devoted to rejected rental applications. Use another color for tenant records, another for financial records, another for property management records, and the last color for maintenance and repair records. Then it will be easy to find the records you need every time you open the drawer. Remember to have your schedules or balance sheets at the front of each folder to save time when you look things up.

Use Your State's Landlord-Tenant Forms

You can find generic copies of certain forms, notices, and landlord-tenant letters in Appendix B. These forms will help you get an idea of what such forms will look like, and the type of information you need to get. But instead of using generic forms, once you know you are serious about landlording, get copies of the forms you need from a rental property owners organization in your state or from one of the Web sites that have specifically tailored documents for each state (see Appendix A). That way you'll be assured that your lease and everything else you use comply with state law. Use these official samples as master copies and duplicate them whenever your supply is low.

Tenant Records

It's impossible to predict what you will need and when. Relying on memory is a mistake, because over time the details will be fuzzy and what you think you remember won't help you in court. The only way to win a lawsuit is to establish a paper trail of documentation. You need names, dates, times, what you said, what your tenant said, and notes of how and why you made your decisions.

You want to save records for both approved and rejected applicants. Keep them on hand for years and find out whether your state mandates a minimum length of time before you can throw them away. In Michigan, for example, it is three years.

Rejected Applicants

For each applicant, set up a separate folder that contains the rental application, results of the credit check if you did one, employment history, notes on your conversations at the showing, and the criteria you used to determine that you would reject the applicant. If you used a worksheet, include that, as well as receipts for fees the applicant paid, such as for the credit check.

File applicants in alphabetical order. You also might want to keep a log of all the people you interviewed as prospective tenants in any given year. Then if you ever have to search specifically for, say, 2004 applicants, you won't have to shuffle through every file folder to find them.

Tenant Files

Keep the originals of the signed lease or rental agreement, riders, the lease package your tenant received upon moving in, the rental application, credit information, and move-in and move-out inspection checklists. Save rent receipts, copies of repair bills, letters, correspondence, and forms. File your requests for entry to the tenant's apartment, the tenant's requests for repairs, and any tenant complaints. Be sure to date everything and write down when and how you repaired broken or malfunctioning items. You'll need to keep annual and semiannual safety and maintenance checklists. Some landlords also keep a logbook of repairs and requests.

Don't forget to store any pictures or videotape taken during the move-in inspection that show the apartment and existing damage. They are evidence of the condition of the apartment at that time, and can be used to prove when damage occurred or to monitor wear and tear of furnishings.

Rental applications, leases, and rental agreements contain a lot of personal information about applicants and tenants. Don't divulge any of it to anyone, whether you know them or not. New federal privacy regulations require doctors, dentists, bankers, and other business owners to keep information confidential. It makes sense to be careful in a business such as yours, as well.

Some landlords like to make a copy of their tenant's rent check each month and attach it to the original receipt for rent—the duplicate goes to the tenant. In addition to assuring accuracy, a copy of the check gives them the tenant's current checking account number and bank. If rent is shared by roommates, copy the second check, too. Store receipts in chronological order and staple them together at the end of the year.

Tenant Schedule

The tenant schedule is a running account of all the tenants who have rented your apartment. Write down their names, telephone numbers, the dates they moved in and out, the due-date for rent, the security deposit they paid, and their bank account and social security numbers. Use this schedule as a handy reference guide and for quick access to the information you most often need.

Property Management Records

The paperwork connected with managing property can be extensive. If you're buying a duplex, you probably have a mortgage or a legal agreement for purchasing the property on a land contract. There are bank records, loan documents, insurance records, tax records, title papers, and reports on such things as termite and safety inspections. Create files or sections for each of these document categories within your property management drawer or binder.

Loan and Note Summary

In the file where you keep all of your loan paperwork, make a list of all of your loans, what each is for, where it is located, the due date for payments, the interest rate, the principal, and the principal balance. Summarizing the information is particularly useful if you have more than one loan. It's information at your fingertips—no hunting required.

Insurance Summary

It will be helpful if you prepare a similar summary sheet listing all insurance policies pertaining to the property. Then when you want to look something up, the information you're most likely to need will be right there. The categories to list include:

- Name of insurance company
- Agent
- Phone number and address
- Type of policy
- Policy number
- Limits paid
- Amount of premium
- When the premium is due
- When the policy expires

Keep copies of your insurance policies. Even the old ones that are no longer in force should be kept for five to seven years.

Financial Records

Everyone has an individual way of doing things, and when it comes to financial records this is especially true. Some landlords store receipts in a shoebox, others have detailed files and books that cross-reference all their records. And, of course, there are those who fall somewhere in between. You'll have to find the system that works best for you. But here are some suggestions that you may find helpful.

Spend a little time at the end of each month filing receipts, logging expenses and income, and recording other pertinent data. Then you'll always know where you stand financially and have good information on which to make sound business decisions. Appendix B includes several worksheets to help you organize and record financial information.

FACT

You'll use income and expense records when you prepare your tax returns. They're necessary if you have to satisfy Uncle Sam during an audit. And they help you understand your cash flow and give you a gauge of whether you're collecting enough in rent.

Expense and Payment Records

Keep all receipts, cancelled checks, and checkbook registers or stubs that pertain to your property. You want all your bills, invoices, credit card statements, and itemized receipts for supplies, services, and repairs. That way you'll know, and be able to prove, exactly how much you are spending each year.

Staple receipts together by category and month. File them chronologically in a file folder or envelope. At start of the new year, put all receipts for the previous year into a large envelope.

Documenting invoices, a procedure used by some large companies, might simplify things for you, too. As you pay your bills, write down the check number on the invoice or, if you paid in cash, put a checkmark next to the dollar amount. Then code the receipt by writing down the ledger sheet category, such as phone or advertising, to which it will be applied. You'll never have to wonder, later, whether or not you paid the bill and then forgot to enter it in your records. You'll know, too, exactly when your payment went out.

Filling Out a Ledger Sheet

Your next task is to write down expenses on a ledger sheet, also known as a rental expense allocation report. Dedicate each row to a separate expense category. Include a column for depreciable expenses and another for deductible expenses. See Appendix B for a sample form to see what categories are commonly included. Some landlords will add additional categories for other fees, such as telephone or Internet service if the tenants don't pay for this themselves. Create a customized ledger sheet for your property and keep records faithfully.

ALERT!

When you fill out your ledger sheet, you should not put down any payments you make to yourself for time and labor. Enter them as personal or time or labor withdrawals, or "draws," in your checkbook, because they are not deductible expenses.

If you pay for everything by check, the checkbook register will confirm entries on your ledger. But sometimes it's easier to pay by cash or credit card. Keep receipts and monthly credit card statements as backup. If you want to use a credit card, get one specifically for your rental business. Many credit card companies send out a summary statement at the end of the year and that makes it easier to see your expense breakdown.

Every time you pay a bill, enter it on the ledger sheet. Each horizontal line should be devoted to one bill. Write down who was paid, the amount paid, the date paid, how it was paid (check, cash, or credit card), and what it was for. If you paid by check, write down the check number for easy cross-referencing with your checkbook register. Also note whether an item is depreciable or deductible.

Monthly Income Record

This sheet, with a column for each of the twelve months, will be used for years to remind you exactly when you last increased rent or any of the fees paid by your tenant. You will simply record the amount of rent you collect each month. The first year or two it might seem unnecessary since you have only one rental unit, but after you've been a landlord for numerous years, you will appreciate having a handy reference that allows you to summarize yearly income and compare one year to another. It also will be useful in determining your cash flow.

Cash Flow Analysis

Cash flow is the money you have left over after you've paid all your expenses. Figuring out your cash flow is the only way you know whether or not you're making a profit. On an income and expense statement, itemize and total all expenses and income for the year (or to date). Subtract your expenses from your income to discover what your cash flow is. This document is similar to the worksheet you use when you prepare your federal income tax return, but much more detailed, and therefore much more useful to landlords or anyone else running a business.

Looking at your cash flow is the only way to determine whether your business is viable or about ready to crash. Everyone in business needs to analyze their cash flow; it's the basis for making sound business decisions. For landlords, that means understanding when they can afford to make capital improvements and whether they can afford to hire someone to do the job.

FACT

Your records will include the money you collected for the security deposit. Remember: it is not income. It is your tenant's money and you are holding it until the tenant moves out. If, however, the security deposit includes the last month's rent, it must be listed as income on your tax return in the year it's received.

Depreciation Schedule

Routine expenses such as repairs, supplies, and anything else you need to maintain your property are deductible items on tax returns. You depreciate capital improvements that increase the value of your property;

they include such things as appliances, a new roof, yard improvements, and the dwelling itself.

The formulas for depreciation are complicated and subject to frequent changes. You want to use the tax advantages of depreciation, but this is one area in which hiring an accountant can be a big help. Remember that listing a depreciable item as a deductible business expense on your tax returns is a huge mistake; it waves a red flag at those IRS personnel deciding which businesses to audit.

Maintenance and Repair Records

Landlords are a prime target for liability lawsuits, as you've learned throughout this book. So it makes sense to do as much as you can to reduce the risk of being called to court. In addition to immediately responding to maintenance and repair calls and complaints, inspect your property thoroughly several times a year and keep meticulous records.

A paper trail of property and safety inspections, your response to complaints and requests, and work and service reports will demonstrate that you're doing everything reasonably possible to keep tenants safe and secure and the premises in good order.

Records Start Immediately

Part of your documentation for repairs and maintenance will be kept with your financial records. The cost of materials, supplies, and equipment you use to fix up your apartment can be deducted from your income, so don't throw out any receipts or invoices. Your expense records also show what you did to repair and improve the unit, the entrance, and the exterior of your building.

Maintenance and repair records also include the inspection checklist your tenant filled out at the start of the tenancy. It shows that everything was in satisfactory condition when he or she moved in. If any problems were noted, it shows that you fixed them right away because your tenant will initial the checklist after the work is completed.

But since repair and maintenance records also include the results of annual and semiannual checklists and inspections, you'll have a way to predict when an appliance or fixture is likely to need replacing. You'll be able to see when what is typically "normal" wear and tear is getting so bad that you'll have to replace a counter or buy a new carpet.

By regularly inspecting the apartment and having records that substantiate the fact that you are vigilant about upkeep and repairs, neither your tenant nor a court is likely to say that you are a negligent landlord.

FACT

Instead of making duplicates of invoices and receipts that will be filed with other financial records, consider starting a repair and maintenance logbook to cross-reference records. With a logbook you'll know at a glance what you had to do and what it cost to repair it. You'll also be able to find the original invoices quickly.

Forecasting Repairs

It helps to know in advance when it will be necessary to replace costlier items, such as appliances, a furnace, or a roof. Your records will show what kind of problem you spotted and how frequently you've tried to repair it. You won't have to rely on memory to figure out when the noise first occurred and how loud it was. If you plan ahead and track things carefully from the time you first note the problem, you'll have a chance to save up for the purchase.

Semiannual Safety Checklist

Twice a year have your tenant inspect the apartment and premises with a safety and maintenance checklist in hand. If he or she sees something that might become a problem, it should be written down so that you can inspect it. Keep the checklist in your file and note when you looked at it and what you did. Make a note of any conversations you had with your tenant about the problem.

Things to look for on a semiannual safety-maintenance checkup include signs that the roof is leaking in the house or garage, mildew, locks that stick or are hard to close, and defective smoke detectors. Ask your tenant if there are any problems with fuses or circuit breakers blowing frequently. You want to know if the hot water supply is too hot or a fan doesn't work. Ask if there's any sign of peeling paint, and if there is, get out your paintbrush.

Yearly Inspection

Once a year go into the unit yourself and, using a move-in inventory checklist, look for signs of wear and tear. If you bring photos taken before your tenant moved in and the original signed checklist, you can compare them to what you observe to see if any noted wear and tear has progressed. You'll also have your original notes handy and won't have to rely on memory as you jot things down on the yearly inspection checklist. Also, using a checklist reminds you to check everything.

If a worn rug is now threadbare, you'll want to replace it immediately so it won't become hazardous and cause an accident. If you have a little more time before it needs replacing, remember to check it more frequently, perhaps in a month or so. Be particularly vigilant about safety issues.

Other things to inspect each year include the screen door, the electrical system, water pressure, and the heating and air conditioning systems. Look at the basement, attic, garage, patio, roof, and exterior of the house. Always check outside locks, smoke detectors in hallways, the stairs, and all handrails. Keep copies of the inspection checklist, your notes, and whether you fixed problems that got worse or whether you decided to monitor the problems for a while longer.

Repair Request Forms

Remind your tenant every once in a while, and certainly during inspections, that you want to keep the building in good repair and that you appreciate being told when something needs to be fixed or could possibly become a hazard. Leave a repair and maintenance request form on the kitchen counter and be sure it includes your home phone and cell phone numbers. Most people put off calling if they have to look up a phone number. You don't want any delays. You want to be notified right away.

QUESTION?

How long should I hang onto old records?
Most people say you should keep financial records for seven years in case Uncle Sam wants to audit you. You might be able to toss other files after three years, but if they're not taking up too much space, hang onto them as long as you can. You can't predict when you will need them to prove your case in an audit or in court.

How to Avoid an Audit

Keeping good records pays in more than one way. With documented income and disbursement records, you can make better business decisions. They'll be an asset at tax time, not only to help you prepare your returns but also to legitimize the information on the returns.

To avoid being audited, always turn in an honest, verifiable account of your business—the deductions you take and the benefits you receive. Be realistic about repairs and improvements to your property. If your deductible business expenses seem outlandish, that might wave a red flag at the auditors and tempt them to look closer. Don't make mistakes when you prepare your taxes, and always pay all of what you owe. Don't play games with the IRS by fudging a little here and a little there on your tax records.

Know exactly what you can claim as deductible business expenses— you don't want to list any money you paid to yourself. Don't confuse deductible business expenditures with those that should be depreciated. Know which things can be categorized as capital improvements and which are considered repairs and maintenance.

When you depreciate property, separate the value of the land from the total value of the property. Land does not depreciate; your building does. Clearly show that you are only depreciating the cost of the dwelling. And use the depreciation tables correctly. (See Chapter 8.) If you're not sure about something, talk to an accountant or another professional who prepares tax returns.

Should You Hire an Accountant?

Unless you have a strong background and skills for working with numbers, get an accountant. You can still do all the paperwork throughout the year, but hand everything over to the accountant so he or she can prepare and file your income tax returns. At the very least, have a professional go over your tax forms to see if you've made a mistake or missed a deduction.

An accountant can also help you prepare a depreciation schedule and knows about changes in tax laws. The laws are complex and constantly being rewritten; it's hard to keep up with everything and therefore easy to overlook possible benefits.

If you don't like working with numbers but still want to keep your own books throughout the year, use a spreadsheet or user-friendly accounting software program written expressly for small businesses. It can give you income, expense, and balance statements and calculate your cash flow.

FACT

Some accounting software is not user friendly. Before you purchase anything, talk to other landlords to find out what they use and recommend. If you get something too difficult, you'll spend countless frustrating hours trying to figure it out. You'd then be better off keeping your records on paper.

Whether you use paper or computer records, if you do a thorough job and hand those records to an accountant at tax time, your tax return will have more credibility, which will do a lot to help you avoid an audit.

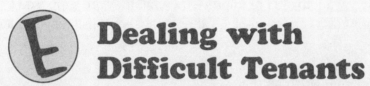

Chapter 19

Dealing with Difficult Tenants

A landlord's nightmare tenants: They have noisy guests at all hours. They never clean house, they rarely take out garbage—and when they do, they somehow get more on the ground than in the container. They paint bedrooms black or dark purple, have mold proliferating in the refrigerator, and litter the hallway with beer cans and bottles. They pay rent late or the check bounces. Do you have to put up with this? Not at all. In this chapter you'll learn what you can do about problem tenants.

Tenant Responsibilities

The obligations and responsibilities in a landlord-tenant relationship go two ways. In return for getting a habitable, clean, safe home, the tenant is supposed to keep it that way and return it in the same condition.

Tenants should not destroy, deface, or take anything from the property. If they want to alter or improve the unit, they are supposed to get their landlord's permission first. Other tenant responsibilities include the following:

- Paying rent when it's due
- Using utilities properly, not overloading outlets
- Fixing anything they or a guest break
- Disposing of trash in a clean, sanitary manner
- Not doing anything to attract bugs or rodents
- Not disturbing other residents or neighbors
- Not using the property for illegal activities
- Not using the property to run a business without landlord approval

In a nutshell, a tenant shouldn't do anything that might reduce the value of the landlord's property. Most of them don't, yet others cause problems. If your tenants are the latter type, there are things you can do about it.

Noisy Tenants

When you hear frequent loud music, parties, or fights in your tenant's apartment, it's a nuisance for you and your neighbors. You don't have to put up with it. You can legally terminate a tenant who behaves unreasonably.

If your tenant makes a lot of noise, first let him or her know that you have received complaints about the disturbances. (Document when and what the complaint was.) Then talk to the tenant. Be courteous and friendly; listen to what he or she has to say and try to solve the problem. Afterward it's a good idea to send a letter saying, "As we discussed earlier…" Keep a copy of the letter for your records.

Your job is to document everything said by neighbors and your tenant that demonstrates how he or she is violating the lease. Ask your neighbors to sign their complaints and date them.

If the problem continues, send your tenant a copy of the lease rules and regulations and/or a written reminder that the lease prohibits disturbing others. Ask the tenant to cease the disruptive behavior and keep noise down. Do this twice, and if the noise still doesn't stop, then send a Notice of Breach with Right to Cure form, also known as a Cure or Quit notice. It, too, gives your tenant a time frame in which to correct or cure the behavior, but it also serves as notice that if the problem is not resolved, the tenant must move or will be evicted. (See the sample form in Appendix B.)

If you have to go to court for an eviction, your documentation will show the judge that you gave your tenant three chances to comply with terms in the lease before you began the eviction procedure. (See Chapter 20 for more information about evictions.)

Tenants Who Harass or Intimidate Neighbors

There's a bit of Jekyll and Hyde in every personality. But if your tenant's dark side gets extreme and includes harassing and intimidating fellow residents and neighbors, you should consider terminating the lease.

Tenants may not be a nuisance or jeopardize the health, welfare, and safety of others, including you and your family or neighbors. They cannot discharge guns. Sexual harassment is also prohibited.

Your lease should include a clause stating that sexual harassment, abusive behavior, threats, racial slurs, or any other kind of intimidation will not be tolerated on the premises or against neighbors.

If a tenant is disruptive, send a warning letter that points out the lease violation. But have your lawyer intervene when the violation constitutes a potential threat to anyone's health and safety.

If anyone complains about your tenant, you should write a letter to the tenant saying that he or she is violating terms of the lease. The letter should state that if the behavior doesn't stop, it can lead to an eviction.

Unless there were threats of violence, talk to your tenant about the complaints and when it occurred. Afterward document the visit by writing down the date, time, what you and your tenant said, and what the outcome was. Then send your tenant a letter reaffirming the discussion. This may be used as evidence in court, should the problem end up there.

If the behavior doesn't stop, send a letter restating what occurred and when it took place. Remind your tenant that he or she is violating the lease and that if the behavior continues, you will begin termination procedures.

If you have to proceed with the eviction, take your documentation to court. Ask your neighbor or anyone else who witnessed the behavior to appear as a witness.

When the Apartment Is Wrecked

Landlords want tenants who call their apartments home. Not all tenants do. They trash the apartment and yard and misuse the property by breaking fixtures and appliances. They can be so unsanitary in their habits that they leave food on counters and in the sink, inviting rodents and bugs indoors to have a feast.

That's why security deposits can be used for repairs and cleaning up trashed apartments after tenants leave. But you don't have to wait until the end of a lease to get rid of objectionable tenants. They can be evicted for decreasing the value of your property.

The ideal tenant will let you know when a faucet needs to be fixed, a door can't be opened because the lock breaks, or the grouting falls out of shower tiles. Tenants should always report problems caused by normal wear and tear. Unless you keep up with your scheduled maintenance checkups, however, you might not learn about damage until they move out.

You won't get an eviction if your tenant simply doesn't keep house up to your standards. If there's no damage or threat to health and safety, the lease protects him or her.

Damage Versus Normal Wear and Tear

Chipped paint, sun-faded curtains, worn countertops, dirty screens are the result of normal wear and tear. Tenants aren't responsible for these things. If you have any doubt, think about your own home. You bump and nick your paint. You have to replace old curtains. After some years even the best Formica countertop looks shabby. And you've got dirty screens at least once a year, just as your tenant does.

Damage includes such things as missing doors, burned or stained countertops and carpets, holes in walls, and chipped or broken tiles. Carelessness, anger, and irresponsible behavior cause damage. Unfixed, they undermine the value of your property.

What Are Your Responsibilities?

As a landlord, you have to pay for repairing items if the malfunction was caused by normal wear and tear. Eventually appliances and fixtures wear out. After years of wear, carpets and linoleum have to be replaced. You also must pay for damage from accidents that are not caused by your tenant or your tenant's guest. It's your responsibility to keep the dwelling functioning in a clean, sanitary, and safe manner. If you're doing your part, though, and the tenant is the one decreasing the value of your property by irresponsible behavior, start the eviction proceedings by sending the tenant a warning letter for lease or rental agreement violations. (See Chapter 20 for more on evictions.)

Tenants Who Get Behind in Rent

A tenant can have a good credit report and income when moving in, but that doesn't guarantee it will stay that way. The economy may become unstable and companies may downsize or move to a cheaper labor markets. If your tenant is laid off, paying rent might become difficult. That's why it's important to have a lease or rental agreement that clearly states what your policy is about when rent is due, whether you allow a grace period, and whether you charge a late payment penalty.

The lease or rental agreement should say how the late payment penalty is applied and what it is. It also should include whether you have a penalty for bounced checks. In establishing a policy keep in mind that if your tenant pays rent, say, two weeks late, it might not solve anything because rent will be due again within ten to fifteen days.

First Step to Take

If your tenant doesn't make the payment on time, go to him or her. Find out why it's late and what day it will be paid. Remind your tenant what's in the lease in regard to late payments.

You can also do this by letter, but either way keep a friendly tone and be professional. Don't become emotionally involved in your tenant's problem. You have your own problems when you're not receiving rent payments on time.

If rent is still unpaid after the predetermined number of days, you'll have to start eviction proceedings.

Garnishing Wages and Income Tax Refunds

Garnishment is a legal process that allows creditors to take a specified sum from a person's wages, income tax refunds, or bank account to satisfy a debt such as back rent. You will need to go through a lower court and it may require that you first have had a money judgment awarded through a court of law. The process may vary from state to state, so get information from your local courthouse or professional landlord's association. It's essential that you know where your tenant works and have his or her social security number; you should have that information on the rental application and the lease.

Garnishing wages is called a periodic garnishment. It will give you a percentage of your tenant's wages until the debt is satisfied. All you have to do is go to your courthouse, file three forms, and pay a small fee. The original filing and fee are effective for only ninety days, however, so you can't do it once and forget about it. It may take several filings before the garnishment goes into effect.

FACT

It's easier to stay detached from your tenant's problem when you aren't friends with your tenant. Even if you sympathize with tenants for being laid off or in another type of difficult financial position, you have to remain detached. Do everything you can to keep your relationship on a business basis.

Garnishing income tax refunds or a savings account is more likely to give you all or nearly all of what you're owed. To garnish funds in a savings account, if your tenant has one, you need the tenant's social security number and the name of the bank. You have to hope it hasn't changed since the rental application and lease were filled out.

You may also garnish income tax refunds to be paid in the next year. But you have to be careful here about following the rules in your state, because deadlines for filing vary. Plan on filing papers in the fall to collect money being refunded in the following year. Don't miss the deadline; if you do, some states will not process the papers and you'll lose out. Other states may be a little more flexible.

Keep in mind that the earlier you file the income tax garnishment forms, the better chance you'll have of collecting money. Some people don't wait until April 15 to mail the IRS forms. If they file early—which is becoming very easy to do online—they could get a refund at the first of the year, before you've filed your forms.

What If Drugs Are Suspected?

Anytime you suspect that a tenant is breaking the law—using your property for an unintended purpose—you should take steps to end the tenancy. If you don't, you are putting yourself and your home in jeopardy with the law and at risk for lawsuits should anyone be injured.

QUESTION?

What kind of behavior is considered illegal?
You should watch for tenants who are involved with drugs, either selling, manufacturing, distributing, using, or processing them. Other illegal behaviors include storing stolen goods or engaging in prostitution.

Regulations for Evicting Lawbreakers

A landlord's liability for criminal activities varies depending on the state. At one extreme, some states demand that landlords evict lawbreaking tenants or they will shut down the building. If you live in Texas, you can be held strictly liable even if you didn't know anything illegal was going on. In Florida you don't even have to go to court; officials can shut down your dwelling if a local administrative board declares your property a nuisance. And New York allows neighbors within two hundred feet of the dwelling to start eviction proceedings themselves.

Some states are more protective of the tenants; New Jersey says that landlords can evict tenants only after they've been convicted of a crime. Texas and North Carolina say landlords can act with only a reasonable suspicion. Find out what the regulations are in your state.

Promote Your Zero Tolerance Policy

Your rental agreement should include a paragraph about not tolerating drugs or other illegal activities on your property. Let tenants know that you will terminate the lease and evict the tenant immediately if anything illegal takes place. Let your neighbors know, as well, that zero tolerance is your standard policy. Then if anyone makes a complaint, check it out thoroughly. Don't put it off.

Keep an eye on whether your tenant has a constant stream of visitors, especially late at night. Discourage it by putting bright lights over exterior doors and in hallways. Drug users don't want to be seen and a tenant selling drugs won't want them to be noticed.

FACT

You take the first step in protecting yourself and your property when you thoroughly screen prospective tenants. However, especially if you have more than four units, keep in mind that former drug abusers are protected by most local and state fair housing laws. Landlords of those properties can only refuse rental if the prospect was convicted of selling or manufacturing drugs.

What You Should Never Do

In anger and frustration it's easy to take that little step that goes over the line between legal and illegal. Know ahead of time what you can't do because if you threaten, intimidate, or retaliate against a difficult tenant, you might find yourself in court with a very unsympathetic judge. State laws prohibit trespass, assault, battery, slander, libel, inflicting emotional distress, and wrongful eviction, and many states permit costly monetary judgments when a landlord is found guilty of these things. Landlords cannot:

- Shut down utilities.
- Change locks to keep tenants out.
- Toss tenants' belongings out on the curb.
- Deliberately let the sewer back up.
- Take anything from the tenant.
- Harm tenants' pets.
- Threaten or intimidate tenants.
- Deliberately make excessive noise.

As frustrating as it is to have a difficult tenant, the last thing you want to do is make things worse by losing your temper, inciting retaliatory reactions, or breaking the law. There are more subtle ways to encourage a tenant to move, preferably before you have to pay money for the eviction proceedings, and it might be worthwhile to try them.

Incentives for Difficult Tenants

If your tenants are being difficult, and you're looking for a way to get them to move without actually evicting them, you can try offering an incentive. For example, if they leave by a designated day, give them back some of their security deposit. Before you make the offer, however, calculate how much of the security deposit you'll need to cover lost rent and damage repair, then compare the overall cost of evicting your tenant to the incentive. Your incentive should be no less than $100.

You can offer to let the tenants store personal property for a month or two at no cost until they have a new place. So what if your basement gets a little crowded or your car sits out of the garage for the duration? Or you can rent a truck for a day so they can take their things to their new apartment.

Some tenants would be happy not to have you report them to the credit bureau. If they have an eviction on their credit report, it only makes it harder to find a landlord willing to give them a new apartment. Incentives like these may very well get them moving. It's illegal, however, to "force" or coerce tenants to leave by locking them out of the apartment, making the apartment uninhabitable, or threatening them. Such behavior can result in your having to pay a hefty fine. (There's more information on what you can't do in Chapter 20.) If incentives don't work, start the eviction process with no further delay.

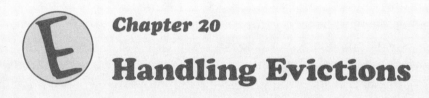

Chapter 20

Handling Evictions

Despite all your care in selecting a tenant, once in a while you have a tenant who just doesn't work out. Rent repeatedly comes in late, lease agreements are ignored, or you discover your tenant uses illegal drugs or creates unsanitary conditions on the premises. Terminating problem tenants is easy if they have a month-to-month rental agreement. It's much more difficult when they have a lease. In this chapter you'll learn how to evict tenants, what notices have to be delivered, and whether you should hire a lawyer.

The Procedure for Evicting Tenants

Tenants can be evicted for many reasons: nonpayment or partial payment of rent, giving false information on the rental application or lease, or lease violations such as unauthorized pets or tenants, subletting the apartment without permission, engaging in illegal activities, and altering the unit without permission. Each state has very strict rules and procedures that must be followed in order to evict a tenant.

Local ordinances may also have requirements that have to be followed. A good source for information in your area would be through a professional organization such as a rental property owners association. You can also find information about local laws online or at your library.

The procedure for getting an eviction is similar in most states; landlords in all states are required to notify tenants first that the lease is being terminated and that they intend to go to court for an eviction. What varies from state to state is the amount of time you must give a tenant to comply with notices before appearing in court.

ALERT!

The content and appearance of a termination notice and how it is delivered may also be very tightly regulated. You must follow the instructions carefully. If you aren't precise, you may delay the eviction or lose your case in court.

There are three steps leading up to a court hearing. If you are evicting a tenant who fails to pay rent, they are to:

1. Give the tenant a Pay Rent or Quit notice.
2. Give the tenant an Unconditional Quit notice.
3. Go to the courthouse to file the forms and pay the fee.

If you are evicting a tenant because of a lease violation, the process is mostly the same, but the first step will be to send a Cure or Quit notice (covered later in the chapter).

Reminder Letter

If you have a tenant who usually pays rent on time, you may want to send a letter asking if he or she overlooked the fact that rent was due "yesterday" before you issue a Pay Rent or Quit notice. Point out that to avoid a late payment penalty, the rent should be paid immediately. You can give the tenant a couple of days. If the rent hasn't come in during that time period, then you should start the process of terminating the lease.

Pay Rent or Quit Notice

The first notice called Pay Rent or Quit, or sometimes Pay Rent or Lease Terminates, gives the tenant three to seven days (depending upon state law) to pay the full amount of back rent owed or else leave the apartment. Most tenants are evicted for nonpayment of rent or continually paying it late. If the tenant then pays the rent, it nullifies the Pay Rent or Quit notice. (You will find samples of this form and most of the others mentioned in this chapter in Appendix B.)

Tenants who pay the money they owe usually get a second chance to establish a good, on-time payment record. If, however, they should fall behind on rent or pay late again within an established time frame, you can proceed with termination and eviction. In other words, you don't have to put up with late payments forever. In most states you can then deliver an Unconditional Quit notice and file for the eviction in court.

FACT

Eleven states allow landlords to go directly to eviction proceedings; tenants do not have to be given a second chance. They are: Alabama, Arkansas, Louisiana, Missouri, North Dakota, Ohio, Pennsylvania, South Dakota, Texas, West Virginia, and Wyoming.

Unconditional Quit Notice

The Unconditional Quit notice (or Notice of Breach with No Right to Cure) tells the tenant that you will no longer accept money for back rent. He or she has to move out; you are starting a legal action for an eviction.

These notices typically are issued after repeated violations of the lease and frequent late rent payments. An Unconditional Quit notice is the last step before you go to the courthouse and file eviction papers.

Cure or Quit Notice

The Cure or Quit notice, also called a Notice of Breach with Right to Cure, is similar to the first step in evicting tenants for nonpayment of rent. But this notice is for lease violations: extensive property damage, illegal activities in the unit, bringing in a prohibited animal, or creating disturbances with frequent loud parties or music.

The notice gives tenants a time frame in which they must "cure" the prohibited behavior. It can be up to thirty days. If the behavior doesn't change, then the landlord can proceed to the next steps toward eviction—the Unconditional Quit notice and filing papers in court. Those processes are similar to what is described for situations of nonpayment of rent.

Tenants with a month-to-month lease can be asked to leave after you give them a thirty-day Notice to Quit. You don't have to give them a reason why you want them to leave or a second chance to correct their behavior. And in most cases, even if you do have a valid reason for their eviction and can prove it in court, it is much easier simply not to renew their thirty-day lease.

Eviction Costs

Evictions are not cheap. A landlord has to pay fees for filing forms in court, possibly get a lawyer, pay the movers, and then add in rent lost for up to three months. There are a few ways to try to recover these costs. If you have a formal court trial, you can try to recover those costs, as well as the fees for serving the complaint, through a Money Judgment.

When your tenant doesn't have resources, you can hire a collections agency to recover the money, but then you'll only get a percentage of what money is recovered—you have to pay them to collect it for you.

If you got a Money Judgment and your tenant is employed, you can garnish the wages (see Chapter 19).

Drug Evictions

In Texas and North Carolina, all you need is reasonable suspicion that your tenant is involved in drugs and you can get rid of that tenant right away. In California you have to go to court, and if the eviction is upheld, your tenant has only twenty-four hours to vacate the apartment. Most drug evictions don't happen quite as quickly in the rest of the states, but they're still faster than regular evictions.

Drug evictions start off with the Unconditional Notice to Quit. In most states, if the tenant doesn't leave after receiving the notice you can then file for an eviction and have a hearing within a couple of days.

FACT

Simply finding out that a tenant has prior criminal convictions does not give you the right to get rid of a tenant who is in compliance with all of the lease provisions. The only way to end that tenancy would be if you discover false statements or information on the lease.

Going to Court

When you are ready to initiate eviction proceedings, go to the courthouse, fill out forms stating why you want to appear before the court, and pay the fee. At the hearing you will present your case and your documented evidence.

Make three copies of the original notices and eviction papers for the court. Also get together other relevant records such as the lease, copies of receipts for rent, warning letters, and your logbook. If the eviction is due to nonpayment of rent, have documentation that shows you gave your tenant a Pay Rent or Quit notice and therefore he or she had time to bring rent up to date. It's essential that you go into the court organized and can quickly demonstrate why the tenant should be evicted.

First Court Appearance

On the date your hearing is scheduled, you must appear in court. Take all of your tenant records—the rental agreement, lease, pet agreement, inventory checklist, correspondence, invoices for repairs and damage, your collection records, and any other notices, photos, or videos. Also bring your logbook of events if you keep one. An eviction usually entails two hearings in court. At the first, you and your tenant will each be given an opportunity to tell your story. The evidence you present will strengthen your case. If the eviction is based on nonpayment of rent, the judge is likely to give the tenant one last chance to pay all money owed before the second court date.

Eviction proceedings can be delayed or speeded up, however. If your tenant doesn't show up, the judge may order the eviction by default. Resolution is also quicker if your tenant is selling or manufacturing drugs. But there are times when the eviction is delayed; tenants can file a motion to delay proceedings and in some instances judges will issue delays.

QUESTION?

Is there any way for me to charge the tenant for court costs?
You can try to recover your out-of-pocket filing and court costs by asking for a formal court judgment that orders the tenant to reimburse you for those expenses.

If your tenant can convince the judge that being evicted will be a hardship, the eviction could be postponed until the tenant's circumstances improve or to give the tenant time to find a new home. The judge can also order a two-week stay; it gives the tenant additional time to get the money together and pay the back rent. Hardships might be determined if the tenant has children, new housing is not available, or the tenant might lose a job because of moving. If the tenant has children who would be affected by the eviction, the judge might order a stay for more than two weeks. When a tenant offers to pay the back rent, the landlord's court costs for filing the eviction, and future rent, that, too, might halt an eviction.

Second Court Appearance

The judge is likely to issue the eviction at the second court appearance. If proceedings were started because of nonpayment of rent and you haven't received the money by the time of the second court appearance, the tenant is likely to receive a Money Judgment, which orders him to pay you a certain amount of money.

The court might allow the tenant to stay in the apartment for another short period if there is a hardship. But in most cases after the second court appearance, your Sheriff's Department will get the eviction order and set up a date on which it will take place. It's generally within two to three weeks.

Tenants sometimes immediately move after the court order. If they don't, the sheriff will hire a moving company—you pay the costs—to remove the tenant's possessions on the day assigned for the eviction.

Do You Need a Lawyer?

Most of the time you can file the paperwork and handle evictions without hiring a lawyer. But each case is different and sometimes legal representation is a good idea. One of those situations is when the unit is in a rent-controlled area. Rent control districts have special rules for evictions and a lawyer can be a big help.

Other times to consider hiring a lawyer are:

- If your tenant hires an attorney
- If the tenant's lawyer files a written complaint or affidavit
- If your tenant contests or appeals an eviction (filed for any reason other than unpaid rent)
- If your tenant files for bankruptcy
- If your tenant appears to have assets, thus giving you a good chance to recover money

How to Avoid Legal Hassles

Evicting a tenant is one of the most difficult situations a landlord can have. By the time you get to that point, you'll be frustrated, to say the least. When rent is owed, you'll probably hear sob stories and tall tales about why it's late or the check bounced. Your tenant may not answer the phone or door even when you know he or she is home. You also have to put up with promises that mean little.

No matter how much you want to get rid of a bad tenant and find a new one, the eviction process is slow and costly. You will likely be losing rent money, and paying to file notices and go to court. But never, ever try to speed up the process by doing something illegal to "persuade" your tenant to move. In some states landlords will be fined $100 per day for turning off a tenant's utilities. Nearly all states forbid coercive persuasion and your tenant can sue you. Guess who will win?

So don't turn off tenants' gas, electricity, or water, block up the sewer, lock them out of the building, or throw their possessions in the street. Above all, don't threaten them.

Some landlords might prefer to have their lawyer send the violation-of-lease letter, but it isn't necessary to pay legal fees for the service. As the landlord, you can handle it yourself.

Handle Yourself Carefully

It takes about three months to evict a tenant. While you're going through the process, your tenant has the right to stay in your unit peacefully. No matter how much you want to be rid of him or her, don't get worked up. Grin and bear it. It's your tenant's home up until the time you've won your court case.

Stay away from your tenant as much as possible. The only time it's okay to meet face-to-face is if you're trying to settle a dispute in a structured setting. If you have to communicate, put it in writing instead of going to talk to your tenant. Make your notes or letters short and to the point. Don't go off on tangents. You want to be focused and not show anger or react to the tenant in person or in a written communication. Keep your message neutral.

Get the New Address

If you can, get your tenant's new address before he or she moves out. You will need that address, and after a tenant leaves it could be very difficult to find him or her. Otherwise try to get the address from the company that moved the tenant. You can try calling your tenant's old telephone number; calls might be forwarded to a new number. You can also call the emergency contact your tenant gave you on the rental application. It's usually a close relative and very often the best way to get the address.

What If They File for Bankruptcy?

Tenants filing for bankruptcy automatically delay evictions and terminations. If your tenant files, you need court approval to terminate the lease or evict the tenant. The security deposit also goes into limbo after your tenant files. You can't use it to repair damage or for back rent without first getting permission from the court.

If you get an automatic stay from a federal court judge, however, a few days afterward, you can continue terminating the lease or evicting the tenant. A stay also allows you to put the security deposit to use.

FACT

Sometimes a security deposit is tapped for repairs or back rent before the tenant files for bankruptcy. If that should happen to you, don't worry about it. It will not matter to the court since you were simply doing what you had to do as a landlord.

If your bankrupt tenant is not behind in rent, oftentimes a court-appointed trustee will allow him or her to remain in the apartment. They believe it only makes matters worse for creditors if the tenant has to leave one apartment and somehow scrape together enough money for the security deposit and initial rent payments for a new apartment. As landlord in this situation, you still have the right to determine whether your tenant has enough resources to continue paying the rent.

When They Abandon Property

Some tenants move out or "disappear," leaving behind furniture, clothing, kitchenware, and other personal items. Obviously you would like to remove these items so you can start cleaning the apartment and finding a new tenant. But states have rules about when and how landlords can dispose of a tenant's belongings. It is essential to find out what these rules are in your area.

It's also a good idea to check your consumer protection agency to see if your state has any other guidelines or regulations to follow regarding disposing of tenants' property. Tenants can sue for liability if their property is sold or thrown out too quickly. So whatever you do, don't jump to conclusions. You have to determine that your tenant really has left and will not be coming back.

It's easier to stay detached from your tenant's problem when you aren't friends with your tenant. Even if you sympathize with tenants for being laid off or in another type of difficult financial position, you have to remain detached. Do everything you can to keep your relationship on a business basis.

Why the Tenant Left Is Important

In most states you have the most flexibility in handling the abandoned property if the tenant left after the lease ended or after receiving a termination notice. But if your tenant was physically evicted, in some states it's important to be careful with what was left behind.

Evicted tenants in most states are notified a couple of days in advance about when to expect the sheriff who will physically move them out. If the tenant "disappears," some states require landlords to try to find them, and to carefully store any property left behind, perhaps in a garage or basement. Eventually landlords will be able to sell or give those items away if the tenant doesn't show up. Other states do not require special handling of abandoned property.

You Can Seize Property to Cover Rent

When your tenant owes you money, you can "seize" the property and put a lien on it. However, don't seize what the courts would call the necessities of life—blankets, seasonal clothes, children's toys. Before selling anything, you have to place a lien on the property. To do that it's necessary to place an ad in your local newspaper describing the property, estimating its value, and saying where it can be reclaimed. That gives merchants time to repossess items on which the tenant still owes money.

State law usually determines how long you have to wait after the notice is published to dispose of anything. Courts in your area may also have rulings that restrict landlords on how quickly they can act. You should find out what the rules are before you place a lien on your tenant's property.

Chapter 21

Keeping Good Tenants

Smart business owners know that the best and most profitable way to make money is by keeping customers happy. So the old saying "The customer is always right" is plain old common sense. It takes time and money to drum up new business. That's especially true if you have only one unit. A vacant apartment has a strong impact on your annual profit. In this chapter you'll learn what you can do to please your customers and keep the good ones as tenants year after year.

Think of Them as Your Customers

When you think of tenants as customers, you're focused on their needs, not yours. Sure, you want to make money from your apartment, but while you do, you want your tenants to be pleased that they're living in it and not elsewhere. Happy tenants have pride in their surroundings. They take better care of their homes, and that saves you money in the long run.

If you are diligent about keeping records, you know exactly what it costs to have a tenant move and to thoroughly clean, paint, and repair the unit. You know what it costs to advertise and how much time you have to devote to showing the apartment, interviewing prospects, doing credit checks, and having a new tenant move in. If you're lucky, you'll find new tenants right away. But the reality is that when a tenant moves out, you're likely to have a vacancy and no rental income for about two months. By doing what you can to keep your tenants happy, you increase the likelihood that they will not move out, and you will not have to deal with the extra expenditures of money, time, and energy.

The Relationship Starts with You

To borrow from the Boy Scout Law, a landlord should be "trustworthy, loyal, helpful, friendly, courteous, kind, cheerful, thrifty, and clean." You can add obedient (to local, state and federal regulations) and brave (when you have to evict a tenant).

Keep a positive attitude and treat your tenants with respect. Listen—and hear—what they say when they talk to you. Be friendly—without being a friend—and show interest when they talk about family or jobs.

FACT

You have bad days, too. Try not to show them to your tenant. If you can't be positive and upbeat one day, postpone talking to your tenant for a day or two. A good night's sleep or a change in the weather may be all it takes to improve your mood.

Show Appreciation

Let your tenants know in small ways that you appreciate their business. Thank them when they help out, whether it's sweeping a stairway, shoveling snow, or simply paying rent on time every month. They'll appreciate knowing that you noticed and care.

Keep in touch. When you see them, ask how things are going, and whether they have any problems in the unit. Tell them again and again in different ways that you want to provide an excellent home and that they can help out by letting you know when maintenance is needed.

Go One Step Further

Do a little more than your tenant would expect from a landlord. It would take only a couple of dollars to provide a replacement package of light bulbs or a plunger for the toilet. You can put a planter or a flat of flowers outside your tenant's door in the spring.

Be concerned about your tenant's safety. Let him or her know if there's been a rash of vandalism or break-ins in the neighborhood. When you tell your tenant about it, ask if you can double-check the door and window locks to see that they're secure. Also look at hall and outdoor lights. Replace them if they're dim or burned out.

Remember that you, as well as your tenant, benefit from your security precautions. He or she will be more alert going to and from the house to the car and about strange noises if you have reported that there are problems in the area. You benefit because your insurance premium will be lower if your agent knows you take every reasonable safety precaution. Tenants who know their landlords are concerned about their welfare are much less likely to sue, so your liability risk will also be reduced.

ALERT!

If there are break-ins in the neighborhood, this is a good time to remind your tenant about renter's insurance. It will cover your tenant's personal property losses that result from theft or other illegal activities. Most policies will also cover losses from your tenant's car.

Tell Tenants about Resources in the Area

Keep a list of social service agencies and phone numbers that can be used if one of your tenants is laid off from work. Many people don't realize that agencies in most communities can be a source of help. They range from food banks to housing assistance to Santa Claus Girls or similar agencies that will give parents a few new toys for their children during the holidays.

Stay Professional at All Times

Try to project a competent, efficient, and businesslike demeanor whenever you are interacting with a tenant. No matter how angry or annoyed you get, never retaliate or try to get even with an obtuse or difficult tenant. Learn how to control your temper; later, blow off steam by going to the gym or taking a long walk. If you instantly reach boiling whenever you have to talk to a tenant, have your spouse or a friend act as intermediary. In those rare instances when you and your tenant don't get along or can't resolve problems, it's best to bring in a neutral third party to mediate.

Watch Your Body Language

Think about your body language when you're talking to tenants—especially those who are pests. Do you have a tendency to roll your eyes? What tone of voice do you use? And do you tend to get sarcastic or cut people down when you're angry? You might be seething inside, but you don't want your tenant to know.

Encourage Dialog

Maintain good communications. Let your tenant know right from the start what your expectations are. Encourage tenants to come to you any time they have a complaint or want to request service or repairs. Ask them to let you know if they see something suspicious on your street.

Sometimes a tenant wants to make an improvement or changes to the apartment. If you have good reason to say no to the request, do it pleasantly. If you can, explain why it won't work or why you've had to establish a policy against it. Don't put tenants down even if you think they've come up with a dumb idea.

Be Personable, but Not Personal

Whenever you see your tenant, remind yourself that he or she is your customer. Without tenants you wouldn't be able to run your small business. Remember each tenant's name and the names of others in their family. Know when they have a birthday and wish them well if you see them that day. When you talk to them, be friendly, courteous, and pleasant. Remember that you're running a business, so treat them the same as you would a business client or a social acquaintance.

FACT

Some landlords like to keep gas heaters and coolers available in case the electricity goes out in a storm or there's a blackout. Others send birthday and holiday cards to tenants. If there's a death in your tenant's family, you might want to show sympathy by sending a card or giving your tenant a small gift of food.

Don't Gossip

Never criticize or gossip about your tenant or talk about your tenant's problems. It might take a while to get back to him or her, but you can be assured it will.

Don't listen to gossip, either. If you have a talkative tenant who goes on and on about nothing when you run into each other, try looking busy. Smile, wave, say "Hi," and keep walking. Emulate the President walking to Air Force One or the White House. It's not difficult to put on a show of having important business or a busy schedule to meet. Most tenants will be content with a cheery greeting and assume you are simply too busy to talk today.

Don't Get Involved

If a tenant tells you about a personal problem, be sympathetic without becoming involved. Don't offer advice, try to solve the problem, or help your tenant. And above all don't get so caught up with what they say that it affects your sound business judgment. Remember, if your tenant loses a job, it might result in an eviction. To conduct your business professionally, you have to stay detached and distance yourself from the problem.

Respect Their Privacy

When your tenant moves into the apartment, it is his or her home. You no longer can enter unless you have permission to do maintenance and repairs or there's an emergency. Your tenant has the right to possess the unit without harassment or interruption and the right to privacy and peaceful enjoyment of the property.

This means you're not knocking on the door or phoning all the time, not peeking or staring out a window when they leave or come home, and not rifling through their mail. You also shouldn't ask personal questions.

Having privacy does not give tenants the right to change locks without asking you first if they can. If they do change locks—with or without permission—they must supply you with a new key. And if you have to enter the apartment for repairs and maintenance, your tenant cannot legally stop you. You need to inspect the unit if you think there's a problem; and if your tenant plans to move, you have the right to show the property while he or she still lives there. Your right to enter applies whether the tenant has a rental agreement or a lease.

FACT

Written notice is not necessarily required for you to enter the apartment. If your tenant tells you verbally that you can go inside, that's good enough. If, however, you occasionally have problems with the tenant, carefully note what day and time permission was granted, and afterward send the tenant an acknowledgment that you were there and what you did.

Did They Really Abandon the Unit?

A landlord has no other rights to enter unless it's permitted through a court order or the tenant has been absent for an extended period of time. Just what extended means may be subject to question. So find out how much time your state or community requires you to wait before you can assume that the apartment was abandoned. And follow the rules exactly.

Your tenant could be on a long extended vacation or might have had to rush to another state to care for an elderly parent, forgetting to notify you. If the property isn't abandoned and if you enter too quickly, you might get caught up in a housing or civil rights complaint.

Asking Permission to Enter

In most situations, you should give your tenant twenty-four to forty-eight hours and a written notice that you must enter the unit for repairs and maintenance. (See Chapter 16.) On the note or form, state the reason why you have to enter, when you'd like to come in, and whether anyone else will be with you.

Remember, if there's an emergency, you can enter without permission if no one is home. Knock first, call the fire or police department, then use your key.

Answer Phone Messages Promptly

Nothing frustrates tenants more than calling a landlord, leaving a message, and not getting a timely response. If the call is about repairs and maintenance and if you've established a pattern of not calling back promptly, your tenant will get irritated and be tempted not to stay on after the lease expires.

Have an answering machine for one of the phone numbers you gave your tenant and listen to the messages every day. If you'll be out of town, delegate the responsibility to a family member or close friend. Your tenant deserves the courtesy of having a real person call back, even if just to say that you'll be back at the end of a week or two.

FACT

You can give the person you designate to pick up calls the authority to call your repair services if a problem needs to be addressed immediately. But since you'll have to pay a fee just to have the serviceperson come to the door, you want to be certain that you trust your helper to make good decisions and that he or she will use common sense before calling anyone in.

If your tenant's message isn't about a repair problem or if it is a repair but both you and the tenant know it can be postponed for a while, respond anyway. Let your tenant know when you'll be able to do the repair or have time to talk things over. Not responding tells your tenant that you don't care, listen, or want to maintain your property.

Think about common courtesy, too. If you're talking to a tenant in person or on the phone, don't take a call on your cell phone or ask your tenant to wait while you answer call waiting. Those interruptions are rude and make your tenant feel less important. You owe your tenants undivided attention.

Emergency Calls

When your tenant signed the lease, you supplied phone numbers where you can be reached day or night. So when you get a call in the middle of the night about an "emergency," you should respond right away. Most tenants call about real emergencies. As you know, others call about every little thing. But you can't risk putting them off.

Even if you have a tenant crying "Wolf" all the time, one day the wolf might really be at their doorstep. You don't want to risk damage to your building or a liability claim after a real emergency from a tenant who's generally a pain in the neck.

Give an Alternate Number

Give your tenants your cell phone number so they can reach you in emergencies or when there are serious problems that they think need the immediate attention of an appliance service, plumber, or electrician. If you don't have a cell phone, consider getting one so that tenants can reach you. Otherwise give them an alternate number to call. Even if you're not home, you'll be able to gauge exactly what is wrong by asking a few questions. If you agree that it needs immediate attention, then you can give your tenant the number of the repair service you usually use.

Give tenants the information they need to deal with certain things when you are not immediately available. Tell them where they can find the circuit breaker box so they can check there first when there seems to be an electrical problem. If they know where to find shut-off valves to the main water supply, it can ward off serious water damage throughout the house should a pipe burst or water overflows a sink or tub because the drain is clogged.

Be Responsive When Repairs Are Needed

Are you vexed when a clerk or a doctor makes you wait forever while serving everyone else, even those who got there after you did? Don't do that to your tenant. When he or she requests repairs or reports that something is wrong, check it out promptly. Make maintenance and repairs a priority.

If it's something serious and beyond your skills to fix, promise you'll bring in an electrician or plumber the next day. When it's a minor problem, tell your tenant you'll have it fixed within the week. Then make sure you meet that deadline.

If, for some reason, there's an unforeseen delay, let your tenant know immediately. Say you're sorry, but it will have to be postponed for a couple of days or a week and that you cannot do anything about it. Let your tenant know that you understand that it's inconvenient; ask if there's anything you can do that might help.

Let your tenant know that you understand how they're feeling and that you are frustrated, too. In the meantime, do what you can to help out. If the freezer isn't freezing, for example, offer to store some of the food in your own freezer. Give your tenant a cooler and buy the first bags of ice. Think about what you'd need in that situation, and how you would want to be helped.

Schedule Periodic Upkeep and Maintenance

You know it's important to do periodic maintenance and upkeep on your property between tenants, but don't take long-term tenants for granted. If they've lived under your roof for a number of years, ask if there's any paint that needs touching up, or how their shades or blinds are holding up. Things wear out and show signs of use. Even if your tenant says everything's fine, he or she will appreciate your thoughtfulness. Moreover, it will be remembered.

FACT

If you have a handyman, painter, or gardener for a tenant, let him or her take over some of your work if that suits both of you. Just remember to get a signed written agreement that includes how you intend to repay your tenant. A rebate on the next month's rent is often welcome.

A Good Reputation Is Worth It

You may think that your reputation as a landlord is not important, but having a good reputation pays off in many ways. By cleaning, repairing, and improving your property, you will be able to find good tenants. They will take pride in their home, take care of the unit, and renew their lease each year. Your own life will be more peaceful because you won't be hunting for new tenants all the time. A stable tenant will minimize the other problems landlords face.

As you establish a reputation for being a responsive landlord, your tenant will be less and less demanding when repairs are needed or an appliance starts making a strange noise. You'll reduce your risk for liability complaints and tenants suing you for damages. You'll also eliminate the cost of evictions.

Your reputation as a landlord will grow. If your tenant does have to move, you can be sure he or she will give your phone number to friends or relatives who are looking for an apartment. Your neighbors, too, are sure to mention that you will soon be having a vacancy and that yours is a good building to live in.

Appendix A: Resources

Internet Sites for Landlords

Legal and Other Important Information

Department of Housing and Urban Development
 ✎ *www.hud.gov*
Government Web site that has a Fair Housing Clearinghouse and information about foreclosures, home improvements, and other housing topics.

Environmental Protection Agency
 ✎ *www.epa.gov*
Government link to information about environmental hazards. You can request copies of EPA brochures here.

FindLaw
 ✎ *www.findlaw.com*
Has links to forms for landlords, property law Web sites, and public and consumer resources, including information about asbestos, bankruptcy, credit and debt, personal injury, real estate, starting a business, taxes, and accounting.

Internet Legal Resource Guide
 ✎ *www.ilrg.com*
Offers legal forms compliant with state law, including leases and credit and collections forms.

The Landlord Forum
 ✎ *www.landlordforum.com*
Offers forms, information about screening tenants, landlord resources, and more.

Landlording Help

✎ *www.landlordinghelp.com*

Has landlording information by state, forms, a discussion group, information about lead-based paint, fair housing material, links to tenant screening, and other resources.

Landlord Portal

✎ *www.landlordportal.com*

Offers free rental listings by state, landlord legal guide, do-it-yourself information, credit and tenant screening, and more information and resources.

Mortgage Investments.com

✎ *www.mortgage-investments.com*

Has free forms for landlords and information about real estate and investing; offers free EPA lead-based paint booklet, free Excel spread-sheets, and a free newsletter.

Mrlandlord.com

✎ *www.mrlandlord.com*

Offers a free newsletter, free rental form, EPA lead-based paint book-let, sample lease, and information about landlord-tenant laws.

Nolo

✎ *www.nolo.com*

Features legal information on line for landlords in every state. Includes a dictionary, Ask Auntie, legal encyclopedia, bookstore, form kits, software, and FAQs—a free e-mail newsletter.

Professional Publishing

✎ *www.profpub.com*

Offers order forms or a loose-leaf sample book that has copies of forms, leases, and records useful to landlords.

Rental Housing On Line

✍ *www.rhol.org*

Offers links to local housing associations, state and national information pages, landlord-tenant laws for each state, and free forms.

U.S. Legal Forms, Inc.

✍ *www.USlegalforms.com*

Offers free forms to landlords.

Apartment Listings

Classifieds 2000

✍ *www.classifieds2000.com*

Lists apartments for rent in the United States. Select a city and specify the number of bedrooms.

ForRent.com

✍ *www.forrent.com*

Offers landlords a place to advertise their single units. Also has listings by state and city, information for owners, and tips about moving.

HomeRentals.net

✍ *www.vacancylist.com*

Lists apartments for rent.

Homestore.com

✍ *www.homestore.com*

Lists campus housing offices and apartments nationwide; includes links to a credit analyzer, mortgage calculator, neighborhood finders, home improvements, and more.

Professional Organizations

Institute of Real Estate Management

A group of certified property managers; offers education programs and services, as well as references.
312-329-6000

National Apartment Association

An organization for owners of multifamily housing.
703-518-6141

National Association of Home Builders Multi-family Council

A registered apartment management program.
800-368-5242, ext. 209

Screening and Background Check Services

Equifax, Inc.

A national credit reporting agency.
1-800-685-1111
www.equifax.com

Experian

A national credit reporting agency.
888-397-3742
www.experian.com

National Association of Realtors

Composed of local association and Realtor boards; has a large library.
312-329-8200
E-mail: *NARLIBRARY@aol.com*

National Apartment Association

A national screening company.
703-518-6141

National Tenant Network

Will let you screen prospective tenants and receive online tenant performance reports.

✍ *www.ntnnet.com*

Rent Grow

Its offices throughout the U.S. offer screening services.
800-736-8476
✍ *www.rentgrow.com*

Tenant Screening Center

A national screening company and credit reporting bureau open all the time.

800-523-2381
✍ *www.tsci.com*

TransUnion

A national credit reporting agency.
800-888-4213
✍ *www.tuc.com*

Appendix B: Sample Forms and Worksheets

Tenant's Checklist (Move-in Form)

INVENTORY AND CONDITION OF LEASED PREMISES: PRE-LEASE

Lessor/Landlord: _____

Lessee/Tenant: _____

Address of leased premises: _____
_____

Term of Lease:
    Begin: [date] _____
    End: [date] _____

The purpose of this form is to catalogue all furniture, furnishings, fixtures, appliances, and personal property upon/in the leased premises that Tenant is responsible for returning in as clean and good condition as on the day of commencement of the Lease, normal wear and tear excepted. In addition, the condition of the premises should be noted when appropriate, including newness and/or condition of carpet, paint, etc.

Landlord should catalogue the presence of, and check and note the condition/working condition of each item in the leased premises. Tenant shall then review and check all listed items, immediately after Tenant moves in, indicating agreement or disagreement with Landlord's assessment, and adding comments as necessary. Tenant shall then sign this document in acknowledgment of the terms hereof and of the presence and condition of the catalogued items, including the following:

Landlord assessment--------------   Tenant assessment (check, or give reason)
[item]   [condition]   [agree] [disagree & reason/comment]

_____
_____
_____
_____
_____

Landlord assessment--------------   Tenant assessment (check, or give reason)

[item]   [condition]   [agree] [disagree & reason/comment]

_____

_____

_____

_____

_____

_____

_____

_____

_____

_____

_____

Inadvertent exclusion of any item from this catalogue does not relieve Tenant of the duty to use the item reasonably and return it in same condition as at inception of this lease, normal wear and tear excepted.

Tenant has reviewed this document and agrees that in consideration of the use and possession of the catalogued items during the term of this Lease, Tenant has checked all items and found them to be present and in the same condition as indicated by Landlord, or else has noted any discrepancy. Tenant further agrees to return said items at the expiration/termination of this lease as discussed above. Tenants, if more than one, agree that signature by one Tenant suffices for agreement by all Tenants.

Signature of Tenant: _____ Date: _____

Tenant [print name]: _____

Signature of Landlord: _____ Date: _____

Landlord [print name]: _____

Tenant's Checklist (Move-out Form)

INVENTORY AND CONDITION OF LEASED PREMISES: POST-LEASE

Lessor/Landlord: _____

Lessee/Tenant: _____

Address of leased premises: _____
_____

Term of Lease:
    Begin: [date] _____
    End: [date] _____

This catalogue should be compared to the Pre-Lease catalogue at the expiration or termination of the Lease. Each item in the Pre-Lease catalogue should be noted below, and its present, post-lease condition noted. If the post-lease condition differs from the pre-lease condition for reasons other than depreciation by reasonable wear and tear, this should be noted. Tenant should then state agreement or disagreement with the new assessment.

Landlord assessment--------------   Tenant assessment (check, or give reason)
[item]   [condition]   [agree] [disagree & reason/comment]

_____
_____
_____
_____
_____
_____
_____
_____
_____
_____
_____

Landlord assessment--------------   Tenant assessment (check, or give reason)
[item]   [condition]   [agree] [disagree & reason/comment]

_____

_____

_____

_____

_____

_____

_____

_____

_____

_____

_____

TENANT SIGNATURE

Tenant has reviewed the premises and the above notations made by the Landlord. By signing below, Tenant warrants the accuracy of the above assessments, or disagrees with those assessments as noted by Tenant in the above spaces.

Tenants, if more than one, agree that signature by one Tenant suffices for signature by all Tenants.

Signature of Tenant: _____ Date: _____

Tenant [print name]: _____

Signature of Landlord: _____ Date: _____

Landlord [print name]: _____

Background Check Consent Form

CONSENT TO BACKGROUND AND REFERENCE CHECK

In consideration of solicitation of my application for employment, or application for lease of premises, I, [print name] _____, do hereby give my consent to [potential employer or landlord]: _____, and the authorized agents thereof, to check the references listed on my application, and to check my background in any way, including but not limited to contacting any and all persons and business entities in order to inquire regarding any and all information relating to myself, provided that said inquiries be limited solely to the purpose of consideration of myself for possible employment or tenancy.

Signed: _____ Date: _____

Print: _____
                      (print name)

Pay Rent or Quit Notice

7-DAY NOTICE TO PAY RENT OR LEASE TERMINATES: RESIDENTIAL

TO: Tenant(s): _____ FROM: Landlord _____

_____ _____

_____ _____

_____ _____

_____ _____

Address of Leased Premises: _____

NOTICE IS HEREBY GIVEN that you are in breach of the Lease Agreement on the above described lease premises due to failure to timely pay rent. Except as provided below, within **seven (7) days** after service of this notice upon you, you must pay in full to Landlord the rent and other charges now due and unpaid, as follows:

$ _____ Rent for _____

$ _____ Late Charges _____

$ _____ Other _____

$ _____ Other _____

$ _____ Total (exclusive of further accruing costs)

Payment will be accepted only by:

☐ cash ☐ money order ☐ cashier's or certified check ☐ personal check

IF YOU FAIL TO TENDER FULL PAYMENT, **your Lease will be terminated** and you must surrender possession of the premises to Landlord. If you fail, within the **seven (7) day** notice period, either to pay the total charges in full, or to surrender possession of the premises, legal proceedings will be commenced against you to recover possession and to recover a judgment for the rent and damages for your unlawful detention of the premises, and all costs of court including attorneys' fees to the extent allowed by applicable law and/or the lease agreement. Surrender of the premises does not relieve you of liability for the outstanding balance.

The **seven (7) day** notice period described herein shall expire at:
_____ O'clock [am/pm], on the _____ day of _____ , 20 _____ .

LANDLORD RESERVES ALL RIGHTS AND REMEDIES UNDER THE LEASE AGREEMENT AND UNDER APPLICABLE LAW, INCLUDING BUT NOT LIMITED TO CONTRACTUAL DAMAGES FOR UNPAID RENT, AND NOTHING IN THIS NOTICE SHOULD BE CONSTRUED AS A WAIVER OR RELINQUISHMENT OF SAME.

Signed, this the _____ day of _____ , 20 _____ .

Signed: _____

       Landlord/Lessor, or authorized agent

Cure or Quit Notice

NOTICE OF BREACH OF SPECIFIC PROVISIONS OF
WRITTEN LEASE WITH RIGHT TO CURE: RESIDENTIAL

TO: Tenant(s): _____ FROM: Landlord _____

_____   _____

_____   _____

_____   _____

_____   _____

Address of Leased Premises: _____

You are advised that you are in violation of the following provision(s) of the lease:

[identify lease provision]

The reason you are in breach of the provision(s) above is the following:

Pursuant to the lease, you are provided with this written notice of the breach. You are given _____ ( ) days from the date of your receipt of this notice to cure the breach, or the lease shall stand terminated and I will pursue eviction remedies.

Signed, this the _____ day of _____ , 20 _____ .
Signed: _____
             Landlord/Lessor, or authorized agent

Unconditional Quit Notice

NOTICE OF BREACH OF SPECIFIC PROVISIONS OF
WRITTEN LEASE WITH NO RIGHT TO CURE: RESIDENTIAL

TO: Tenant(s): _____ FROM: Landlord _____

_____   _____

_____   _____

_____   _____

_____   _____

Address of Leased Premises: _____

You are advised that you are in violation of the following provision(s) of the lease:

[identify lease provision]

The reason you are in breach of the provision(s) above is the following:

Pursuant to the lease, you are provided with this written notice of the breach and termination of the lease due to the breach. Due to the nature of the breach and in accordance with the lease provisions, there is no right to cure this default. The lease is therefore terminated effective _____ ( ) days from the date of your receipt of this notice. Please vacate the premises and provide the keys to me by the termination date.

Signed, this the _____ day of _____ , 20 _____ .
Signed: _____

Landlord/Lessor, or authorized agent

Notice of Outstanding Charges

Date: _____

To: _____
   _____
   _____

Your payment for outstanding charges has not been received as of the above date. Please send a separate check or money order (do not combine it with the rent payment) upon receipt of this letter to avoid further charges. Your payments will be applied as follows: First to late charges, second to other charges due, and third to rent.

Description of Outstanding Charges:

Additional Information

Late Charges: _____   _____

Utilities: _____   _____

Other: _____   _____

Rent: _____   _____

Total Due: _____

Your payment should be sent to:

—Owner/Management

                    Phone:

Landlord's Ledger Sheet

RENTAL EXPENSE ALLOCATION REPORT

LOCATION:			YEAR	
Category	Date	Description	Tax Amt	Book Amt
Accounting/Legal				
Advertising				
Depreciation				
Electricity				
Insurance				
Maintenance/Cleaning				
Mileage				
Mortgage/Interest				
Other Interest				
Natural Gas				
Repairs				
Supplies				
Taxes				
Water				
Other Expenses				
Subtotal Taxes				
Mortgage Payment				
Down Payment				
Subtotal Books				
Total Expenses				

Monthly Income Record

MONTHLY INCOME RECORD

Year

PROPERTY	JAN	FEB	MAR	APR	MAY	JUNE	JUL	AUG	SEP	OCT	NOV	DEC
Subtotal												
Other Income												
Subtotal												
Total												

Cash Flow Analysis

Gross Income:

Estimated Annual Gross Income _____

Other Income _____

Total Gross Income _____

Less Vacancy Allowance _____

Effective Gross Income _____

Expenses:

Taxes _____

Insurance _____

Water/Sewer _____

Garbage _____

Electricity _____

Licenses _____

Advertising _____

Supplies _____

Maintenance _____

Lawn _____

Snow Removal _____

Pest Control _____

Management—Offsite _____

Management—Onsite _____

Accounting/Legal _____

Miscellaneous _____

Gas _____

Telephone _____

Budget for Replacements _____

Total Expenses _____

Net Operating Income _____

Debt Service:

1st Mortgage _____

2nd Mortgage _____

3rd Mortgage _____

Total Debt Service _____

Cash Flow: _____

Index

THE EVERYTHING SERIES!

BUSINESS & PERSONAL FINANCE

Everything® Budgeting Book
Everything® Business Planning Book
Everything® Coaching and Mentoring Book
Everything® Fundraising Book
Everything® Get Out of Debt Book
Everything® Grant Writing Book
Everything® Homebuying Book, 2nd Ed.
Everything® Homeselling Book
Everything® Home-Based Business Book
Everything® Investing Book
Everything® Landlording Book
Everything® Leadership Book
Everything® Managing People Book
Everything® Negotiating Book
Everything® Online Business Book
Everything® Personal Finance Book
Everything® Personal Finance in Your 20s & 30s Book
Everything® Project Management Book
Everything® Real Estate Investing Book
Everything® Robert's Rules Book, $7.95
Everything® Selling Book
Everything® Start Your Own Business Book
Everything® Time Management Book
Everything® Wills & Estate Planning Book

COOKING

Everything® Barbecue Cookbook
Everything® Bartender's Book, $9.95
Everything® Chinese Cookbook
Everything® Chocolate Cookbook
Everything® College Cookbook
Everything® Cookbook
Everything® Dessert Cookbook
Everything® Diabetes Cookbook
Everything® Easy Gourmet Cookbook
Everything® Fondue Cookbook
Everything® Grilling Cookbook

Everything® Healthy Meals in Minutes Cookbook
Everything® Holiday Cookbook
Everything® Indian Cookbook
Everything® Low-Carb Cookbook
Everything® Low-Fat High-Flavor Cookbook
Everything® Low-Salt Cookbook
Everything® Meals for a Month Cookbook
Everything® Mediterranean Cookbook
Everything® Mexican Cookbook
Everything® One-Pot Cookbook
Everything® Pasta Cookbook
Everything® Quick Meals Cookbook
Everything® Slow Cooker Cookbook
Everything® Soup Cookbook
Everything® Thai Cookbook
Everything® Vegetarian Cookbook
Everything® Wine Book

HEALTH

Everything® Alzheimer's Book
Everything® Anti-Aging Book
Everything® Diabetes Book
Everything® Hypnosis Book
Everything® Low Cholesterol Book
Everything® Massage Book
Everything® Menopause Book
Everything® Nutrition Book
Everything® Reflexology Book
Everything® Stress Management Book

HISTORY

Everything® American Government Book
Everything® American History Book
Everything® Civil War Book
Everything® Irish History & Heritage Book
Everything® Middle East Book

HOBBIES & GAMES

Everything® Blackjack Strategy Book
Everything® Brain Strain Book, $9.95
Everything® Bridge Book
Everything® Candlemaking Book
Everything® Card Games Book
Everything® Cartooning Book
Everything® Casino Gambling Book, 2nd Ed.
Everything® Chess Basics Book
Everything® Crossword and Puzzle Book
Everything® Crossword Challenge Book
Everything® Cryptograms Book, $9.95
Everything® Digital Photography Book
Everything® Drawing Book
Everything® Easy Crosswords Book
Everything® Family Tree Book
Everything® Games Book, 2nd Ed.
Everything® Knitting Book
Everything® Knots Book
Everything® Motorcycle Book
Everything® Online Genealogy Book
Everything® Photography Book
Everything® Poker Strategy Book
Everything® Pool & Billiards Book
Everything® Quilting Book
Everything® Scrapbooking Book
Everything® Sewing Book
Everything® Woodworking Book
Everything® Word Games Challenge Book

HOME IMPROVEMENT

Everything® Feng Shui Book
Everything® Feng Shui Decluttering Book, $9.95
Everything® Fix-It Book
Everything® Homebuilding Book
Everything® Landscaping Book
Everything® Lawn Care Book
Everything® Organize Your Home Book

All Everything® books are priced at $12.95 or $14.95, unless otherwise stated. Prices subject to change without notice.

EVERYTHING® KIDS' BOOKS

All titles are $6.95

Everything® Kids' Animal Puzzle & Activity Book
Everything® Kids' Baseball Book, 3rd Ed.
Everything® Kids' Bible Trivia Book
Everything® Kids' Bugs Book
Everything® Kids' Christmas Puzzle & Activity Book
Everything® Kids' Cookbook
Everything® Kids' Halloween Puzzle & Activity Book
Everything® Kids' Hidden Pictures Book
Everything® Kids' Joke Book
Everything® Kids' Knock Knock Book
Everything® Kids' Math Puzzles Book
Everything® Kids' Mazes Book
Everything® Kids' Money Book
Everything® Kids' Monsters Book
Everything® Kids' Nature Book
Everything® Kids' Puzzle Book
Everything® Kids' Riddles & Brain Teasers Book
Everything® Kids' Science Experiments Book
Everything® Kids' Sharks Book
Everything® Kids' Soccer Book
Everything® Kids' Travel Activity Book

KIDS' STORY BOOKS

Everything® Bedtime Story Book
Everything® Bible Stories Book
Everything® Fairy Tales Book

LANGUAGE

Everything® Conversational Japanese Book (with CD), $19.95
Everything® French Phrase Book, $9.95
Everything® French Verb Book, $9.95
Everything® Inglés Book
Everything® Learning French Book
Everything® Learning German Book
Everything® Learning Italian Book
Everything® Learning Latin Book
Everything® Learning Spanish Book
Everything® Sign Language Book
Everything® Spanish Grammar Book
Everything® Spanish Phrase Book, $9.95
Everything® Spanish Verb Book, $9.95

MUSIC

Everything® Drums Book (with CD), $19.95
Everything® Guitar Book
Everything® Home Recording Book
Everything® Playing Piano and Keyboards Book
Everything® Reading Music Book (with CD), $19.95
Everything® Rock & Blues Guitar Book (with CD), $19.95
Everything® Songwriting Book

NEW AGE

Everything® Astrology Book
Everything® Dreams Book, 2nd Ed.
Everything® Ghost Book
Everything® Love Signs Book, $9.95
Everything® Meditation Book
Everything® Numerology Book
Everything® Paganism Book
Everything® Palmistry Book
Everything® Psychic Book
Everything® Reiki Book
Everything® Spells & Charms Book
Everything® Tarot Book
Everything® Wicca and Witchcraft Book

PARENTING

Everything® Baby Names Book
Everything® Baby Shower Book
Everything® Baby's First Food Book
Everything® Baby's First Year Book
Everything® Birthing Book
Everything® Breastfeeding Book
Everything® Father-to-Be Book
Everything® Father's First Year Book
Everything® Get Ready for Baby Book
Everything® Getting Pregnant Book
Everything® Homeschooling Book
Everything® Parent's Guide to Children with ADD/ADHD
Everything® Parent's Guide to Children with Asperger's Syndrome
Everything® Parent's Guide to Children with Autism
Everything® Parent's Guide to Children with Dyslexia
Everything® Parent's Guide to Positive Discipline

Everything® Parent's Guide to Raising a Successful Child
Everything® Parent's Guide to Tantrums
Everything® Parent's Guide to the Overweight Child
Everything® Parenting a Teenager Book
Everything® Potty Training Book, $9.95
Everything® Pregnancy Book, 2nd Ed.
Everything® Pregnancy Fitness Book
Everything® Pregnancy Nutrition Book
Everything® Pregnancy Organizer, $15.00
Everything® Toddler Book
Everything® Tween Book
Everything® Twins, Triplets, and More Book

PETS

Everything® Cat Book
Everything® Dachshund Book, $12.95
Everything® Dog Book
Everything® Dog Health Book
Everything® Dog Training and Tricks Book
Everything® Golden Retriever Book, $12.95
Everything® Horse Book
Everything® Labrador Retriever Book, $12.95
Everything® Poodle Book, $12.95
Everything® Pug Book, $12.95
Everything® Puppy Book
Everything® Rottweiler Book, $12.95
Everything® Tropical Fish Book

REFERENCE

Everything® Car Care Book
Everything® Classical Mythology Book
Everything® Computer Book
Everything® Divorce Book
Everything® Einstein Book
Everything® Etiquette Book
Everything® Great Thinkers Book
Everything® Mafia Book
Everything® Philosophy Book
Everything® Psychology Book
Everything® Shakespeare Book

RELIGION

Everything® Angels Book
Everything® Bible Book
Everything® Buddhism Book
Everything® Catholicism Book

All Everything® books are priced at $12.95 or $14.95, unless otherwise stated. Prices subject to change without notice.

Everything® Christianity Book
Everything® Jewish History & Heritage Book
Everything® Judaism Book
Everything® Koran Book
Everything® Prayer Book
Everything® Saints Book
Everything® Torah Book
Everything® Understanding Islam Book
Everything® World's Religions Book
Everything® Zen Book

SCHOOL & CAREERS

Everything® After College Book
Everything® Alternative Careers Book
Everything® College Survival Book, 2nd Ed.
Everything® Cover Letter Book, 2nd Ed.
Everything® Get-a-Job Book
Everything® Job Interview Book
Everything® New Teacher Book
Everything® Online Job Search Book
Everything® Paying for College Book
Everything® Practice Interview Book
Everything® Resume Book, 2nd Ed.
Everything® Study Book

SELF-HELP

Everything® Dating Book
Everything® Great Sex Book
Everything® Kama Sutra Book
Everything® Self-Esteem Book

SPORTS & FITNESS

Everything® Fishing Book
Everything® Fly-Fishing Book
Everything® Golf Instruction Book
Everything® Pilates Book
Everything® Running Book
Everything® Total Fitness Book
Everything® Weight Training Book
Everything® Yoga Book

TRAVEL

Everything® Family Guide to Hawaii
Everything® Family Guide to New York City, 2nd Ed.
Everything® Family Guide to RV Travel & Campgrounds
Everything® Family Guide to the Walt Disney World Resort®, Universal Studios®, and Greater Orlando, 4th Ed.
Everything® Family Guide to Washington D.C., 2nd Ed.
Everything® Guide to Las Vegas
Everything® Guide to New England
Everything® Travel Guide to the Disneyland Resort®, California Adventure®, Universal Studios®, and the Anaheim Area

WEDDINGS

Everything® Bachelorette Party Book, $9.95
Everything® Bridesmaid Book, $9.95
Everything® Creative Wedding Ideas Book
Everything® Elopement Book, $9.95
Everything® Father of the Bride Book, $9.95
Everything® Groom Book, $9.95
Everything® Mother of the Bride Book, $9.95
Everything® Wedding Book, 3rd Ed.
Everything® Wedding Checklist, $9.95
Everything® Wedding Etiquette Book, $7.95
Everything® Wedding Organizer, $15.00
Everything® Wedding Shower Book, $7.95
Everything® Wedding Vows Book, $9.95
Everything® Weddings on a Budget Book, $9.95

WRITING

Everything® Creative Writing Book
Everything® Get Published Book
Everything® Grammar and Style Book
Everything® Guide to Writing a Book Proposal
Everything® Guide to Writing a Novel
Everything® Guide to Writing Children's Books
Everything® Screenwriting Book
Everything® Writing Poetry Book
Everything® Writing Well Book

We have Everything® for the beginning crafter!
All titles are $14.95.

Everything® Crafts—Baby Scrapbooking
1-59337-225-6

Everything® Crafts—Bead Your Own Jewelry
1-59337-142-X

Everything® Crafts—Create Your Own Greeting Cards
1-59337-226-4

Everything® Crafts—Easy Projects
1-59337-298-1

Everything® Crafts—Making Cards with Rubber Stamps
1-59337-299-X

Everything® Crafts—Polymer Clay for Beginners
1-59337-230-2

Everything® Crafts—Rubber Stamping Made Easy
1-59337-229-9

Everything® Crafts—Wedding Decorations and Keepsakes
1-59337-227-2

Available wherever books are sold!
To order, call 800-872-5627, or visit us at *www.everything.com*.
Everything® and everything.com® are registered trademarks of F+W Publications, Inc.